A DIRTY U.S. GOVERNMENT SECRET

By
ANTHONY P. KEYTER

Library of Congress Control Number

LCCN: 2025944446

International Standard Book Number

ISBN: 978-1-967866-19-9

Front cover photo of Lady Justice
by courtesy of Bob Speel
Website: www.speel.me.uk

Dedicated to all honest workers, noble institutions,
and moral entities who faithfully labor in love
to secure just government and the rule of law.

Table of Contents

To ignore crime and injustice is to condone it.

To condone crime and injustice is to perpetuate it.

To perpetuate crime and injustice is to be party thereto.

The law affirms that providing

protection to criminals is a crime …

and failing to identify them is a crime.

And so began my odyssey.

Preamble

The story you are about to read is not fiction. What follows is not just a history of events, but a testimony of lived experience. A lived experience in a nation that prides itself on democracy, but shields itself with secrecy, intimidation, retaliation, and cover-up. It is the account of a government willing to hide its failures and its serious crimes, while ordinary citizens are left to pay the price. Here lies the evidence of wrongdoing, concealed from the public eye, and now finally brought forward.

My factual story recounts an exhaustive effort to find justice and protection of the laws against the malevolent deeds of a group of malfeasant United States judicial and government officials. When the law finally takes its proper course, as inevitably it must, many senior US Government officials who knowingly and willfully engaged in that malicious conduct could potentially face harsh punishment for their lawlessness - including prescribed sentences of life imprisonment or even the death penalty. This statement is not expressed lightly.

From the outset of this narrative, I want to make it clear that I wish no such fate upon any United States government official implicated in the events revealed in this book. I wish to state with absolute sincerity that I have no enemies among the US Government officials who seek to do me harm, amongst the officials who have attempted to take my life and continue with their plot to do so, even as I write this story. I hold no animosity or vengeance within my heart towards them. I hold only love, as I do for all.

However, I do observe gross violations of the nation's laws and of moral law - God's higher laws for humanity. Those violations should be addressed and opposed, for lest we condone and, by that condoning, foster and encourage such immoral behavior - such godless behavior. Those amongst us who place themselves in a

1

position of authority over others, proclaiming the welfare of their subjects at the center of their hearts, are relied upon to honor their undertaking and oath to serve their fellow countrymen.

Everyone who violates the law must face the consequences of their actions. Presidents, politicians, prosecutors, policemen, judges, and other high government officials involved in the lawlessness described herewith are not above the laws of this country – nor above moral law. And every violator in this matter will be brought to justice before the courts of the United States - that I have vowed.

But this book is not about revenge. It is about truth and law. And truth, when revealed, is a weapon more powerful than secrecy itself. The intent of this account is to share my harsh experience with the community so that others who might tread this same road behind me do not suffer the same indignities and injustices at the hands of mean government officials, and may benefit from my experience.

Before commencing to describe those harsh and unjust experiences that constitute the essence of this book, I will divert momentarily from the central theme of the narrative. I will first endeavor to provide an appropriate perspective on the life, the characteristics, the modes of thinking, and some of the events that shaped the one who endured those indignities and injustices - and who took up the 'ceremonial sword of justice' to oppose them.

****

Throughout my life, there never was more than a sensible and practical interest or involvement in government, party politics, or law. I was, I suppose, somewhat of a side-line observer in these fields of human endeavor. For instance, the only prior exposure to the courts I had before this saga was a court argument against an unjust traffic ticket, which secured the annulment of that ticket. My interests and activities in life lay elsewhere. My proclivity tended to be for the outdoors, for sport and adventure, and for nature. It is

2

my passion to wander the mountains, finding beauty and harmony in their majesty and inspiration in their solitude, both in the summer sunshine and in the winter snow. I love to play my guitar and sing along. My life's devotion and career, however, was in matters of aviation.

As a fighter pilot, test pilot, and survey pilot, I was technically oriented and interested. I loved the exhilaration of high-performance jet flying and the thrill of test flying. I also loved the technical challenge of solving complex aerodynamic stability and control problems caused by some newly developed weaponry slung under the wings of a fighter aircraft. Later, as a senior instructor pilot for the Boeing Company in Seattle, I honed an avid appreciation and interest in the man-machine interface, in an effort to safely and efficiently integrate trainee pilots into the complex cockpits of modern jet-liners. I also developed an acute appreciation for the cultural influences upon flight safety, inherent in the diverse crews from far-flung countries whom I instructed.

To me, life has been a captivating journey. Although not without its challenges, life's experiences have nevertheless always been enriching in so many fascinating aspects. From an early age I have had the urge to explore, to travel, to venture, and to commune with nature. In short, to experience the joy through the very best of what a 'love of life' can offer the dedicated searcher, under whatever surprising circumstances he may find himself in. That early impulse continued into adulthood and throughout the years.

I was born and raised in South Africa, on a continent that I love. According to the family genealogy, my ancestors came from Paderborn, Germany, and, as farmers, settled in the Stellenbosch area in South Africa in 1788. Despite growing up without a father (he died when I was young), I was blessed with a wise and loving mother and grandmother and enjoyed an exceedingly happy and carefree childhood. Blessed also, I was to have an older sister to pave the way and a twin brother, Barry, who has been a best friend throughout my life. In an era without television, computer games, cell phones, and the like, as boys, we lived an active outdoor life of exploration and self-created amusement in an environment of freedom, without license to behave sans restraint.

Mother was a trained psychologist and worked for the South African Government, first at the Department of Labour and later at the Department of Information. She was a gentle, loving soul, and yet she could also be very firm when she needed to set the boundaries of discipline. My father was a South African Air Force fighter pilot and instructor, who saw combat in North Africa during World War II. We unfortunately never got to know him well before he passed away, but both sons inherited his passion for flying.

Straight after high school, in 1966, we were drafted into the South African Army (into the same infantry training unit) for one-year compulsory military training. The next best thing to flying for us was to join the paratroopers in order to live out our passion for the skies. The training at No. 1 Parachute Battalion was rigorous and tested our mettle to the full, yet it was an exhilarating time served at that elite airborne unit. At the end of our national military service, at the close of our 18th year of age, as Active Citizen Force second lieutenants, the twin brothers each commanded a platoon of 30 paratroopers and had 15 proud parachute jumps to our credit.

After paratroopers, a rare opportunity opened up for me to receive flight training at an army air reconnaissance squadron. Only one training slot was available and twin brother Barry was to stay with the paratroopers as part-time soldier for a while longer. He followed into the Active Citizen Air Force some five years later. So, by June 1967, at age 19, I could proudly pin paratrooper wings to the right breast of my uniform tunic and Army Air Reconnaissance flying wings to the left breast. I continued in the Active Citizen Force until 1979, first flying the Cessna 185 in the Army, and later the Harvard (North American T-6) and then Impala jet strike fighter in the South African Air Force. In the interim, Barry had joined the same Active Citizen Force squadron and received his flying training part-time on the Harvard and later on the Impala strike fighter. For many years we flew as 'weekend warriors' (part-time) while we each pursued our respective university studies and, later on, our civilian careers. I studied physics and astronomy as majors, and Barry studied business economics and accountancy.

After initial army training and before university, together we toured Europe for six months (with proceeds from our casual part-time dance band). Initially, we hitchhiked and later bought a used scooter for a few dollars, which carried the two of us plus a backpack and a guitar each. We covered the continent from North Cape in Norway through almost all Western European countries (except Portugal) down to Greece, mostly camping out or staying in youth hostels as we traveled along. It was a very rewarding experience. Apart from the cultural diversity, interesting sights, and rich history of Europe, the six-month journey brought with it an invaluable lesson in tolerance, respect, and acceptance of different peoples, cultures, creeds, and modes of thinking, which was to stand us both in good stead throughout our lives.

In March 1974, at age 26, we scraped together all the spare money we had and bought an old Tiger Moth, an open cockpit World War II era biplane, which we owned (together with a close friend) for the next 26 years. It brought great pleasure, and we used to fly aerobatics for fun and in competitions. We did aerial stunting for feature films and wing walking just for excitement – without parachutes, of course.

Other sports in which we were active included skydiving, scuba diving, snow skiing, water skiing, mountaineering, and hiking, and our main sport at the time: kayaking. Together we kayaked a number of South African rivers and took a few long excursions over the years. The longest of those expeditions was 425 miles over 22 days down remote regions of South Africa's longest river, the Orange River. There were many exhilarating episodes while

5

kayaking South African rivers, and some very close calls would involve crocodiles and hippopotamuses on the Olifants River.

These were some of the activities that we were fortunate enough to share as twin brothers and which brought adventure and added a zest for life. Along the way, there were many close shaves and narrow escapes - and a few broken bones as well. Some escapes, I will sheepishly admit, occurred by pushing the limits of healthy adventure well beyond the envelope of prudence. Yet, if ever the spirit of the brothers was ever dampened in any way, it was not for very long.

****

Though already flying as a part-time military pilot for several years since 1967, in 1972, after university, I began my civilian flying career as a flight instructor and soon progressed to survey flying for a South African mining company. It was interesting and technical work, utilizing a variety of remote sensing equipment, including an infrared line scanner, magnetometer, and multi-spectral cameras. We would sometimes spend exacting flying hours at low level, 200 feet above the ground, on a radio altimeter, with the magnetometer trailing on a cable 65 feet below the aircraft. At other times, we could be found at 25,000 feet, mapping with the multi-spectral camera during daylight hours or using the infrared line scanner at night. The work took me across most countries in Southern Africa, all the way up to the equator. Besides the magnificent countryside, I gained an acute insight into the plight of the African people in many areas across those regions.

The neighboring country of Namibia is a dry but spectacularly beautiful piece of Africa. During one of our high-altitude missions over this magnificent terrain, the fuel indicators (magnetic float switches) of our Dornier Skyservant airplane froze up, indicating fuel in the tanks, which we never had, and resulted in a dual engine failure through fuel starvation. It was a long glide back to Eros

Airport in Windhoek, but to the relief of our four-man crew, we made it with altitude and airspeed to spare. Sadly, that fine aircraft was later lost due to the very same, uncorrected cause during a night infra-red line scanner mission over mountainous terrain in Namibia. With excellent flying skills demonstrated by a fellow survey pilot, and with some good luck thrown in, the flight crew walked away from the wreckage without major injury.

After the most enjoyable stint as a survey pilot, I flew some charter and a few months on an executive jet before joining a commuter liner on a Douglas DC-3 (Dakota) aircraft. What an enjoyable time that was. We had an early morning flight from Johannesburg to the Kruger National Park game reserve, with a late afternoon return. After refueling at our destination at Skukuza camp, which was my job as co-pilot, there was plenty of time to take a leisurely game drive in that magnificent game park before flying back home late afternoon, while circumventing huge thunderstorms on the Drakensberg escarpment en route.

From the commuter liner, I progressed to a freight company flying Lockheed Hercules L100 aircraft for the next five years on African, European, and other international routes. A favorite trip of mine in those years was the European destinations, which had a stopover in Las Palmas in the Canary Islands. There, I learned to scuba dive on our lay-overs, and I kept my diving log active that way for a number of years.

In parallel to my civilian flying career, I maintained an active status in the South African Air Force, flying as a Citizen Force pilot for them every Saturday when I was not away on a trip with the freight company. For fun flying on days off, our Tiger Moth biplane was always available. I never seemed to get enough of the joy of flying from those three sources.

As the South African Border War with Angola built up to a climax, at the end of 1979, I left the freight company to serve with the South African Air Force full-time, this time as a test pilot with the rank of major. The work was technical and demanding and involved experimental, production, and maintenance test flying on jet fighters and transport aircraft, including Mirage III, Mirage F-1, Impala strike fighter, and the DC-3 transport aircraft. Experimental testing included flutter and weapons development testing. Production testing was undertaken at Atlas Aircraft Corporation factory in Johannesburg, where the Impala light strike fighter was built under license from Aermacchi in Italy. I later became Base Commander of a detachment of the Test Flight and Development Centre serving the live weapons range. The 22-man detachment was stationed at the airport outside the small town of Upington, at the southern tip of the Kalahari Desert. There was not much air traffic into or out of this remote rural community and the skies 'belonged to me,' as it were, making for wonderful flying and a great tour of duty.

****

Mid 1984, at the height of my test flying career, I left the South African Air Force to pursue a Master's Degree in space science at the University of Houston in the USA. The graduate campus at Clear Lake is situated next to the Johnson Space Center, and what better place to study that subject matter than at a campus where nearly all the students and lecturers in class were associated in one way or another with the space program? It was a stimulating time.

During those study years, I simultaneously put my flight test experience and technical knowledge to use and instructed on flight simulators at 'FlightSafety International.' After completing the Master's Degree in Houston (to my delight, with straight A's), I joined the National Test Pilot School in Mojave, California, as a test pilot instructor for a period of about three years. There, I taught flight test techniques and theory of flight test to both military and civilian test pilot students from the United States and abroad. The time spent there was also most satisfying, and I taught a broad array of flying maneuvers on a wide variety of aircraft. On one such flight, I was teaching spin-analysis to a Taiwanese Air Force colonel when we had an engine failure. Fortunately, we had just climbed up to 11,000 feet to start our series of twelve consecutive spins. We thus had sufficient altitude in hand to glide back to Mojave Airport and, for the second time in my flying career, a dead-stick landing without power.

Always aiming further, from the National Test Pilot School in Mojave, California, I applied to the Boeing Company, where I was accepted as an instructor pilot. I was to spend the next seventeen years of my flying career with the Boeing Company in Seattle.

****

And so, with this background information on activities, interests, and a brief mention of some experiences, I have endeavored to give the reader some perspective on my personal life and an insight into some of the things that have impelled and shaped my mindset and my being. And it was not government or law ... *that* was thrust upon me!

By 1989, at age 41, I had a good and steady flying job with Boeing to last me until retirement, or so it seemed at the time, in a prosperous land of opportunity, free from government tyranny or oppression, or so it appeared at the time. The United States is, after all, seen universally as an honorable nation, a land of laws where the 'rule of law' holds sway and the Constitution holds supreme. The nobility and *pre-eminence* of that benevolent document cannot be doubted. And government officials swear before God and the nation to uphold the tenets of the Constitution – and that gives one confidence.

There are many government institutions and laws and rules in place that are meant to check the lawful and ethical behavior of officials, and to discipline them when they step out of line. Also set in place to prevent abuse of government power is a doctrine of

9

separation of powers between lawmakers in Congress, judges in the Court System, and Administration officials under the President and his Cabinet. Foolproof government, it would appear, in which the separate branches hold some independence to check on each other, and yet cooperate and function effectively and efficiently to render the necessary services to the public, whom they are there for to serve.

Consequently, in good faith, on May 14, 1992, I became a United States Citizen and swore my loyalty to this country by taking the *'Naturalization Oath of Allegiance to the United States of America.'* It was a big day, a proud day, to become a small fragment of that "one nation under God, indivisible, with liberty and justice for all." Note: Liberty and justice for all.

As a quid pro quo, in return for my oath of allegiance, the United States of America was to bestow upon me the fundamental human rights enshrined in the Constitutional 'Bill of Rights,' as it does for all its citizens. Amongst those cherished freedoms and 'inalienable rights' promised me on that special day of naturalization as an American citizen, were the right to due process of law and the right to equal protection of the law. Note, again: Equal protection of the law. In the interceding years, the fidelity to those noble principles, and the trustworthiness of the United States and its officials were inadvertently but conclusively to be put to the test.

Through the years I have had many close calls, which nearly ended my life prematurely while flying and pursuing sport, adventure, and excitement. Of the many narrow escapes over the years, one or two random examples I have mentioned. Yet, it never occurred to me that one could also be killed simply by obeying a United States law: statute 18USC4. I emphasize that declaration in case it did not register upon the mind of the reader. That law demanded that I report to some judge, my knowledge of serious crimes committed by senior government officials. Those reports

10

precipitated what can indisputably be described as *'state-supported tyranny in the land of the free.'* That tyranny involves judges, congressmen, and other high administration officials - and consecutive Presidents of the United States.

Allow me, then, to share *that* adventure story with you as well.

Chapter 1
Protection of the Laws

How would one bestow upon the population 'the equal protection of the laws' as promised by the United States Constitution?

Extract from Chapter 1.

JUSTICE

The Preamble to the United States Constitution nobly states:

> *"We the people of the United States, in order to form a more perfect union, **establish justice,** ensure domestic tranquility, provide for the common defense, promote the general welfare, and secure the blessings of liberty to ourselves and our posterity, do ordain and establish this Constitution for the United States of America."*

In theory, and in the eyes of those untouched by personal experience with the law, the United States of America has an adequate system of justice. In practice, however, and for those touched by its harsh realities, the United States justice system hopelessly fails to dispense with *'justice'* as intended by the Constitution and the laws of the country. Despite the best intentions of the 'founding fathers' when they drafted the United States Constitution, with the passage of time, something has gone dreadfully awry in the practical application of the laws.

What do we mean by the term *'justice'?* The Concise Oxford Dictionary defines 'justice' as behavior and treatment that is morally right and fair; or, the administration of the law or authority in maintaining that. Is the concept of being morally right and fair, which remains so elusive to man, not just our best human interpretation of a divine principle? If that be so, what is that divine principle?

Surely, *'justice'* is the outworking of a natural law: the law of *cause and effect*. This universal law being a higher decree of the idea which in Western Christian theology is captured in the words: *'what we sow, so also shall we reap'*. In the East, that same concept is simply called *'karma'*. That is to say, for good or for ill, we reap the fruits of what we have caused to be. In its positive form, good deeds have their rewards. In its negative form, in the field of human interactions, that divine principle indisputably pertains to the payment of debt in the exact measure as such debt is incurred when good human relations are transgressed.

All the great religions of the world and all the great judicial institutions concerned with the morality of man embrace this very concept in one form or another: the harmonizing of injury in exact measure to the harm inflicted. In other words: the balancing of the 'scales of justice'.

Included in the institutions to which I refer is the United States judicial system, with its Constitution and its system of laws and punishment that addresses violations of those laws, as reflected in the 'United States Code' (USC). Yet, in the practical application of the laws of the United States, notable and indefensible exceptions are arbitrarily made to the divine principle of *'justice'.*

PROTECTIONS OFFERED BY THE US CONSTITUTION

In America, the highest law of the land, the United States Constitution, states in part in the 14th Amendment:

> *"... No state shall make or enforce any law which shall abridge the privileges or immunities of citizens of the United States; nor shall any state deprive any person of life, liberty, or property,*

14

without due process of law; **nor deny to any person within its jurisdiction the equal protection of the laws".**

How would one bestow upon the population *'the equal protection of the laws',* as demanded by the 14th Amendment to the United States Constitution?

In a few simple words: you would design a system with policemen who would police the actions of persons who appear to violate the laws. The policemen would investigate and, having gathered evidence of transgressions, they would take the violators to the prosecutors. The prosecutors would prepare the case and present it before the judges. In turn, the judges, having the law in front of them, would say: "You have not obeyed what is expected of you under this law" and would sentence the offenders accordingly. And punishment in exact measure to the severity of the offense would act as a lesson and a deterrent to the offender and to other delinquents alike. Unless justice is exacted in every instance where there is a violation of a right or a law, such violation will continue with impunity, and something that is wrong comes to be seen as being right, and *that* becomes the norm.

The laws would have come from the legislators who would have sat and pondered and debated long and hard on all the causes and ramifications before enacting the laws. Laws based on reason and good judgment - and the protection provided by enforcing those laws upon the general population and upon public officials alike - is what keeps a nation free from anarchy and government tyranny. That is how the populace would benefit from the *'equal protection of the law'* clause of the Constitution.

TYRANNY

Now, what happens, for instance, if a judge does not obey the law and is allowed to get away with it? Before long the other judges see what's happening and neither do they obey the laws when it suits them. And why would they when their colleague is allowed to take free rein? However, overseeing the legal system would be a state governor or a president to *'take care of the faithful execution of the laws'* in keeping with the system of checks and balances enshrined in the United States Constitution and in the American form of democracy.

But what happens, say, if the President of the United States himself does not obey the laws and, whilst knowing of the delinquent judges, willfully neglects to 'take care of the faithful execution of the laws' as his Constitutional duty demands? Soon, the legislators would follow that example, and *they* too don't obey the laws. And the prosecutors would follow the lead of president and legislators, and on a whim prosecute only those that they wish to prosecute, getting even with perceived adversaries, but letting favored friends go free. And the policemen, the lowest members on the totem pole in the justice system, will still police – but not those above them on the totem pole per se, but only those below them: the public. And in that, you have a system designed for tyranny upon the populace. Anarchy from the police on upwards in the hierarchy - and tyranny from the police on downwards.

Of course, there are degrees of intensity. Tyranny upon a population has many faces and torture can take on many forms. One system may employ mental oppression only, while another might stoop to physical oppression as well. Yet, the agony enforced upon the human psyche by these two forms of cruelty is the same. Here, as the author, I speak from harsh personal experience, having been subjected to such tyranny firsthand on a number of occasions over the preceding two and a half decades. Without the faithful application of the laws upon official misconduct, the population of the United States, or any other western-style democracy for that matter, is no more *free from covert tyranny* than those in more overt dictatorships of present-day Africa or the Middle East or Far East, for example.

The only thing that key officials in the justice system have to do in order to sanction, to perpetrate, and to proliferate that tyranny, is to *do nothing* with regard to official misconduct or crime. They simply have to withhold any law enforcement action and neglect to perform their peremptory judicial or statutory duties. When officers from several departments that make up a justice system cooperate to turn a blind eye to crimes committed by government officials against the people, it is certain to entrench oppression upon a populace - no matter how free a society outwardly appears to be. And such are the circumstances that give rise to this real-life story.

The 'Rule of Law', respect for the law, and above all a compulsion to apply the laws logically and fairly upon *all offenders* throughout the full spectrum of society, whether they be government officials or ordinary citizens - these are essential ingredients for a benign, civilized, and law-abiding society. On the other hand, a lawless bureaucracy leaves hardship and a scarred population. Such hardship, suffered at the hands of disrespectful and merciless United States officials, is in essence no different from that suffered by the populations of pre-war Iraq under Saddam Hussein, or Afghanistan under the Taliban.

The justice system of the United States, which masquerades as one of arbitration amongst men, is neither a system of *justice* nor of *law*. It serves neither the state nor the people. A system that permits and fosters the corruption demonstrated in these pages is profoundly defective. It is a system based upon deceit and dishonesty by litigants, by lawyers, and by judges alike, where judges can and do breach the law without reserve and with total impunity.

Moreover, the corrupt United States justice system and courts do not operate in a vacuum. Rather, they operate hand in glove with a debauched and corrupt executive and legislative branch, in which the higher aspirations expressed in the Constitution have fallen casualty to the darker energies of the prevailing system. The noble objectives of great philosophical minds - those that bring the greater principles to humanity - have been dexterously usurped by malfeasant government officials with lesser and darker intentions. The United States of today has a self-serving system of government that serves officialdom and the passion of man for money and for power over others. This system, as it now functions, cannot produce the results that tens of millions of Americans yearn for.

Theoretically, all the laws are in place to ensure a law-abiding and benevolent society, just as, theoretically, the Federal Emergency Management Agency (FEMA) was in place to cope with a disaster such as the flooding of New Orleans during Hurricane Katrina in 2005. Yet, despite all the rhetoric, the United States has an oppressive and autocratic government; a government at war … with its own people. It is a governmental system that is used to serve and protect the interests of officials and abused to suppress the very people it was designed to serve. The case presented herewith demonstrates that warfare.

The United States Constitution has, in this case, failed to provide the American people the protections promised in the Bill of Rights. The laws have failed to stem a massive insurrection against the laws of the United States by government and judicial officials. In the events recounted in this book, unlawful obstructions of justice by officials have made it impossible to enforce the laws of the United States through the ordinary course of judicial proceedings.

This extensive criminal conspiracy within the government and the courts of the United States 'so hinders the execution of the laws that the American people are deprived of the rights, privileges, immunities, and protections named in the Constitution and secured by law'. The constituted authorities have, in many cases, willfully refused to protect those rights and have denied the 'equal protection of the laws' secured by the Constitution. The doctrine of separation of powers and the system of checks and balances, designed into our democracy to guard against tyranny, have miserably failed the American nation. The American people are as much at the mercy of the politicians of the day as are the people under the rule of more overt dictatorships.

These assertions are not the wild, unsubstantiated claims of the emotionally disturbed or mentally unstable. To wit, these statements are based upon and formulated from a posteriori observations, experiences, reasoning, deduction, and evidence - painstakingly gathered, meticulously documented, and compiled over a period of twenty-five years. That evidence, comprising some 55,000 pages, is bound in a technical exposition by the same author, intended for scholars and researchers, titled: *"The Defeat of Justice: A Treatise on the Practical Application of the Laws in the USA"*. The treatise unambiguously points to an unmitigated failure of the United States judicial system and fatal flaws in our democracy. An overview of the treatise is presented in *Appendix 3*.

It is this systemic aberration that has to change. It is this war between a callous and corrupt United States government and its people that has to end. A new, more benign system *has* to be found. The forces that lie as cause of the suffering must be combated. A more benevolent system of justice must be introduced, which can provide succor where today there is a great deal of suffering; a system that will provide kindness and empathy where today there is overwhelming deceit, malice, callousness, and above all ... lawlessness *in* the system and *by* the justice system.

Legal scholars and inspired minds alike must reach for a more benign jurisprudence premised upon the truer principles of justice that will serve the nation better than the system in force at present.

This account aims to provide impetus for that change in some small way, by illuminating and revealing:

- o The willful failure to provide protection of the laws to ordinary citizens when a crime has been perpetrated against them by a government official;
- o The widespread, but irregular, protection by felonious officials of their lawbreaking colleagues;
- o The inherent malevolence of the many officials involved in this particular case and the arbitrary nature in which they apply the laws in practice, throughout the American justice system today; and
- o The appalling price paid by the public for such delinquency.

There is one more illuminating point to make: this book provides insight into what effort it would take to bring the needed change to the corrupted government establishment existing today.

Chapter 2
The Kangaroo Court

The colloquial term 'kangaroo court' can loosely be described as a mock court, a sham legal proceeding, an unfair, biased, informal, or hasty judicial proceeding without regard for human rights or legal principles or the law.

Extract from Chapter 2.

THE LEGAL MILIEU IN THE UNITED STATES

The 'founding fathers' of America enshrined noble principles in the United States Constitution - principles of freedom, justice, and the protection of individual rights. However, in the application of these principles, the administration of the laws has fallen far short of the mark. The lofty principles established by the United States Constitution have been usurped by officials with more sinister aims. In the great American law schools, the principles of justice and law still hold true and pure. Yet, beyond the halls of learning, those fundamental principles have been perverted and corrupted in a myriad of ways. The United States of today is not the benign society that the founding fathers aspired to create through the higher values enshrined in the US Constitution.

Two sets of standards have developed in the execution of the laws - one set applicable to the general populace, the other applicable to those in authority. U.S. government officials in positions of authority who abuse their positions and violate the law may generally do so with impunity. This has become the norm and there is no effective antidote available to the common man against this phenomenon. The US system of government and certain laws, in fact, protect such abusers from culpability. This further encourages immoral and corrupt behavior amongst officials.

21

US officials who are tasked with administering the laws, simply fail to take action against offenders in their midst. This proves to be a most common and effective method of protecting a law-breaking peer from prosecution. This collusion amongst officialdom, to assist colleagues to escape criminal and civil accountability, is widespread throughout all three branches of the United States government: executive, legislative, and the judiciary. The profound malevolence permeates through every level of government: city, county, state, and federal. The phenomenon translates into a certain brand of tyranny - the tyranny of a democratically elected government wrought upon its own people.

On the face of it, this indictment might appear implausible. However, the veracity thereof is amply substantiated by the facts elaborated in a *'Dossier of Crimes'*, and in thousands of pages of evidential documents surrounding the broader case and filed with the US courts. The dossier comprises some 2,400 pages of prima facie evidence meticulously gathered over 25 years and describes the *impunity* with which some 15,000 criminal conspirators from the United States (mostly US Government and State officials and a few co-conspirators from industry) and further afield, have committed innumerable offenses and have attempted to kidnap and murder a witness to their crimes. The *'Dossier of Crimes'* is frequently referred to in this narrative and is a source of information that meticulously details the criminal transgressions of officials. A short review of the dossier and where it can be accessed is presented in *Appendix 3 – An Overview of Evidence.*

Every criminal endeavor starts somewhere and starts with someone. The major unlawful enterprise dealt with in this discourse, involving sedition, insurrection against the laws, murder, and attempts to kidnap and murder a witness, as it does, has its unassuming origins in the Superior Court of the State of Washington, in a simple *'no-fault'* marital divorce case. But don't get me wrong. The subject matter of this narrative, with its potential to shake the foundations of jurisprudence in America, I would venture to say, is not about marital dissolution. However, mention of the unpretentious origin of the impending precipitous upheaval might be appropriate at this juncture.

TRIAL BY KANGAROO COURT

The colloquial term 'kangaroo court' has loosely been described as 'a mock court, a sham legal proceeding, an unfair, biased, informal, or hasty judicial proceeding without regard for human rights or legal principles or the law'. It is a contrived court, where violations and manipulations of procedures, precedents, and due process are so gross that fundamental justice is denied, and which usually ends in harsh punishment. The outcome of a trial by kangaroo court is essentially determined in advance, usually for the purpose of ensuring conviction by going through the motions of procedure or by ignoring any defense. A kangaroo court's proceedings deny the right to due process of law in the name of expediency.

In my use of the term 'kangaroo court', there is no intent to be disrespectful to the noble institution of the United States courts. Rightly must one have respect, as I do, for the very necessary institution which is designed to provide justice and arbitration amongst men. But then, when we show our respect, is it not the court's responsibility to act respectfully and honorably?

The United States Code, in statute 18USC401, defines *'contempt of court'* as follows:

> *"A court of the United States shall have power to punish by fine or imprisonment, at its discretion, such contempt of its authority, and none other, as (1) Misbehavior of any person in its presence or so near thereto as to obstruct the administration of justice;*

(2) Misbehavior of any of its officers in their official transactions; (3) Disobedience or resistance to its lawful writ, process, order, rule, decree, or command".

Bear this definition in mind when deciding for yourself *who, in fact,* stands in contempt, disobedience, and resistance to the court's lawful process, order, rule, decree, and command, so as to obstruct the administration of justice. Crimes committed by the people who populate and administer the court system can hardly command our respect, only our contempt in cases such as this one.

If, by way of example, your mother was a prostitute, could you have respect for such a mother who taught her children immorality? If your father was a drunkard who beat his children when inebriated, could you have respect for such a father? And, if the judge you stand before was a criminal in terms of the law, could you have respect for him or her? *Of course not.* One should not respect, tolerate, and condone immorality and criminality merely because it was perpetrated by someone in authority.

Every citizen living in the United States has, by law, amongst others, the inalienable rights to lawful ownership of property, to due process of law in the courts, and a right to equal protection under the laws enforced by the justice system. Every judge of the United States takes an oath or affirmation to support the Constitution of the United States and to faithfully and impartially discharge the duties of a judge to the best of their ability. Despite these constitutional protections, I was maliciously stripped of almost all my lawful assets and a sizeable portion of my future income by *illegal* government action in the Superior Court of Washington State, Pierce County.

In the first week of January 2000, after some 19 years of matrimony, I made the difficult and heartrending decision to end my

24

marriage to Maureen (née Pasifakis) due to irreconcilable differences in temperament. It was a childless marriage and the marital dissolution was anticipated to be a simple *'no-fault'* procedure. That expectation was patently in error, for, at that time, I knew nothing of the hellholes they call the American courts. But that was soon to change.

My personal sense of responsibility and fairness insists that, if there are two people who need to feed and there is only one apple to share, a dissection straight down the middle is the only evenhanded thing to do. Even a child could come to that simple conclusion. Prior to the Washington State Superior Court Case (number 00-3-02932-1), an amicable and fair 'separation agreement' was reached, and signed by both parties, for the division of assets and spousal maintenance in our marital dissolution. That legally binding agreement provided for a 50/50 split of all assets between husband and wife, and further allowed for a generous difference in award in favor of my wife, which constituted an upfront lump-sum amount in lieu of monthly maintenance payments.

The maintenance paid upfront resulted in an 'agreed' difference in asset distribution between the parties of: *35% to the husband and 65% of the estate to the wife.* In addition, an *'ante nuptial contract'* served as the default contract to safeguard each party's personal property. Both parties were fully capable and qualified to support themselves. There was a moral obligation upon both partners to be fair - and fairer to each party we could not have been in our signed and settled separation agreement. With that, Maureen was passed into her own care with love and a whisper of caution. The situation that was to follow was entirely of her own making and, for sure, it caused my heart to bleed.

That was the moment when we moved out of the arena of horse-trading and into the arena of what is right and what is wrong. That was the juncture where the greed of Maureen's callous lawyer entered into the milieu, casting aside the signed agreement between the parties and unashamedly taking the case to court in order to motivate a greater share for his client and, more importantly, *more fees for himself.* At that pivotal point the scales of justice lost their poise and tipped into immorality and criminality. A retrospective glance across that point of inflection, twenty-five years later, and the situation it created, provides acute insight into the potential major consequences, for good or for evil, of the seemingly innocuous decisions we make daily. A point to remember - always.

The judge presiding over the marital dissolution, Marywave Van Deren, at first fraudulently allocated 90% of the estate to Maureen, plus maintenance until I retired six years hence, despite both parties being able-bodied and amply qualified to work and to earn their keep. The token 10% portion of the estate allocated to me was later illegally *reduced to zero* by Judge Van Deren six months after the trial, with 100% of the assets going to Maureen, and nil to me. The inequitable judgment disregarded the legal pre-marital contract (which was filed as a deed in the country of our origin) and dishonestly set aside the equitable and signed settlement agreement reached between the parties, notwithstanding it being a *'no-fault'* divorce.

Two clear factors led to that unjust distribution of assets. Firstly, from the time Maureen's lawyer, Michael J. Turner, coerced her into dishonoring the settlement agreement (in his pursuit of lawyer's fees), they both kept up a steady barrage of fraudulent and perjurous statements throughout the court case. Secondly, for reasons of her own, the judge *entered the arena and,* in extreme prejudice against me, and fully aware of the perjury by Maureen and her attorney, exploited that perjury. In cunning deceit, Judge Marywave Van Deren added her own numerous fraudulent misrepresentations to conceal the facts and to cover her tracks, in order to motivate the grossly unfair, unwarranted, and *illegal* judgment.

CRIMES IN AND BY THE COURT

'Fraud' is defined as wrongful and criminal deception intended to result in personal financial gain or loss to another. It is the unlawful and intentional making of misrepresentations that causes actual prejudice or that is potentially prejudicial to another. Fraud is regarded as criminal in its essence and involves moral turpitude. It consists of false representations deliberately made with the intention of being acted upon, to the detriment of another, as was so evident in this case. The essence of fraud is that this intention is tainted with deceit.

In juxtaposition, *'misrepresentation'* is a willful perversion of the truth, deliberately made with the intent to deceive, resulting in the actual or potential prejudice to another. The misrepresentation can take place expressly or implicitly; is false in fact; is dishonest opinion or conduct; is a concealment of the truth or a half-truth, or the omission of facts or evidence. Statements made knowingly or without honest belief in their truth, made recklessly, careless whether they be true or false, fit this description.

Between the three conspiring parties in the court (Maureen, her attorney Michael Turner, and Judge Marywave Van Deren), 245 counts of perjury were identified and documented during the trial - 64 of them coming from the judge, giving rise to massive fraud. As exhibited in this case, fraud was the *'theft by false pretenses'* of legally held possessions and property through criminal deception. Those possessions and property were protected by the United States Constitution, by a binding settlement agreement, by an antenuptial contract, and by several Washington State laws. The three conspiring parties participated in that criminal deception with the same intent, namely: to take de jure (rightful) property and income

27

from one party, without lawful means, and to give it to another. In other words: to steal. Each was motivated by benefit and reasons of their own.

The fraudulent misrepresentations uttered by the three acting in collusion were known by them to be false, were material to the divorce case, and resulted directly in prejudice and enormous financial loss. I was left destitute, without home or furniture or household goods, with only my clothes and a very few (but not all) personal items, and with half my income going to Maureen as maintenance payments. She was also allocated the full share of my (401K) pension and my financial security plan (a financial plan for pilots in case of loss of flying medical certificate). That outcome was unjustified, was unfair, and in one malevolent sweep destroyed all that I had worked for during my life. Many years of acute financial hardship were to follow for me. Twenty-five years, as of the time of writing - and enduring.

The case was characterized by profound criminality committed by the three conspiring parties. Maureen violated several laws on a number of counts, including fraud and theft on three counts; perjury on 181 counts; false representation concerning title; conspiracy against rights and deprivation of rights; and burglary to steal documents, a crime to which she later confessed under oath. Maureen's attorney, Michael Turner, violated 11 laws on several counts, including fraud and theft, perjury, his oath of office, and conspiracy against rights. Judge Van Deren violated some 36 Washington State and federal laws on numerous counts, to arrive at her fraudulent judgment. Those breaches are enumerated herewith for illumination of the interested reader (RCW referring to the Revised Code of Washington):

> *Fraud - RCW 9, 9A (regarding Ante Nuptial Contract) and theft - RCW 9A.56.030; Fraud - RCW 9, 9A (regarding Settlement Contract) and theft -*

RCW 9A.56.030; Fraud - RCW 9, 9A (regarding Discovery Request) and theft - RCW 9A.56.030; Fraud- RCW 9, 9A (regarding Judge's Ruling) and theft - RCW 9A.56.030; Rendering criminal assistance - RCW 9A.76.080; False representation concerning title - RCW 9.38.020; Perjury and false swearing - Inconsistent statements -RCW 9A.72.050; Statements of what one does not know to be true - RCW 9A.72.080; False swearing - RCW 9A.72.040; Marital contract - RCW 26.09.070; Separate property of husband - RCW 26.16.010; Separation contract - RCW 26.09.070; Unfair distribution of assets - RCW 26.09.080; False report by public official - RCW 42.20.040; Failure of duty by public official - RCW 42.20.100; Official Misconduct - RCW 9A 80.010; Rights of Married Persons in General - RCW 26.16.150; Regarding Foreign Law - RCW5.44.050; False Representation - RCW 9.38; Intent to Defraud - RCW 10.58.040; Maintenance Orders - RCW 26.09.090; Payment of costs - RCW26.09.140; Perjury RCW 9.72; Theft - RCW 9A.56.030; Oath of Office - US Constitution; 14th Amendment, US Constitution; Article 3, Washington State Constitution; International Law of Contract; Changing of divorce decree; Fraud (regarding motion for relief) - RCW 9 and 9A; Perjury (regarding motion for relief) - RCW 9.7; Oath of Office (regarding motion for relief) - RCW 2.04.080; Failure of duty (regarding motion for relief) - RCW 42.20.100; Conspiracy against Rights, US Code, Title 18, Chapter 13, Section 241; Deprivation of Rights, US Code Title 18, Chapter 13, Section 242; Obstruction of Justice, 18 USC § 1505.

In an endeavor to prevent further offenses and to seek protection of the laws, criminal charges were filed with the courts, with state and local police and prosecutors, and with state officials. Grievances were tabled at the Washington State Bar Association and

Commission on Judicial Conduct. *No corrective action was taken.* The relevant authorities simply swept the criminal charges under the carpet and ignored the criminal offenses despite incontrovertible evidence thereof.

An appeal against the undeserved judgment was abandoned when a number of attorneys who were consulted all advised that there was little or no chance in the Washington State court system to have the judgment overturned. Judges are provided great latitude, they all agreed. However, the latitude to split assets in a marital dissolution may be one thing; the *latitude to break the law* is another matter entirely. Post-trial relief from the personal financial ruin which the dissolution generated was thereafter sought through some 13 separate motions (petitions) to the court, without success and without any softening of the court's malice.

Thus, the greed of a lawyer had neatly dovetailed with the vindictiveness of an ex-wife and had found their soul-mate in a malevolent female judge. Of morality, there was none. Of justice, there was none. It was hard to fathom that a person whom you address as *'your honor'* could act so dishonorably - a person whom the community looks up to, pays respect to, pays the salary of, and entrusts with the important task of providing justice and arbitration, and administering the laws. The motivation for Judge Van Deren's iniquitous actions is yet to be determined in full through investigation, but is strongly believed to be associated with campaign funds paid by Michael Turner to Judge Van Deren's public election campaigns. In returning the favor and settling the 'bribe', she was quite willing to prostitute herself and to break the laws. The Judge's rationale is easy to understand: because she could - with impunity.

Thus ended the trial in the Washington State kangaroo court in the matter of Keyter versus Keyter. Those who have experienced injustice in one form or another know the distress and suffering it leaves upon the human psyche. Nevertheless, in a short time it became clear to me that I would remain the victim only if I acquiesced to the injustice perpetrated by the Washington State Superior Court; and if I failed to rise up against the iniquity. It was a simple choice to make in a common dilemma so eloquently phrased by Shakespeare: *"Whether 'tis nobler in the mind to suffer the slings and arrows of outrageous fortune; or to take arms against a sea of troubles, and by opposing, end them?"*

The judgment in the marital dissolution needed to be corrected. Stolen money and stolen property needed to be returned to their rightful owner. The thieves needed to be apprehended and punished for their misdeeds so as to prevent future occurrences. The 'contempt of court' *demonstrated by the judge, for the rules and laws of the court, for her oath of office, and for due process of law,* needed to be addressed.

I thought to myself that for her premeditated injustice, vindictiveness, callousness, nay, lawlessness, Judge Marywave Van Deren deserved to be hauled into court. But wait a minute, there is an oxymoron, a contradiction in terms. She was already in court, having sworn before God and the nation to do right. The entire government establishment is rightly or wrongly geared to protect judges from any negative consequences of their actions, whether those actions were legal or illegal. What to do then? Lie down and die or take the US Constitution at face value as it proclaims 'equal protection of the laws' for all United States denizens. Thus, I pondered the weighty question: What will it take to bring a judge to justice? What indeed?

The answer to that puzzling question lies in the pages ahead. It is not as simple or easy as one would rationally want to think.

CIVIL CLAIM FOR DAMAGES

In an effort to recoup some of the disastrous losses sustained and to address the multiple crimes of burglary, perjury, fraud, theft, and common law violations committed in the divorce case, a civil complaint for damages was filed against my ex-wife in the Washington State Superior Court, Pierce County (case no. 04-2-13977-1). Amongst her co-conspirators named in the criminal charges filed together with that civil case were her attorney, Michael J. Turner, and Judge Marywave Van Deren. In violation of court rules of procedure, the presiding judge in the damages suit, Sergio Armijo, a contemporary of Judge Van Deren, dismissed the case without delineating a reason and without addressing the criminal charges filed in the case – and without giving me a chance to speak to make my case as pro se litigant, acting on my own behalf. My thoughts on Judge Sergio Armijo, were: "Nice man, wrong principles, corrupted by the system. Not so nice a system, good principles, corrupted by man".

An appeal was thus filed in the Washington State Court of Appeals (case number 2737-6-II). The Appeals Court Judges were notified of the crimes that had not been investigated or prosecuted and were requested to tend to the criminal allegations according to their judicial duties and the court rules. However, the Appeals Court judges similarly chose to neglect those duties to the state and to the public, and instead acted to protect the troika of conspirators from prosecution – likely, because Judge Van Deren had been promoted up to the appeals court by that stage and was a colleague on the bench. The Court of Appeals similarly dismissed the civil claim in contravention of several laws and court rules.

By now, there were several judges who had demonstrated their willingness to violate the laws in order to protect a malfeasant colleague. It is just so easy. Recourse to the Washington State Supreme Court was not possible as there was no prospect of a fair hearing in that court. That was demonstrated when the State Supreme Court Justices had earlier been presented with the criminal charges filed in the lower court and had determinedly ignored the criminal conspiracy underlying the civil case, without investigation into any of the crimes. Furthermore, the State Supreme Court Justices had fraudulently forwarded money to Maureen, which had been *placed in their trust*. Yes, the Washington Supreme Court Justices had committed fraud with money held in trust.

Accordingly, an appeal was filed in the United States Supreme Court. The Petition for Certiorari was accompanied by the *'Dossier of Crimes'* which document described to the US Supreme Court, the crimes committed by Maureen Keyter, attorney Michael J. Turner, Judge Van Deren, together with several state officials who had a duty to investigate and/or prosecute but who had instead illegally assisted the trio to escape punishment. These cases were fought pro se, without the assistance of a lawyer. No lawyer was willing to take on a case against their own colleagues or known judges. And, of course, I had no money to hire an attorney.

In an effort to keep the account of official wrongdoing, which was detailed in the *'Dossier of Crimes'*, out of court, the US Supreme Court Clerk, acting on behalf of the justices, refused to file the certiorari and supporting criminal dossier on fraudulent grounds. The false argument employed by the US Supreme Court Clerk stated that the petition was filed *too late*. In reality and in truth, the court (and I) were in possession of documentation stamped with the filing date, which physically verified that the petition was filed within the proper time. Such blatant dishonesty by the US Supreme Court Clerk was only the beginning of an unbroken procession of deceitfulness still to be experienced. Thus, the stage was set for the widespread obstruction of justice associated with this case that was to follow in the courts and in the government departments of the United States 'state and federal government'.

Some early illustrations of that foiling of justice by government officials in Washington State are presented below. The few incidents mentioned here are commonplace examples of official misconduct, seemingly inconsequential in nature until it is realized where that misconduct can lead when such 'trivial' incidents are ignored and allowed to accumulate. Insignificant as they appear to be, they are indicative of a very broad pattern of dereliction of duty when it comes to addressing official misconduct within the United States Government.

SYSTEMIC FAILURE TO PROVIDE PROTECTION OF THE LAWS

City of Gig Harbor Police

The Police Department of the City of Gig Harbor, where I live, prides itself on providing high-quality service to the community. The Gig Harbor Police claim to understand the importance of what they do and claim to have a strong sense of duty and pride when it comes to protecting and serving the people in their community. Their stated mission is to continually provide exceptional law enforcement services to their citizens. To demonstrate their commitment to their profession, they ostensibly subscribe to values and beliefs of integrity, respect, trust, honesty, and compassion; and publicly undertake to live up to their commitments. Yet, in addressing this case, their deeds fell far short of their hollow words when measured against the practical application of their imperative law enforcement duties.

On January 21, 2003, attempts were made to file a criminal complaint in the case at the offices of the Gig Harbor Police Department. The charges were presented in the *'Dossier of Crimes'* and included the criminal offenses of burglary, perjury, fraud, and theft, which were committed in Gig Harbor during the marital dissolution proceedings. Allegations against public officials who had sanctioned the criminal offenses were also included in the well-documented charges and included official misconduct, rendering criminal assistance, failure of duty by public officials, false statements by an official, and more.

From the outset of the meeting with the police, the officer who served me, Officer Entze, was dismissive and unaccommodating in his demeanor. He flatly rejected the dossier, stating that 'there was another person like me in Gig Harbor who was *bothering* the Police Department'. He also stated categorically that he would not file the criminal charges. Officer Entze was requested to hand the dossier to the Police Chief. He scoffed that he would not do so, turned, and just walked away whilst leaving the somewhat confidential 'Dossier of Crimes' behind lying in a public antechamber.

Gig Harbor Police simply refused to file the charges against public officials. No investigations were initiated by the Gig Harbor Police into any of the offenses reported to them in the 'Dossier of Crimes', including the later charges of murder, and attempted murder of a witness. No 'protection of the laws' was provided, as the US Constitution demands. There can be no pride or integrity, or respect, or trust, or compassion, as claimed by the Gig Harbor Police, in the willful failure of *essential* police duty. The City Police denied fundamental rights to a complainant and thereby transgressed the laws on official misconduct, rendering criminal assistance, failure of duty by a public official, and so on.

City of Tacoma Police

On January 17, 2003, I met with the Assistant Chief of Tacoma Police, Catherine Woodard, at the Tacoma Police Offices in Tacoma, Washington. I informed her that I intended to file criminal charges contained in the 'Dossier of Crimes' with the Tacoma Police. During the lengthy discussions that followed, Assistant Police Chief Woodard made intense attempts to drive me away.

Only after persuasive demands by me to allow the filing of the charges did she finally condescend to the request and arranged for a police officer to take my statement and the dossier. Almost a month went by before I received a telephone message on February 13, 2003, from Sergeant Odey of the Tacoma Police Department. The Tacoma Police disposed of the criminal charges with the following communication:

> *"As you previously already know, Gig Harbor Police Department, Pierce County Prosecuting Attorney's Office, and the Governor's Office, all have explained to you that there's nothing that they can do, I'm just letting you know as well that the Tacoma Police Department is of the same opinion, there's nothing that we can do for you, and at this point we're going to close the case, there's nothing we can do for you, as I said sir. If you have any questions, you're free to call me back. The area code is 253 591 5992, but I'll tell you just the same, at this point your matter is closed and there's nothing we are going to be able to do to help you out, sir, thanks, bye".*

The Tacoma Police refused to investigate the multiple and obvious offenses committed by public officials and reported to them in the 'Dossier of Crimes', and conspired with the other law enforcement agencies to deny the constitutional right to protection of the laws.

Pierce County Sheriff

In a letter dated February 13, 2003, Pierce County Sheriff Paul Pastor was requested to act to prevent impending criminal acts in the ongoing marital dissolution case. The letter to the Sheriff described the circumstances surrounding imminent offenses by Judge Marywave Van Deren in one of her court proceedings.

A hearing was set for relief in the judgment, and the original judge, Marywave Van Deren, was to hear the motion. However, Judge Van Deren was a party to the fraud that formed the basis of the motion for relief. Washington State Law debarred her from presiding in the hearing since she was a party to the action, had a direct interest in the action, and had no capability to offer a fair and impartial hearing. She had been requested to recuse herself on several occasions through 'affidavits of prejudice', but had refused to excuse herself from the case - thus keeping her foul little secret, *secret*. Proceeding with the hearing would have violated the law (RCW2.28.030), which states that a judicial officer shall not act as such in a case in which he/she is a party to or has an interest in.

Knowing of the impending crime by the judge, the Sheriff replied that they would not be taking any action regarding the impending crime. As a result, the statute RCW2.28.030 *was* violated by the judge and the crime was committed (followed by many others besides) *with* the Sheriff's knowledge, sanction, and complicity therein, in blatant denial of the victim's right to protection of the laws.

Washington State Patrol

Circa February 5, 2003, the 'Dossier of Crimes' was first filed with the Washington State Patrol. The 850-page dossier of that date provided details and facts relating to 169 criminal offenses committed by 27 officials of Washington State Government, and two others. The crimes were of a serious nature and included charges of burglary, perjury, fraud, theft, official misconduct, rendering criminal assistance, and tampering with evidence.

On February 13, 2003, I met with Washington State Patrol Officers Lt. Lameroux, Lt. Davis, and Sergeant Dahl in the state capitol of Olympia, concerning the allegations contained in the dossier. During the discussions, the Patrolmen made false statements regarding their law enforcement duties, denying their public responsibility and falsely stating that it was not their duty to investigate those crimes. They said that they did not want the dossier and requested that I leave and take the dossier with me. They threatened that they would dispose of the evidence contained in the dossier if I didn't leave and take it with me.

When I refused to accept the return of the dossier, stating that the criminal allegations remained filed with them, Lt. Davis got very angry and quickly stepped up close to me in a physically threatening manner, in an attempt to intimidate me to take the dossier and to remove evidence of official wrongdoing from their premises. The malevolence exhibited by Lt. Davis proved to be only the first sign of the physical aggression that was to follow in official resistance to my pursuit of justice. He stated furiously and loudly: *"You mean you're not going to take the files back?"* I reiterated my point of view in the affirmative. After this threatening episode and considerably heated debate, the Patrol Officers, upon my insistence, recognizing that they were in the wrong, eventually conceded to look into and investigate the criminal charges.

Six weeks passed after our meeting without investigations into official wrongdoing being initiated. I then called for a further meeting, and during that next meeting on March 28, 2003, Lt. Davis and Sergeant Dahl informed me categorically that they *had not* investigated and that the Washington State Patrol *would not investigate*, demonstrating willful dereliction of their law enforcement duties.

Prosecutors and the Bar Association

Pierce County Prosecutors and the Washington State Bar Association, who were subsequently requested to address the criminal conduct of officials and a lawyer, were unperturbed and derelict in *their* duty to stop the ongoing crimes. They simply swept the allegations under the carpet and failed to take peremptory action. The reason given at the time was that it was not in the general public's interest to prosecute.

Let us then measure if their statement was indeed true in what follows in this narrative – that it was not in the general public's best interest to prosecute the little criminal endeavor. Incisive action could have stopped any proliferation of this matter in its tracks. Let us see whether assisting law-breaking officials in order to hinder and prevent their apprehension, trial, and punishment, is indeed in the general public's best interest. *But of course, it is not. How can it be?*

These initiating incidents formed the foundation of what proliferated into a widespread criminal enterprise to foil the application of the laws upon malfeasant government and industry officials, by any means available – including violence. All I did was to relentlessly pursue justice as I identify with that elusive concept and the law compelled me to do; and then to meticulously document the unfolding saga in the Dossier of Crimes, as the criminality perpetrated by government officials propagated.

Chapter 3
Development of the Case

In this matter, the cover-up of crimes committed by law-breaking government officials was absolute. Yet, my case is not unique, but merely a reflection of what happens across the United States, day after day, in court upon court, and in administration upon administration - city, county, state, and federal... However, providing protection to criminals is a crime, and failure to identify criminals is a crime.

Extract From Chapter 3.

EXHAUSTIVE MEASURES

Following the offenses committed in the marital dissolution case and in the cover-up by Washington State officials, exhaustive measures were taken to seek justice and restitution for the initial crimes and to animate the law enforcement process to deal with a deluge of subsequent crimes amongst government officials. All without success. In ensuing efforts over the next 25 years, I unrelentingly made in excess of 14,000 written requests to some 15,000 US officials (addressed as individuals and/or as groups) - from the most junior police officer to the highest authorities in the land. With every letter, I thought: *this one* will reach a heart and change a mind. But I woefully underestimated the darkness I had to penetrate.

The numerous written requests for protection and enforcement of the laws were directed to officials from 627 different, but pertinent, institutions of government tasked with law and order. Those institutions are listed in *Appendix 1*. The institutions include state and federal police departments, state and federal prosecutors, state and federal judges, judiciary committees, judicial conduct commissions, ethics boards, bar associations, state and federal attorneys general, and state and federal legislators and executives.

Requests for protection and enforcement of the laws were also addressed to the courts. In all, 62 court cases have been filed in state and federal courts, including the United States Supreme Court. The 62 court cases are listed in *Appendix 2*. In the early cases, I sought redress for the illegal seizure of de jure property, and in all cases, I sought the protection of the law against *ongoing* harmful criminal acts, through some 352 proceedings in the 62 court cases. Those rights are ostensibly secured to every United States citizen, including me, through the promise of the 5th and 14th Amendments of the US Constitution. In all cases, that constitutional right was denied. The cases were eventually combined into a single petition to the US Supreme Court for "Due Process and Protection of the Laws". The case remains active and pending, but suppressed by the Chief Justice and Associate Justices.

Apart from the initial marital dissolution case, all 61 subsequent court cases were fought 'pro se (representing myself in court) without the benefit of a lawyer. At first, I could not find a lawyer who was prepared to tackle official misconduct in the marital dissolution case, and for all 61 later cases, I did not have the finances available to hire an attorney. Although my life's devotion was in matters aviation, and although I held a strong preference to live in harmony with all in my environment, sometimes fate brings one in contact with injustice and obliges one to oppose the wickedness. Sometimes one has to fight resolutely for that which one knows to be right - after due consideration of what is right. Consequently, it was necessary for me to study the technicalities and the vagaries of the law. The unexpected and inexplicable conflicts in American jurisprudence caught me by surprise. The arbitrary nature of the application of the laws leaves the layman agape.

Corruption in Government and Judiciary

The exhaustive measures taken in pursuit of justice are also reflected in 240 criminal complaints detailed in the *'Dossier of Crimes'*. These complaints are meticulously documented and detail the official wrongdoing throughout the proliferation. *Prima facie* evidence of the crimes committed by government officers was provided to the authorities and to the courts on numerous occasions, and in each of the 62 court cases. Each official or judge to whom the criminal complaints were presented had the capacity, the authority, and a statutory duty, to address the offenses. However, *every official and judge* willfully failed to perform their legal duties to investigate and prosecute, or administer the law, or to initiate the same.

In *every instance*, my appeals for justice and protection of the laws were rejected with callous indifference, in favor of a cover-up of government and judicial wrongdoing, and in protecting the law-breaking officials from prosecution. In *every instance*, my rights, ostensibly protected by the Constitution and the laws, were scorned, and my appeals to the authorities were rejected with contempt, many times over. In *every one* of the 62 interrelated court cases (which addressed different groupings in, or different aspects of, the criminal conspiracy), the courts not only failed to deal with the deluge of crimes presented to the courts, but actively suppressed the shameful issue.

From the outset, I wish to be clear with my use of the word *'conspiracy'*. I do not use it as in the pop culture term "conspiracy theories". Rather, my usage and meaning are as per the legal definition given in statute 18USC371, which states:

> ***Conspiracy to Commit Offense:*** *If two or more persons conspire either to commit any offense against the United States, or to defraud the United States, or any agency thereof in any manner or for*

any purpose, and one or more of such persons do any
act to effect the object of the conspiracy, each shall
be fined under this title or imprisoned not more than
five years, or both.

I trust this clarification will suffice throughout this narrative.

In this matter, the cover-up of crimes committed by law-breaking officials has been absolute. Yet, my case is not unique, but merely a reflection of what happens across the United States, day after day, in court after court, and in administration after administration - city, county, state, and federal. In practice, government officers who break the law at the expense of the common man are unassailable. But, to ignore crime and injustice is to condone it; and to condone crime and injustice is to perpetuate it; and to perpetuate crime and injustice is to be party thereto. The law affirms that providing protection to criminals is a crime ... and failing to identify them is a crime. And so began my odyssey.

Misprision / Obstruction / Conspiracy

The United States Code statute on misprision of felony (18USC4), amongst many other statutes, obligates officials to deal with felonies and other crimes which have been brought to their attention:

Misprision of Felony, statute 18USC4: *"Whoever,*
having knowledge of the actual commission of a
felony cognizable by a court of the United States,
conceals and does not as soon as possible make
known the same to some judge or other person in
civil or military authority under the United States
shall be fined under this title or imprisoned not more
than three years, or both".

In this matter, officials should either have initiated the investigations or prosecutions on their own volition, or alternatively, they should have passed the information on to somebody in authority who would have addressed the crimes. Each official involved failed to perform that legal duty and violated the statutes on misprision of felony, as well as the legal requirement to report or investigate crimes involving government officers. (See statute 28USC535). (For the interested reader, a presentation of statutes frequently quoted in this account appears in *Appendix 4 – Extract of Statutes.* In addition, some statutes are presented in the text or as footnote).

> ***United States Code, 28USC535 (b)*** *(Reporting of offenses of government officers) states: "Any information, allegation, or complaint received in a department or agency of the executive branch of the government relating to violations of title 18 involving Government Officers and employees shall be expeditiously reported to the Attorney General by the head of the department or agency, unless (1) the responsibility to perform an investigation with respect thereto is specifically assigned otherwise by another provision of the law".*

By the same reasoning, each official who failed their duty, obstructed and impeded the due and proper administration of the law and violated the statute on obstruction of justice. (18USC1505[1]). Every official was thus a principal offender due to his own substantive violations of law. By their criminal conduct, each official, knowing that criminal offenses against the United States had been committed, assisted other offenders in order to hinder or prevent their apprehension, trial, and punishment, and became an

---

[1] 18USC1505 - Obstruction of Justice
In relevant part: "Whoever corruptly… influences, obstructs, or impedes … the due and proper administration of the law under which any pending proceeding is being had before any department or agency of the United States … shall be fined under this title, or imprisoned not more than 5 years…"

accessory after the fact to the crimes of the initial and later offenders. (18USC3[2]).

Each official also furthered the aims of the broad-ranging conspiracy to commit offenses, and the conspiracy against rights, and joined in with the objectives to obstruct the course of justice. As a result, each official became a co-conspirator in the crimes of the other offenders. Thus, a staggering number of crimes have been documented according to the dictates of the law.

Yet, the initial crimes cannot be disputed. The laws are clear and have not been obeyed. Unimpeachable evidence of the numerous felonies is provided in the *'Dossier of Crimes'*. For instance, burglary has been confessed to under oath by the perpetrator; perjury is clearly discernible in conflicting statements under oath; a judge acknowledges in court transcripts the illegal removal of crucial court evidence - tampering with evidence.

Other serious crimes associated with this criminal conspiracy include: conspiracy against rights; conspiracy to commit an offense; tampering with a witness; retaliation against a witness with intent to kill; and attempted kidnapping with intent to kill.

Details and *prima facie* evidence of the crimes committed by the approximately 15,000 conspirators from the United States (as recorded in the *'Dossier of Crimes'*), have been presented to government authorities and the courts on some 700 occasions. At the time of writing, no investigations or prosecutions have been conducted on any of these known felonies. The undeniable evidence has also been presented to the US Supreme Court on some 34

---

[2] 18USC3 – Accessory after the Fact: Whoever, knowing that an offense against the United States has been committed, receives, relieves, comforts or assists the offender in order to hinder or prevent his apprehension, trial or punishment, is an accessory after the fact.

occasions, but on each occasion the conspirators removed those criminal dossiers from the Supreme Court Records.

Perversion of justice can have no clearer and more debased an example. The 15,000 or so United States government officials involved in the criminal conspiracy hold pertinent positions in state and federal governments. Amongst state officials are police chiefs, prosecutors, attorneys general, secretaries of state, legislators, and governors. Also included are state judges from all levels of state courts. Amongst federal government officials involved in the criminal conspiracy are FBI agents, US Attorneys General and US Attorneys, federal judges, including the Chief Justice, generals and admirals of the Armed Forces, and consecutive Presidents and Vice Presidents of the United States.

APPEAL TO CONGRESS

Since February 2003, and in every intervening year until publication in 2025, Congressmen have been kept informed of the escalating criminal endeavor within the government and requested to exercise their oversight duties concerning the corruption in the courts and in the Administration. Amongst my 330 letters over the intervening years to Congressmen and to several congressional committees (including the judicial committees of both House and Senate), on October 3, 2004, I wrote to all United States Senators:

Dear Senator,

Re: Your Obligations Regarding Crimes
Committed by Government Officials

Crimes have been committed against the United States by officials of the Federal and State governments. You have been informed that, although these crimes were presented to the proper authorities, none of the crimes involving officials have been investigated or prosecuted. Evidence was presented to you of specific crimes, together with information on the location of a more inclusive "Dossier of Crimes" which fully describes this affair. The dossier details 1.6 million crimes by corrupt officials bent on obstructing the conduct of justice.

As a person in authority under the United States, you have been requested to see to the administration of the laws regarding these crimes. To date, your statutory duties have not been accomplished as the wave of criminality in government continues unabated. In the event that the impact of this tyranny upon the populace has escaped you, I include for your sober attention my "Statement to Congress" of July 15, 2004, which was made available to you at either of the Committees on the Judiciary.

Kindly ensure the termination of this ongoing conspiracy to obstruct the normal course of justice and take care that the laws of the United States are applied fairly to the common people and to government officials alike. I remain disposed to furnish you with any additional information you may need to accomplish your obligations to the people of this nation. Sincerely...

There was no investigation or any other reaction from Senators to the filing of comprehensive information on the escalating criminal conspiracy within the government and the courts of the United States. It was simply of no concern to them. Their re-election to Congress was not threatened by it.

THE CASE AGAINST 230 GOVERNMENT OFFICERS

On December 20, 2004, a civil suit was filed in the US District Court of Western Washington against 230 malfeasant government officers involved in the matter.

Anthony P. Keyter vs. 230 Government Officers

U.S. District Court, Western District of Washington, Case #3:04cv5867. The case sought to redress harm and loss caused as a consequence of their dereliction of statutory duties, violation of criminal statutes, and violations of the common law rights of a citizen. Criminal charges were filed against 230 government officers for violation of the following laws as principal perpetrators or accessories after the fact:

1. 14th Amendment, US Constitution
2. Article 3, Washington State Constitution
3. Conspiracy against Rights, 18 USC § 241
4. Conspiracy to commit an offense, USC 18 § 371
5. Deprivation of Rights, 18 USC § 242
6. Misprision of Felony, 18 USC § 4
7. Obstruction of Justice, 18 USC § 1505
8. Accessory after the Fact 18 USC § 3 to initial crimes:
9. Burglary - RCW 9A.52.025
10. Perjury - RCW 9.72
11. Fraud - RCW 9, 9A
12. Intent to Defraud - RCW 10.58.040
13. Theft - RCW 9A.56.030
14. Tampering with Physical Evidence - RCW 9A.72.150
15. Rendering criminal assistance - RCW 9A.76.080
16. Failure of duty by public official - RCW 42.20.100
17. Failure of judge to recuse - 2.28.030
18. Official Misconduct - RCW 9A 80.010
19. False report by public official - RCW 42.20.040
20. Oath of Office
21. Legislative Declaration - RCW 42. 52. 900
22. Perjury - RCW 9A.72
23. Perjury - Inconsistent statements -RCW 9A.72.050
24. Statements of what one does not know to be true - RCW 9A.72.080
25. False swearing - RCW 9A.72.040
26. False Representation - RCW 9.38
27. False representation concerning title - RCW 9.38.020

28. Separate property of husband - RCW 26.16.010
29. Separation contract - RCW 26.09.070
30. Unfair distribution of assets - RCW 26.09.080
31. Rights of Married Persons in General - RCW 26.16.150
32. Regarding Foreign Law - RCW5.44.050
33. International Law of Contract
34. Maintenance Orders - RCW 26.09.090
35. Payment of Costs - RCW 26.09.140
36. Changing of divorce decree after trial

The court was also petitioned to compel the delinquent government officers to perform their duties to the American public and, in particular, to me as plaintiff. Amongst the defendants were high-level Washington State officials: legislators, four police chiefs and several police officers, county prosecutors, the incumbent and past Attorneys General, the Secretary of State, and the incumbent and former Governors of Washington State. Also implicated in the case and included as defendants were the Washington State Chief Justice and several other judges from the Washington State Courts.

The case was characterized by a significant level of criminality by judicial officers, defense attorneys, and defendants alike, in order to shield the 230 malfeasant government officials from criminal and civil prosecution. For example, the defendants in the case committed numerous counts of perjury in their efforts to have the case prematurely dismissed before trial. Furthermore, defense attorneys for Washington State officials (Attorney General Christine Gregoire, her successor Rob McKenna, and their Assistants), acted ultra vires and in conflict of interest. They were compelled by law to prosecute the defendants for crimes committed, yet defended the malfeasant officers in this civil suit based on those very same crimes - a conflict untenable in law.

Further criminal charges were filed with the court against the defendants and their attorneys for that perjury and other violations associated with the conduct of the case in the District Court. Judge

R.J. Bryan, who initially presided, was removed from the case following a motion to disqualify him for failing *his* judicial duties and failing to address the crimes perpetrated by defendants. He was replaced by an out-of-state judge from Montana, Judge Charles C. Lovell. However, Judge Lovell rendered criminal assistance to the accused officials on a grand scale, helping them escape justice by:

- o Allowing the defendants' blatant perjury to stand in Court.
- o Allowing motions submitted illegally to be heard (and granted) by the Court.
- o Allowing defendants' counsel, who were acting ultra vires and in conflict of interest, to continue their unlawful representation.
- o Failing to compel defendants, who were in breach of the law, to obey the law and to perform their duty to the United States of America and to society.
- o Failing to perform his legally mandated duties in terms of the criminal statutes 18USC3041, 18USC3046, and 18USC3060 – namely, issuing a warrant of arrest and convening a preliminary hearing to determine whether there was probable cause to believe that offenses had been committed against the United States.

An additional motion was submitted to disqualify Judge Lovell for the above-mentioned irregularities. Judge Lovell illegally ruled on his own disqualification, finding himself innocent of any prejudice or wrongdoing, and dismissed the case without addressing the underlying crimes. In his judgment, Judge Lovell perjuriously and fraudulently misrepresented the facts of the case on 47 counts in order to provide legal respectability to the illegal dismissal. The counts were documented. He unambiguously demonstrated how simple and easy it is for a judge to violate the laws with impunity.

The case was presented on appeal to the 9th Circuit Court of Appeals, in Case # 05- 35717. Its sojourn through the 9th Circuit was likewise marred by an all-out effort by 9th Circuit judges to protect the malfeasant officers from criminal and civil prosecution. The 9th Circuit judges irregularly denied all motions and injunctions presented; they criminally neglected to address the deluge of criminal offenses filed with the court pursuant to statute 18USC4; they affirmed the illegal District Court ruling despite knowing about the blatant misrepresentations by the District Judge; and they dismissed the appeal case. In a further endeavor to find restitution and to have the criminal charges addressed by the judicial system, the case against the 230 malfeasant government officers was appealed in the United States Supreme Court on August 14, 2006, in Case # 06-284.

The Supreme Court was also requested to compel the malfeasant officials to obey the laws which they were in breach of, and to require those officials to perform their legal duty to the United States and to society. Once more, *the Supreme Court* was put to the test to see whether the highest judicial authority in America would bring justice to bear upon law-breaking officials, or whether the Supreme Court Justices would likewise join in with the illegal protection of the 230 criminal, but unassailable, government officials.

Once more, *the institutions of the American nation* were put to the test to see whether the institutions could or would deal with an insurrection against the laws and authority of the United States - an insurrection perpetrated by its senior officials. Both the Supreme Court and the nation's law-enforcement institutions failed spectacularly. On October 27, 2006, the Supreme Court Justices fraudulently and illegally denied the case. They fraudulently decided the case without the benefit of four pertinent documents, which had been corruptly removed from the case records beforehand, *with their knowledge.* I told them. The actions of the Supreme Court Justices were illegal on several grounds, including failure to perform peremptory judicial duties to tend to the underlying crimes committed by the government defendants.

Criminal charges were filed *in the case* against the US Supreme Court Justices for violating several criminal statutes, as per my duty under statute 18USC4. These charges, together with another round of criminal complaints against the defendants, were also thieved from court records. In broad daylight. A petition for rehearing was filed on November 16, 2006, in order to address the theft of court records and other offenses and to secure due process of law. However, the Justices denied the petition despite having no legal capacity to rule on the case because of their own direct involvement in the profound criminal misconduct in the case.

As demonstrated in every phase of this matter, the lawlessness amongst state and federal officials runs deep. The assistance rendered to one another to escape prosecution is absolute. The malfeasant officers involved are the very officials entrusted to enact the laws, to enforce the laws, and to administer the laws. They are the governors, legislators, policemen, prosecutors, and judges - in whom we have readily placed our trust and welfare. With this impasse, the fatal flaws in the government and judicial system of the United States stand acutely exposed.

IN CONFLICT WITH OUR PATRIOTISM

As a patriotic people, we like to believe that we live in the best country in the world. We like to believe in the oft-quoted notion of 'American exceptionalism'. Like naïve children, we want and need to believe in our government; we want to believe in our leaders. We don't like to see all that we have faith in criticized and torn down. We need our heroes. We need them to be just and honest and selfless, serving the American people and the common good to the very highest they are capable of. After all, they took an oath before God and the nation to do exactly that. We need them to be exceptional people in the performance of their tasks *and* in their daily lives.

One would like to believe that the rhetoric of our leaders is truthful, is candid: that we are indeed a land of laws, as they claim, where the rule of law is absolute; where freedom from government tyranny holds sway. We cherish our 'freedom', sing songs about our freedom, flaunt it to the rest of the world. Any emerging evidence that counters these deep-seated beliefs and norms leaves us perplexed, even angry, and is usually discarded without intellectual investigation lest we upset our happy, but illusory, existence. These traits portray deep-rooted human nature. What a let-down it would be if we in fact found our leaders to be no different than the common man, with the same human frailties and shortcomings as we all have.

Yet, here, before my astonished eyes, a very different scenario was starting to emerge. A picture of our national institutions that few of us would dare to look at or admit to – a picture even fewer would have the proclivity to tackle head-on in an effort to rectify. This offensive reflection of the nation which was emerging out of the murk of my personal ordeal was totally incongruent with the idea of a benign country holding world leadership in all things important to right living: human rights, human dignity, justice and fairness, freedom from oppression, and holding the high ground concerning morality.

Sadly, at this stage of my odyssey, I had not seen the worst of it yet - not by a long way. The worst was yet to come!

Chapter 4
President Bush Supreme Court Conspiracy

"The role of the courts has been one of considerable corruption, manipulation, and politics in this matter presented to you. Your resolute action will be required to lay the foundations of a more just, equitable, and caring mechanism for the resolution of human conflict."

Extract from Chapter 4.

APPEALS TO PRESIDENT BUSH

When all the available remedies had been exhausted through the normal avenues of justice and I nevertheless failed to animate the United States legal system to deal with the harmful criminal offenses of government officials, I addressed myself to President George W. Bush with the request that he see to the faithful execution of the laws in terms of his constitutional duties, viz: *"The President ... shall take care that the laws be faithfully executed"*. (US Constitution, Article II, Section 3).

Through 87 letters and the Dossier of Crimes, President Bush was informed of the mounting subversive and criminal conspiracy by government officials and of the large-scale breakdown in the faithful execution of the laws of the United States. The President was informed that all evidence and investigation of their crimes had been corruptly suppressed and that an illegal cover-up of a large parcel of criminal offenses had taken place. He was provided with all the necessary evidence in order that he might take the appropriate corrective action regarding the faithful execution of the laws.

President Bush Supreme Court Conspiracy

Amongst the 87 written appeals to President Bush for protection of the laws, at the beginning of that process, on September 2, 2003, I wrote:

Dear President Bush,

Re: Request for Presidential Action
in the faithful execution of the laws

During my recent divorce case, the presiding judge violated dozens of laws and illegally seized my entire estate from me.
The taking of property without lawful means is theft. That theft by a high official acting on behalf of the government was brought to the attention of 195 Officers of Washington State, all of whom had a responsibility to investigate and/or prosecute, or to initiate investigation and prosecution of the malfeasance and crimes. None of these officers performed their legal duty in regard to this case, but instead chose to willfully withhold the administration of justice and to provide protection to the malfeasant officer.
Providing protection to a criminal is a crime. The offenses of state officers thus implicated were then presented to the following divisions within the US Department of Justice: the FBI in Seattle, the US Attorney in Seattle, the Assistant Attorney General, Criminal Division, and the Assistant Attorney General, Civil Rights Division. Attorney General Ashcroft was also informed. None of these federal officers performed their duty to ensure that the multiple and unmistakable crimes against me were investigated and prosecuted, nor saw to it that property illegally seized from me was returned to me.
I provide for your information the "Dossier of Crimes," which was previously sent to each of these divisions, which details the crimes committed and demonstrates unequivocally the defeat of justice. My

prior correspondence and requests to you on this topic are also included for your aide memoire. This tyranny and aberration of good government must not be allowed to continue with your knowledge and consent. Ultimately, the responsibility to see to the proper administration of justice pertaining to this case lies with the President of the United States. I am therefore requesting that you take care that the laws of this country are faithfully executed. Sincerely....

DERELICTION OF DUTY AND THE CASE AGAINST BUSH

Despite his peremptory duties under the Constitution and the criminal statutes, and despite the numerous requests over several years to perform that duty, President Bush willfully failed to take any action at all, but instead elected to join in the cover-up of the growing criminal endeavor within the government. His willful dereliction of Presidential duty 'to take care that the laws were faithfully executed', complemented and abetted the actions of the malfeasant government officials:

President Bush joined with and furthered the aims of the scheme against the rights to ownership of rightful property, due process, and protection of the laws - in violation of the criminal statute 18USC241[3] – Conspiracy against Rights.

- o The President's denial of those rights, by failing to uphold constitutional rights when he had an express duty under the

---

[3] 18USC241 - Conspiracy against Rights: In relevant part: "If two or more persons conspire to ...oppress...any person in any State...in the free exercise or enjoyment of any right or privilege secured to him by the Constitution or laws of the United States...they shall be fined under this title or imprisoned not more than ten years".

circumstances of this case, further violated the criminal statute 18USC242[4] – deprivation of rights.

- o In suppressing and covering up the crimes of government officials, instead of addressing them through investigation and prosecution by the Department of Justice, President Bush obstructed justice in violation of statute 18USC1505.

- o Knowing that offenses against the United States had been committed, and assisting the offenders in order to hinder and prevent their apprehension, trial, and punishment, rendered the President an accessory after the fact to the offenses of the lawbreaking officials, in violation of 18USC3.

(As a reminder to the reader, an extract of statutes is presented in *Appendix 4*).

The President's sanction of the subversive conspiracy within the government and the courts placed him directly in breach of the Constitution, the criminal statutes, and the common law duties of every citizen. As a consequence, on November 24, 2003, a civil suit was filed against President Bush in the US District Court, DC (case number 03-cv-2496), for ongoing harm caused directly by his dereliction of duty. The case further sought a court order to compel President Bush to obey the law and the Constitution, and to initiate investigation and prosecution of the offenses, or to see to the same.

The President's response to the lawsuit was to wrongfully employ the machinery of state to thwart the normal course of justice in the case and to evade civil (and criminal) culpability by illegal

---

[4] 18USC242 - Deprivation of Rights: In relevant part: "Whoever, under color of law.... willfully subjects any person in any State... to the deprivation of any rights... secured by the Constitution or laws of the United States, ... shall be fined under this title or imprisoned not more than one year".

means. The President knew that if due process was administered, as to ordinary citizens, he could face substantial restitution and likely a prison sentence of several years. Judicial officials willingly obliged and rallied to render assistance to the President to enable him to evade justice, with total disregard for the law, confident that they, in turn, would be shielded from culpability by 'the system' and by the President. At the behest of President Bush:

- The Secret Service was dispatched to harass and intimidate me as a petitioner in the case against the President. Following a visit to my home by the Secret Service, to warn me off continuing to seek justice, the US Marshals were next employed to intimidate me by another visit to my home and to menacingly discourage me from pursuing the lawsuit.

- The FBI was employed to initiate illegal interception of all my communications and to plot to neutralize me as a witness to the crimes filed in the court cases.

- The US Attorney appearing for the President violated a court order and the law. The US Attorney defended the President in a civil suit premised upon crimes which he was obligated by law (28USC547) to prosecute.

The Federal District Court Case against President Bush met with unceremonious and illegal dismissal by the presiding judge, Judge Emmet G. Sullivan. The judgment submitted by the District Court was illegal, because: a) criminal acts and omissions, which had a most pertinent impact on this case, were swept under the carpet and concealed; b) contrary to the normal administration of justice, criminal offenses committed by President Bush, upon which the civil claim was based, were dismissed by the Court without investigation or prosecution; c) contrary to the normal administration of justice, criminal offenses committed by the defense team were dismissed without investigation or prosecution; d) contrary to the normal administration of justice, underlying crimes in the broad conspiracy by government officers to obstruct justice, were dismissed without investigation or prosecution; e) the judgment was rendered on a 'Motion for Dismissal' which was illegitimately submitted in breach of a court order; f) the judgment was rendered by a judge who was acting in contravention of the law for not arresting the offending officials and not setting a preliminary hearing as was required from him under law (See *Appendix 4,* statutes 18USC3041, 18USC3046, and 18USC3060).

The judgment was contrived to favor and protect President Bush and the other government officers implicated in the crimes, while justice and law played no part therein. The District Court judgment was thus appealed to the US Court of Appeals for the D.C. Circuit in case no. 04-5324. In their turn, the Court of Appeal judges willfully failed to deal with the criminal offenses and joined in the endeavor of President Bush, Judge Sullivan, and other law-breaking officials, to conceal the escalating number of criminal offenses. In so doing, the Appeals Court judges violated the statutes themselves.

Every omission of duty by government officials in the case impeded the proper functioning of government and obstructed the normal course of justice as set out in the Constitution, the laws, and the court rules. Every willful failure of duty denied the rights to justice and protection of the laws to one who was directly at the receiving end of the lawlessness. And every criminal act was meticulously documented in the 'Dossier of Crimes' and lodged with the relevant authorities and the courts, as demanded by statute 18USC4 – only to be swept under the carpet once more. And that is how the matter kept proliferating and escalating. I was relentless in my pursuit of justice; and government officials were relentless in their cover-up of the burgeoning number of crimes.

The unceremonious dismissal of the case against President Bush from the US District Court and from the D.C. Circuit Appeals Court, sans addressing the escalating underlying criminal conspiracy, was appealed to the United States Supreme Court. Circa that time, there were two further court cases which addressed the criminal neglect of government officials to deal with the deluge of crime within their ranks. Those cases also met with strong obstruction in the administration of the laws. Petitions for justice were made to the United States Supreme Court in all three cases, since chiseled upon the marble edifice of the Supreme Court are the compelling words: *"Equal Justice under Law"*. Under this auspicious banner, the following three initial cases, which pitted the common man against the might of a lawless American establishment, were presented to the US Supreme Court:

    a. *Anthony P. Keyter vs. George W. Bush*, Supreme Court Case No. 05-140.

    b. *Anthony P. Keyter vs. 230 Government Officers*, Supreme Court Case No. 06-284.

    c. *Anthony P. Keyter vs. McCain et al.*, Supreme Court Case No. 06-1069de

CRIME IN THE UNITED STATES SUPREME COURT

Defeat of Justice

Unsurprisingly, the criminal endeavor by politicians, lower court judges, law enforcement, and other officials to obstruct the course of justice, advanced uninterruptedly into the US Supreme Court. The Supreme Court deliberately failed to address the corruption in the government and the courts, and willfully failed to attend to a large number of criminal offenses placed before it in all three of the above cases against government officials, which were active at that time. In their turn, the Supreme Court Justices lent their considerable (but corrupt) power to advance the aims of the criminal conspirators, to obstruct the administration of the laws, and to defeat the course of justice. All three initial cases were characterized by significant criminality in the court so as to protect President Bush and the other senior government officials implicated, from civil and criminal prosecution.

Fraudulent Judgments

In each instance, the Certiorari petitions to the Supreme Court were fraudulently and illegally denied without the benefit of all the relevant documentation and without the justices performing obligatory judicial duties to address the underlying crimes. A mandamus petition was filed in the case against President Bush requesting a Supreme Court Order to command the President to obey the laws. The mandamus petition was ostensibly deliberated and then fraudulently denied by the Justices (according to correspondence from the court), yet all the copies of the petition had already been stolen from the courthouse within hours of being filed and were never available for deliberation by the Justices. Few in this country would credit the Supreme Court and its Justices with such deceit. These are some of the most noble men and women we produce as a nation. Sadly, there are many more documented examples to be conveyed.

Chief Justice John Roberts assured dismissal of the case *Anthony P. Keyter vs. George W. Bush* from the Federal Appeals Court whilst he was a judge in that court. He also assured suppression of the US Supreme Court case once he became Chief Justice - in both cases, without due process of law. His actions in assisting President Bush to escape prosecution in the DC Appeals Court may well have led to his being chosen as Supreme Court Chief Justice shortly afterwards, as a return favor from President Bush.

Rendering Criminal Assistance

The failure of the Supreme Court Justices to act upon evidence of multiple and serious felonies presented in court documents and in the Dossier of Crimes, protected and rendered criminal assistance to known felons. The justices thereby obstructed the due and proper administration of the laws and violated statute 18USC1505 concerning obstruction of justice and statute 18USC4 concerning the reporting of crimes. Urgent motions for injunction, seeking court protection from ongoing theft of records and other crimes in each of the three related Supreme Court cases, were simply not addressed. This neglect sanctioned further criminal misconduct by officials and violated the statute concerning accessory to crime, 18USC3. (For verbiage of statutes, see *Appendix 4*).

Violation of Laws Disqualifying a Judge

Motions for recusal and/or disqualification of the justices were submitted to the Supreme Court when it became clear that they were colluding in the criminal conspiracy underlying each of the three cases. However, the justices failed to recuse themselves, acted under a severe conflict of interest, which was indefensible in law, and rendered judgments to dismiss the very cases that implicated them in crime. The justices thereby shielded themselves from investigation, impeachment, and prosecution. It must be noted that Chief Justice Roberts did in fact recuse himself from two of the deliberations; however, on other applicable occasions he did not. The laws governing the recusal of judges, 28USC144[5] and 28USC455[6], expressly prohibit acting under such conflict. What

---

[5] 28USC144 (Recusal of Judges)
"Whenever a party to a proceeding in a court makes and files a timely and sufficient affidavit that the judge before whom the matter is pending has a personal bias or prejudice either against him or in favor of any adverse party, such judge shall proceed no further therein, but another judge shall be assigned to hear such proceeding."

[6] 28USC455 – Disqualification of a Judge
"(a) Any justice, judge, or magistrate of the United States shall disqualify himself in any proceeding in which his impartiality might reasonably be questioned."

worth does any law have if it is not obeyed by the judges, who are there to administer the laws in strictness?

Shielding of Criminal Offenders

Criminal Complaints and other unambiguous evidence regarding felonies associated with the three initial Supreme Court cases were filed with the Supreme Court Police. A number of those felonies were committed *in the Supreme Court*. However, the Supreme Court Police failed to act against the offenders, instead providing a protective umbrella for the ongoing lawlessness of theft of court records, intimidation, and retaliation against a witness.

Tampering with / Illegal removal of Court Evidence

In all three related Supreme Court cases at that time, which are listed above, all incriminating evidence implicating President Bush and other senior government officials in crime was illegally removed from Supreme Court Records. Subsequent attempts to re-file the stolen documents repeatedly met with the same offense. In the civil case against President Bush, 41 out of 47 documents filed in the case and incriminating George W. Bush in crime, were stolen from the court records. In the case against 230 Government Officers, four incriminating documents were corruptly and repeatedly removed. In the case against Senator McCain, Vice President Cheney, Chief Justice Roberts, and other senior officials, six pertinent documents were corruptly removed. These documents were re-filed and repeatedly removed in violation of the law regarding theft of court records.

On 34 occasions to date, the criminal dossiers and the evidence they contain were illegally removed from the Supreme Court Records. Subsequent to the initial three cases, the Supreme Court simply failed to docket or to provide a case number for eleven further Supreme Court appeal cases that were to follow and that sought to address aspects of the extensive criminal conspiracy.

These criminal acts transpired with the full collaboration of the Supreme Court Justices, with the co-operation of the Clerk and his personnel, and under the protective umbrella of the Supreme Court Police. All these entities were kept fully informed of the criminality in the Supreme Court. These acts of pilfering of records violated the statute on theft of court records, 18USC1506, on numerous counts.

> ***Theft of Record, statute 18USC1506*** *– states in relevant part: Whoever feloniously steals, takes away, alters, falsifies, or otherwise avoids any record, writ, process, or other proceeding, in any court of the United States, whereby any judgment is reversed, made void, or does not take effect...; -- Shall be fined under this title or imprisoned not more than five years, or both.*

Retribution

Because of my unrelenting persistence to find justice, the government conspirators resorted to witness-tampering (18USC1512) and retaliation against me (18USC1513). That witness tampering and retaliation is described anon in a little more detail. This was done with the clear intent to prevent my attendance in official court proceedings and to prevent further testimony against the law-breaking government officers, including the ring-leaders: President Bush, Chief Justice Roberts, Attorney General Gonzales, and FBI Director Mueller. In a further display of abuse of power and of state machinery, President Bush ordered the illegal interception of all my communications in violation of the tenets of the Patriot Act. The Court willfully neglected to address the offenses, and the Supreme Court Police deliberately failed to protect a litigant from retaliation by government officials.

SUPREME COURT CLERK'S OFFICE PARTICIPATION

The events at the US Supreme Court on the morning of February 8, 2006, are important details in my personal story, since those events were the prelude to violent crime that was later committed by US government officials with impunity. Therefore, the events will be described in detail so as to be both accurate and informative in terms of the later history.

On the morning of February 8, 2006, at around 9:20 am, I left the Hyatt Hotel in the District of Columbia, where I was staying for a few days, and went straight down to the US Supreme Court Clerk's office. There, I checked the contents of the correspondence file *and* documents file in case number 05-140 – the case against President Bush. Out of 47 documents filed in that case, as already mentioned, 41 had been illegally removed from the court, and the Supreme Court Justices were denied sight thereof. *All missing documents* contained details of crimes committed by government officials.

I asked the Clerk's Assistant who brought the files to the front desk (name unknown) to verify the contents with me against my own list of what should have been there. This he did, but when I asked him to sign the prepared sheet showing the discrepancy of missing documents, he called in a more senior Clerk's Assistant, Mr. Calvin Todd, who had worked with me before on the documents. Mr. Todd was initially reluctant to sign the prepared list of discrepancies; however, he went through the file with me and then went to print a docket sheet. Together, Mr. Todd and I confirmed that there were many items missing from the record, and he later signed the discrepancy sheet.

While we were standing there working together, a more senior person in charge had walked by and Mr. Todd and he had some interaction, which unfortunately was not audible to me. The senior in charge, Mr. Kemp, then left and went back to the far side of the Clerk's Office. After finishing up with Mr. Todd, I said that I would like to discuss the discrepancy in the records with the Chief of Supreme Court Police, Mr. Ross Swope, and requested Mr. Todd to lead me there and to take the records over. We had a crime on our hands: theft of Supreme Court records in the George W Bush case – and I had the incriminating evidence in my hand. Mr. Todd said he would not accompany me to the Chief of Supreme Court Police and that I should ask Mr. Kemp on the other side of the Clerk's Office, whom he had spoken to earlier, to accompany me. I then went across the aisle and had a talk to Mr. Kemp (he sat in the left-hand side office, and apparently was the 'Supervisor on Duty'). Mr. Kemp came forward to meet me and I requested for him to escort me to the Chief of Supreme Court Police and to bring along the file of case no. 05-140, in order to report the theft of court record to the Supreme Court Police Chief and to show the incontrovertible evidence thereof. Mr. Kemp simply refused to assist. He obstructed by saying I needed an appointment (to report a crime) and that he would not take me to see the Chief of Supreme Court Police. The concealment and cover-up of crime (theft of court record) and obstacles thrown in the way of addressing that crime had already started. Government officials protect one another from the consequences of wrongdoing. They were certainly not going to protect the crime victim. Oh no. They were hell-bent on protecting President George W. Bush from the consequences of his crime of theft of court records.

Supreme Court Police Participation

I then left the Clerk's Office and approached two policemen on duty in the center passage-way near the information office. Their names were Officer Moore and Officer Gordon. I made the same request to them: I said that I needed to talk to the Police Chief and asked if they would kindly accompany me to see him. They naturally asked what it was about; was there anything they could do? I replied that it concerned crimes in the Supreme Court, and I needed to report this to their chief. Moore said I need an appointment. I said phone, then, to see if the chief was available. He went to phone.

When he put down the phone, he said the chief was busy, and I needed an appointment. I said it was an urgent matter. He said a supervisor will come to talk to me. I then said there is one thing he can do for me, and that is to secure the records in case number 05-140, because there has been tampering with the record. He prevaricated and said he could not leave his post. I said there are others that can do either job, and that he has a radio to contact them. He just scoffed at me. He was very clearly making excuses. I then asked Officer Gordon to go secure the case records, and he said he can't because he is under training. Clearly, they refused to accede to the request for me to report the crime to the Chief of Supreme Court Police.

One of the officers spoke on the phone and must have called for backup. In short succession, I found myself surrounded by approximately 10 menacing and hostile police officers, who formed themselves in a half-moon formation in front of me. Other officers cleared Supreme Court visitors out of the hallway. Three stepped forward and asked, "What's the problem?" They understood I'm making demands to see their chief. Amongst the belligerent officers were Sgt Jeff Smith, Officer Krista Jaffe, and Officer Jeff Banazak.

Entirely taken aback, I attempted to explain to the threatening police officers that I was a Supreme Court litigant and needed to report crimes associated with my case to the Supreme Court Police Chief. That's all. Sgt Jeff Smith barked: "That's not possible; we're here to speak to you". Under very hostile conditions, I briefly tried to explain who I am and what it's about. They were jumpy and not friendly – in their eyes, I was the intruder and the 'criminal'. Eventually, we agreed to a proper discussion, and they led me to a basement room in the Supreme Court. The larger platoon dispersed and left three or four officers to deal with the matter.

Perversely, my attempts to report to the police the theft of court records in the case against President Bush instead invoked threatening treatment upon me as a litigant *by the police*. In the basement room, meeting with the smaller group, I more or less spoke along the lines of the notes I had prepared for the Chief of Police. I shared with them the incontrovertible evidence I had. At one stage in the tense conversation with the policemen, I subconsciously straightened my tie, which prompted one of the officers to reach for his gun – clearly as an intimidation tactic, demonstrating their hostile intent.

Then, for a short while, they relaxed a bit more than their earlier onslaught. However, soon there came a time in the discussions when they got hostile again. That happened around the time when they were confronted with unassailable evidence that their President, and mine, had engaged in crime that would put the common man in prison for five years. The evidence was clear, but they did not want to see it. I asked to meet with Clerk's Assistant Gail Johnson and the Clerk, William Suter, who had been dealing with the matter, to ask them the pertinent questions that would further prove the point. Again, they said that was not possible; they would not allow that (of course, because that would prove the crime!).

Officer Krista Jaffe left to talk on the phone to Clerk's Assistant Gail Johnson, and came back saying that Gail said she received one of the items under discussion, a mandamus petition, on the 28th of September, 2005, and sent it back on the 28th because it was late. At that time, I pointed out to the police in the discussion group that, if it was *now confirmed* by the Clerk's office that the mandamus petition was sent back on the 28th, how come the court (all the Justices) denied that same mandamus petition on the 3rd of October, 2005, five days later? "Were all the justices involved in the crime, or just the clerk's office?" I asked. They did not answer me - but they did stare at me! They could not answer, without incriminating one group or the other: the justices and/or the clerks.

Other unassailable evidence that was shared with the Supreme Court Police was the contents of the correspondence file and the list of 37 pieces of correspondence that were received by signature confirmation, but that did not appear in the court file. The police themselves were forced into a corner where they did not want to be: to admit criminal wrongdoing by the Clerk's Office and by President Bush and his lawyers.

It was clear that they were trying to argue away the evidence, saying things like: "Officer Krista (Jaffe) is not a lawyer" – meaning neither she nor anybody else amongst them could explain away the unambiguous evidence of a crime having been committed. Other comments were: "We must cut this short because Krista has another appointment; there is nothing further they can do for me". With that, they ushered me out of the courthouse. It was a most humiliating and unpleasant experience. But that's what you get for obeying the law (statute 18USC4) and reporting blatant crime committed by a top United States Government official.

Reflecting upon the hostile incident afterwards, it became clear to me that the Supreme Court Police, already informed of the situation, had been forewarned by the Clerk's Office, since they were primed to put every obstacle in the way of filing a formal criminal complaint for theft of record in the case against President Bush.

Such is the coordination in wrongdoing amongst officials in the various departments of government. The significant events that were to follow this incident further demonstrated the depth of depravity in the United States government and ended all illusions I might have had of finding *"Equal Justice under Law"* in the United States Supreme Court. Nonetheless, that slogan remains chiseled in stone upon its marble edifice in memorial to the golden age of rhetoric and dishonesty; and commemorative of a dark age for the noble principles of truth and justice.

A Dirty U.S. Government Secret

We are a nation of laws, I have often heard it said. There are laws that cover all aspects of human misbehavior. But are they equally applied to all deviants? Or are they arbitrarily applied upon some people and not others? Sometimes, and not other times? My duties under the statute on misprision of felony, 18USC4, demanded that I report known crimes in the US Supreme Court, quote:

> **Misprision of Felony, Statute 18USC4:** *"Whoever, having knowledge of the actual commission of a felony cognizable by a court of the United States, conceals and does not as soon as possible make known the same to some judge or other person in civil or military authority under the United States shall be fined under this title or imprisoned not more than three years, or both".*

Duties prescribed by law, for the Clerk and Assistants, the Supreme Court Police, and later the nine justices who were informed, were blatantly violated. Amongst those obstruction of justice crimes of these groups, perpetrated at the behest of and on behalf of President George W Bush, were breaches of statute 18USC1512:

> **Tampering with a Witness, Statute 18USC1512, in relevant part:**
> (b)Whoever knowingly uses intimidation, threatens, or corruptly persuades another person, or attempts to do so, or engages in misleading conduct toward another person, with intent to —
> **(1)** *Influence, delay, or prevent the testimony of any person in an official proceeding;*
> **(2)** cause or induce any person to—**(A)** *withhold testimony, or* **withhold a record**, *document, or other object, from an official proceeding;***(B)** *alter, destroy, mutilate, or conceal an object with intent to impair the object's integrity or availability for use in an official proceeding; ....*

(3) *hinder, delay, or prevent the communication to a law enforcement officer or judge of the United States of information relating to the commission or possible commission of a federal offense…;*
shall be fined under this title or imprisoned not more than 20 years, or both.
(c)Whoever corruptly—
(1) *alters, destroys, mutilates, **or conceals a record, document**, or other object, or attempts to do so, with the intent to impair the object's integrity or availability for use in an official proceeding; or*
(2) *otherwise obstructs, influences, or impedes any official proceeding, or attempts to do so,*
*shall be fined under this title or imprisoned not more than **20 years**, or both.*

The Supreme Court Clerk and Assistants, the Supreme Court Police who had a role in the events, and later the nine justices who were informed and were requested to act pursuant to their duties, but failed, were all guilty of corruptly concealing and obstructing the filing of the criminal complaint of theft of court record. They should have been fined or imprisoned for not more than 20 years, or both – according to statute 18USC1512.

President Bush remained determined to squash the criminal complaint of 'theft of court record', and his next moves proved that he was not shy to employ violence to achieve his ends: protecting himself against prosecution for crimes he committed. In the next phase of their obstruction of justice, President Bush and his henchmen approached my employer at the time, the Boeing Company, to act as proxy for the president and to perform his foul deeds – naturally, with repayment in kind included in the deal.

Boeing obliged, as we see in the next chapter, and has been a part of government criminality ever since.

Chapter 5
The Bush / Boeing Attempted Murder

Neither Nixon's Watergate nor Clinton's disgrace will compare with the ignominy wrought upon the nation when this episode comes to light, as inevitably it must.

Extract From Chapter 5.

When the Boeing Company had its 100th birthday in 2016, it was still going strong. More accurately put, Boeing was doing better than ever. Designer and manufacturer of rockets, missiles, rotorcraft, and satellites, the company is, of course, best known as one of the largest aircraft manufacturers in the world. It designs and builds both military and commercial jet aircraft and employs about 170,000 people worldwide. Boeing is a major defense contractor and has been the largest exporter in the United States, monetarily. Boeing's sales in its feeble year of 2024 were $66.5 billion. This figure was $77.7 billion in 2023, with a backlog in orders of around $521 billion. By all accounts, Boeing is a hugely successful, much-needed, and desired company.

But there is another, more insalubrious distinction that sets this mighty aerospace giant apart. The Boeing Company has hidden a dark and dirty secret in the passing years since 2006. Boeing lies squarely at the center of a virulent criminal enterprise active within the United States Government: the seditious conspiracy and insurrection against the laws described in this chronicle. Boeing is part and parcel of, and criminally culpable in, the crimes perpetrated by government officials, which are detailed herewith. Boeing has facilitated some of those violent crimes (attempted kidnapping and murder of a court witness, for instance) while acting as a proxy for a high government official, namely, former President George W. Bush. As co-conspirator and co-perpetrator, the Boeing Company imputes its own serious offenses to its government partners in crime - and vice versa. These legally accurate statements are not made frivolously. I shall expand on the details presented in Chapter 4 and will endeavor to show how the close, but corrupt, relationship between government officials and Boeing officials has had a disastrous effect upon the well-being and security of the public-at-large. Criminality within the Boeing Company amongst its officials, has been covered up, condoned, and sanctioned by successive US Presidents, Administrations, and Congressmen, and by a number of Court Judges, including the US Supreme Court Justices - thereby plunging all of them into what can accurately and legally be described in terms of the United States Code, as an *organized crime network* engaged in serious racketeering activities.

I was an employee of the Boeing Company in Seattle for nearly 17 years, from July 1989 to March 2006. As Senior Instructor Pilot (operating at management level), I enjoyed the esteem of the company in that professional position. I was qualified to fly most Boeing aircraft in recent production, including Boeing 737, 747, 757, 767, and 777 aircraft. Apart from being an instructor, I am also a trained test pilot and am experienced in testing jet fighters and transport aircraft alike; and am an (inactive) member of the coveted Society for Experimental Test Pilots. Although instructing was my primary task at the Boeing Company, I also flew many production test flights at the Boeing factory, as well as some experimental test flights, like stall testing on the Boeing 737-500. My 17 years spent at the Boeing Company were very satisfying years from a personal and professional standpoint - and I was happy and eager to continue doing what I loved to do until retirement. However, the President of the United States at the time, George W Bush, had more sinister events in mind for his resolute opponent in Supreme Court case number 05-140.

BOEING RETALIATION AGAINST A COURT LITIGANT

Ordered by President George W. Bush

One day after the humiliating Supreme Court Police encounter described in Chapter 4, on Friday, the 9th of February 2006, a 'Petition for Rehearing' (which had been blocked the previous day), was filed in the US Supreme Court in the case against President Bush, together with the Criminal Complaint which addressed the extensive theft of court records. These documents significantly increased the risk of public exposure and prosecution of President Bush and his co-perpetrators.

Within 24 hours of those documents being filed in the US Supreme Court, President Bush and his agents initiated a criminal plot to retaliate against me with the intent to kill me as the primary witness to their crimes - so as to prevent my testimony and thwart the course of justice and administration of the laws. The execution of that plot commenced in the Supreme Court under Chief Justice Roberts and Chief of Police Ross Swope. In clear abuse of power, the plot unfolded through the halls of the White House, the DOJ, the FBI, and the Federal Aviation Administration, and through the offices of my employer, the Boeing Company in Seattle.

Under orders from President Bush, White House aides contacted the Boeing Company for assistance. Upon my return to Seattle from Washington DC, acting at the behest of and on the behalf of President Bush, officers of the Boeing Company embarked upon a devious attempt to inveigle me to an area away from my normal workplace, there to unlawfully seize me - kidnap me - in collaboration with and in execution of the plot to murder me. Considering the cunningness and the speed with which the plot was executed, it was clear to me that the criminal scheme had been hatched beforehand and was primed to be executed at an appropriate time and at a moment's notice. That moment had arrived.

I was requested to meet with the Boeing Chief Pilot (Mike Coker, at that time) and Personnel Manager Linda Enebrad, on the 13th February 2006, just days after the US Supreme Court incident. At that meeting, they advised me that I was suspended from my position at Boeing with immediate effect; that I was accused of 'bizarre behavior' at the US District Court in DC on the 7th and 8th of February 2006, and that I was to see a counselor, Kevin King. These names are mentioned here since each of them played a definite role in the kidnapping and murder attempts. From that step in their hasty plot, I was to be sent to a psychiatrist, whose name is also known.

Boeing Chief Pilot (Training), Mike Coker, and Personnel Manager Linda Enebrad were never able to tell me what that 'bizarre behavior' was, despite my repeated requests. It was very clearly a contrived story. Yet, they gave me absolutely no chance to explain my trip to Washington, DC, and my whereabouts on the dates of the false accusations. If they were at all interested, they would have known that I was never at the District Court on either of the dates of the supposed bizarre behavior. On the 7th of February, I was in my hotel room preparing notes for the Supreme Court meetings. On the prime date of the 8th of February 2006, I was meeting with the US Supreme Court Police. It was all a well-organized setup by Boeing, acting at the behest of George W Bush, but it was amateurishly executed to get me to the psychiatrist. What did they have waiting for me at the psychiatrist? Pray tell. As a pilot from the time that I was 19 years old, I have undergone mandatory fitness tests and flight physical examinations annually since then, and twice a year in my years at Boeing. I had an impeccable physical and mental fitness record, bar for accidents and broken bones. I was a perfectly normal pilot and instructor pilot. One week prior to the Bush incident, on

28th January 2006, I was still trusted by Boeing to give flight training on a new Boeing 777 aircraft for 3 hours and forty minutes, to some international customer flight crew, as the instructor being the only 'qualified' pilot on board. One week later, they were into their criminal conspiracy with George W. Bush.

I recognized the deception, the objectives, and the dangers very early and declined to walk into the Bush/Boeing trap. Boeing became frantic as a result of my refusals, since they were all hell-bent on getting me to that psychiatrist. And for what? For doing my duty under statute 18USC4 and reporting the theft of 41 out of 47 documents filed in the Bush Supreme Court case! Boeing officials threatened over and over again to fire me if I did not comply and go to see their psychiatrist – the 'trigger puller' - which I obviously did not do, for it was clear to me from their deceit that my life was in danger.

Chief Pilot Mike Coker and Personnel Manager Linda Enebrad called for at least two further meetings with me, with an ominous change noticeable in their strategy. Each meeting was to be at a location away from my normal workplace. One was at an odd location on a remote corner of the factory premises in Renton, obviously out of sight of any people. I declined to meet with them there. The next proposed 'meeting place' was at the entrance of another Boeing office building, a way off from my normal workplace. Both meeting places I viewed with great suspicion. Whereas, my office desk was an estimated twenty paces from Mike Coker's office, which was the obvious place to meet for a 'genuine' meeting. I was not fooled into exposing myself to be trapped under such conditions. What did they plan to do at those remote locations?

Mike Coker and Linda Enebrad were not practiced common criminals - yet. Coker tried his best to act nonchalant and aloof in our meetings. Linda Enebrad, normally a very composed professional, was decidedly uncomfortable and tense, even stuttering at times, in the role she was requested and expected to play, apparently against her will. It made her very nervous and uncomfortable. In my analysis, they both knew that they were engaged in foul play. Linda Enebrad certainly was one dead giveaway in their criminal plot, a strong piece of evidence that left me in no doubt as to their malevolent intentions.

In the meantime, I escalated the saga to the highest levels within Boeing. Nothing happened without me keeping CEO McNerney, the Vice Presidents, and the Board of Directors informed of Boeing's very suspicious and deceitful moves. In that way, they were all party to the malevolent happenings driven by President Bush and his henchmen. No one at those company levels could claim ignorance or innocence. Strong indications are that Boeing was offered an attractive contract or compensation to facilitate this iniquitous conduct – that compensation was very likely the new USAF tanker aircraft contract - and the Boeing Board acquiesced to the request.

On March 10, 2006, my employment with Boeing was illegally terminated in retaliation against my filing of criminal charges against President Bush in the US Supreme Court case 05-140 – and for my resistance in complying with their kidnapping and murder attempts. These acts violated the statute on kidnapping, 18USC1201:

> ***Kidnapping, statute 18USC1201:*** *In relevant parts:*
> *(a) Whoever unlawfully seizes, confines, inveigles, decoys, kidnaps, abducts, or carries away and holds for ransom or reward or otherwise any person, except in the case of a minor by the parent thereof, when---(2) any such act against the person is done within the special maritime and territorial jurisdiction of the United States;---such person shall be punished by imprisonment for any term of years or for life; --- **(c) If any two or more persons***

77

*conspire to violate this section and one or more of such persons **do any act to effect the object of the conspiracy**, each shall be punished by imprisonment for any term of years or for life.*

The acts of Boeing also violated the statute on retaliation against a witness, 18USC1513[7].

The first attempt to kidnap and murder me (initiated by officers of the Boeing Company under the direction of the FBI) failed and resulted in further criminal charges being filed by me, which in turn led to a second assassination attempt. In their effort to prevent information relating to these federal offenses from reaching the public, a second attempt was undertaken through the Federal Aviation Administration (under a request from Bush and Boeing and again under the direction of FBI agents).

The second kidnap attempt was also abortive, since it again was easy to see through their ongoing sinister objectives and moves. However, those attempts succeeded in destroying my livelihood and 17-year career as Senior Instructor Pilot with the Boeing Company - thereby purposefully targeting my financial ability to conduct the court cases, in violation of 18USC1513(e)[8]. The Boeing Company

---

[7] 18USC1513(a) - Retaliating against a witness, victim, or an informant: In relevant parts:
(a)(1) Whoever kills or attempts to kill another person with intent to retaliate against any person for-- (A) the attendance of a witness or party at an official proceeding, or any testimony given or any record, document, or other object produced by a witness in an official proceeding; or (B) providing to a law enforcement officer any information relating to the commission or possible commission of a Federal offense ... shall be punished as provided in paragraph (2): The punishment for an offense under this subsection is ... B) in the case of an attempt, imprisonment for not more than 20 years; ......

[8] 18USC1513(e) Whoever knowingly, with the intent to retaliate, takes any action harmful to any person, including *interference with the lawful employment* or livelihood of any person, for providing to a law enforcement officer any truthful information relating to the commission or possible commission of any Federal offense, shall be fined under this title or imprisoned not more than 10 years, or both.

made no secret about the fact that their actions were a direct result of, and were linked to, the iniquitous Supreme Court actions of President George W. Bush. The Federal Aviation Administration was used to fraudulently prohibit me from using my flying license, thereby destroying my ability to earn a living in my profession.

The first two foiled kidnap and murder attempts were respectively commanded, facilitated, and directed by President Bush, Chief Justice Roberts, Attorney General Gonzales, and FBI Director Mueller. Unconcealed and overt audio tapes of conversations with Boeing managers and FAA officials clearly indicate the conclusions on intent and reveal the intense involvement of Attorney General Gonzales and agents from his Justice Department. A grim threat remains, and there is a high likelihood of further retaliation against me on behalf of the seditious conspirators.

Murder may sound like a strong accusation, but many more details and evidence of the malicious murder plot are known. However, for good reason, these details are withheld from publication until such time as formal investigations are initiated and completed. The perpetrators have time and again demonstrated their strong inclination to go back and to cover up their tracks and destroy any evidence or trace of their misdeeds. The willful refusal to investigate, by law-enforcement agencies who have the duty to do so, should be a clear enough indication to the discerning reader that things are dreadfully amiss concerning this entire malevolent episode.

CONSPIRACY TO KIDNAP AND MURDER

Charges were filed against President Bush and his co-conspirators for conspiracy to kidnap and murder.

18USC1111 – Murder
In relevant part: (a) Murder is the unlawful killing
of a human being with malice aforethought. Every
murder perpetrated by..... attempt to perpetrate
murder, kidnapping, treason .... or perpetrated
from a premeditated design unlawfully and
maliciously to effect the death of any human being
other than him who is killed, is murder in the first
degree.   Whoever is guilty of murder in the first
*degree shall be **punished by death or by***
imprisonment for life.

18USC1117 - Conspiracy to Murder
If two or more persons conspire to violate section
1111, 1114, 1116, or 1119 of this title, and one or
more of such persons do any overt act to effect the
*object of the conspiracy, **each shall be punished** by*
imprisonment for any term of years or for life.

AIR INDIA PARTICIPATION

Besides *the Boeing Company* and President Bush and his government agents, a third party was directly involved in the kidnapping and murder attempts, namely, *Air India.* During the latter half of 2005 and the first half of 2006, officials from Air India pressured and incited Boeing to act to silence and prevent my witness against lawlessness within Air India. Air India sought to suppress a damning Flight Safety Report authored by me in my capacity as Senior Boeing Instructor Pilot, and sought to suppress knowledge of their violations of the Indian Aviation Act.

In an illegal conspiracy to violate the law, the Boeing Company acquiesced to the incitement by Air India in order to facilitate and protect its 11 billion US Dollar aircraft deal with Air India at that time. *That incitement occurred* simultaneously *with the pressure and incitement by President Bush upon the Boeing Company to facilitate retaliatory action against me.* Thus, the incitement by Air

India upon the Boeing Company merged with the incitement by President Bush upon Boeing. Boeing's malevolent responses to that dual incitement are not distinguishable. The suppressed flight safety warnings were later to play a crucial role in the death of 158 passengers and crew of Air India Flight IX-812.

In addition, the President of Boeing Commercial Airplanes at the time, Alan Mulally, was a key figure in the kidnapping and murder plot. He later joined the board of *The Ford Motor Company* and implicated that company's board members in criminality.

DE FACTO IMPUNITY AGAINST ARREST

The kidnap and murder attempts have not been investigated or prosecuted - neither by the Department of Justice nor the FBI, nor by any other law enforcement agency or state or federal court - despite having been provided with the information, certain evidence, and numerous appeals. Exhaustive measures thus failed to bring President Bush and his co-conspirators to justice before the courts of the United States and failed to secure protection against further attempts upon my life. These malevolent officials in their high positions were granted *de facto 'impunity'* against arrest for attempted murder and numerous other serious felonies. In direct conflict with the 'equal protection of the law' clause of the Constitution, the Department of Justice's policy thoughtlessly stipulates that a sitting President may not be indicted for any crime. That includes murder. The common man and the public at large effectively have no practical antidote or protection against such assault upon the public peace and safety by government officials in high positions.

SEDITIOUS CONSPIRACY

The United States statute addressing seditious conspiracy (18USC2384), clearly states:

"If two or more persons in any State or Territory, or in any place subject to the jurisdiction of the United States, conspire to overthrow, put down, or to destroy by force the Government of the United States, or to levy war against them, or to oppose by force the authority thereof, **or by force to prevent, hinder, or delay the execution of any law of the United States,** *or by force to seize, take, or possess any property of the United States contrary to the authority thereof, they shall each be fined under this title or imprisoned not more than twenty years, or both".*

None of the participants acted alone in the criminal activities briefly described herewith. The complicity (18USC2[9]) and/or accessory role (18USC3[10]) of each of the known criminal conspirators in my attempted kidnap and murder as a key witness to their crimes is evident from their failure of legal obligation to address that crime. They should have dealt with it either as responsible United States citizens according to 18USC4, or as officials pursuant to their oath of office and their specific duties associated with their position of authority under the United States.

The criminal acts described above furthered the common aims of, and were of mutual benefit to, *all* known conspirators. The illegal removal of the criminal dossiers and other incriminating evidence from the Supreme Court Record suppressed information concerning the crimes of *all* the conspirators. The illegal removal of the mandamus petition in the Bush Supreme Court case saved *all* the

---

[9] 18USC2 – Principals: (a) Whoever commits an offense against the United States or aids, abets, counsels, commands, induces or procures its commission, is punishable as a principal. (b) Whoever willfully causes an act to be done which if directly performed by him or another would be an offense against the United States, is punishable as a principal.

[10] 18USC3 – Accessory after the Fact: Whoever, knowing that an offense against the United States has been committed, receives, relieves, comforts or assists the offender in order to hinder or prevent his apprehension, trial or punishment, is an accessory after the fact.

conspirators from a court order enforcing criminal investigation and resultant prosecution. The attempts to kidnap and murder me, if they had succeeded, would have wiped (or if the conspirators do succeed, it will wipe) all pending court proceedings against Boeing and all other conspirators clean off the slate. It is the *combined action* by conspirators that has served to defeat the course of justice so absolutely - one conspirator or group performing one part of the criminal act, another performing the other part of the act. For instance, one group of conspirators commits the crime of retaliation against a witness with the intent to murder, while the others illegally protect those law-breaking colleagues by refusing to investigate or prosecute the crime. (Statute 18USC371).

This cooperative endeavor amongst the conspirators, to commit offenses against the United States or to assist in the commission thereof, was amply demonstrated during the period March 13 to 25, 2006. I was informed that meetings were held between representatives of the different groupings of conspirators, under the auspices of former US Attorney General Gonzales, to plot their evasion of criminal culpability for crimes committed, to render criminal assistance to one another, and to plot further retaliatory action against me.

From a study of the case against President Bush, it is evident that United States Government power lies firmly in the hands of the iniquitous and is used to enforce a definite brand of tyranny upon the populace and to conceal a deluge of criminal activity by corrupt officials. 'Just government power' is usurped to serve immoral, selfish, and party interests, but not the interests of the American people. It is truly difficult for me to comprehend how educated and developed human beings, capable of holding such high office as president of a leading nation, can stoop so low and demonstrate such moral depravity as to plot and to attempt, with malice aforethought, the assassination of a fellow countryman simply because of his lawful pursuit of justice.

A Dirty U.S. Government Secret

In juxtaposition, the brutal murder by Saudi Arabian state actors, of a prominent Saudi dissident and journalist for the Washington Post, Jamal Khashoggi, in Istanbul, Turkey, on October 2, 2018, shocked the conscience of the civilized world. Such savagery, likely ordered by high Saudi government officials, left the world repulsed and disgusted. The Saudi Royal family, of course, denied ordering or sanctioning the killing or the dismemberment of his body, yet it was reported that seven of the fifteen Saudi suspects arrested were personal bodyguards of the Crown Prince. What then is the difference between the repulsive killing of a journalist opposed to the Saudi Royals, and the deeds of the acting United States 'king (for eight years), George W Bush, in the attempted killing of his Supreme Court opponent? The only difference is this: the Saudi killers were successful on their first attempt and were apprehended under immense public pressure; whereas, in three successive but foiled attempts, the assassins dispatched by George W. Bush in early 2006 were not successful. Neither Nixon's Watergate nor Clinton's disgrace will compare with the ignominy wrought upon the nation when this episode comes to light, as inevitably it must.

To date, more than 15,000 US government and industry officials have conspired to, by force, prevent, hinder, and delay the execution of the laws of the United States, in violation of the law prohibiting seditious conspiracy. Remember that this all originated from that initial incident where a single judge made the choice not to follow the law.

And yet the escalating saga steadily gets worse. Attempted murder led to mass murder. The subsequent crimes build upon the previous crime, as we shall see unfolding in the next chapter concerning the Boeing mass murder - with US Government permission.

Chapter 6
Boeing and the Crash of Air India Flight IX-812

The series of events that led to the deaths of the 158 innocent people constitutes murder in the first degree, perpetrated by those officials who suppressed the vital flight safety warnings. I, for one, cannot read the law in any other way.

Extract From Chapter 6.

During my career as Senior Instructor Pilot for the Boeing Company, I represented Boeing on assignments to 35 different customer airlines in some 30 different countries across the globe, usually in flying assignments lasting one or two months at a stretch. The work included simulator training, flight training, delivery flights of new aircraft, and line flying training of crews on the customer's new Boeing aircraft and routes worldwide. As one would expect, the training was heavily oriented towards flight safety and towards procedures that would facilitate a safe standard. Accordingly, I also performed several safety audits of airlines and of air crews during their normal route-flying operations.

It was a very satisfying occupation, providing me with stimulating and sometimes very demanding flying, and flying has been my lifelong passion. Simultaneously, the job presented an excellent opportunity to study and gain insights into the diversity of peoples and cultures; and of modes of living and thinking across the world – issues in which I hold a deep interest. By necessity, the challenging work honed an avid concern for flight safety as well as an acute awareness of cultural differences and how that translated to the hi-tech cockpits of modern airliners. And how that aspect influenced safety.

The challenges of flying large commercial jets with crews who were new to that specific type of aircraft were more demanding in some countries and some airlines than in others. Many aspects of flight operations contributed to the challenges. Sometimes, it was the usual and innocuous mistakes of pilots learning to fly a new type of aircraft that gave cause for attention and challenged the instructor. Often, the sudden and unpredictable errors of inexperienced or ill-equipped and ill-adapted trainee pilots required urgent corrective action lest disaster ensue. At other times, the challenges were obstinately imposed by an overly demanding airline management, bent on profit and indifferent to the governing rules of the air, the mechanical fitness of aircraft to fly, or the margins between the safety of flight and certain tragedy.

Unfortunately, the latter was found to be the case when I worked with Air India training flight crews on their new Boeing 777 and Boeing 737 aircraft during 2005. On that assignment, I submitted a flight safety report that warned of impending disaster if the observed frequent violations of the air rules were allowed to continue. My credentials, mentioned earlier in Chapter 5, were stated for no other reason than to aver with confidence that I consider myself qualified to have issued the stern flight safety warnings to Air India and to the Boeing Company during the prelude to the fateful events under discussion in this chapter.

At the time when I issued the flight safety warnings, they were met with censure and retaliation against me, imposed by my trusted employer, the Boeing Company, at the behest of and in conjunction with Air India. As fate would have it, that retaliation escalated, overlapped, and dovetailed neatly with retaliation against me by President George W. Bush, who was at the time my opponent in US Supreme Court Case No. 05-140, as was mentioned in Chapter 5.

But for providence, that retaliation against me would have taken my life. Others, who were in due course directly affected by the retaliation against me, were not so fortunate and paid with their lives.

THE DEATH OF 158 PEOPLE IN INDIA

When a person intends to kill subject 'A' but instead kills subject 'B' in the attempt, that person is guilty of the murder of subject 'B' in terms of both the United States Code and the Indian Penal Code. Attempts by President Bush to kill me, in order to silence my testimony in the courts of both America and of India, were directly responsible for the suppression of vital flight safety information pertinent to Air India flight operations. As has been mentioned, all investigations into those assassination attempts by President Bush were squashed by the powers that be, including being squashed by President Obama, who followed Bush into the White House.

That violent suppression of my dire flight safety warnings was, in turn, responsible for the deaths of 158 passengers and crew of Air India Flight IX-812. The series of events that led to the deaths of the 158 innocent people constitutes murder in the first degree, perpetrated by those officials who suppressed the vital flight safety warnings. I, for one, cannot read the law in any other way. However, the events, the facts, and the pertinent laws are provided below for your edification. You, the reader, are invited to consider your own verdict on the matter.

CULTURE OF LAWLESSNESS

During 2005, India's national air carrier, Air India, embarked upon the renewal and expansion of its fleet of aircraft. To this end, Air India placed orders for the supply of new aircraft from the Boeing Company in a business deal worth more than 11 billion US Dollars. The training of Air India's flight crews for the new aircraft was undertaken by Boeing Company flight instructors. In my capacity as Senior Instructor Pilot at Boeing, I was involved in that training on both Boeing 737 and Boeing 777 aircraft types over a period of two and a half months in India.

Throughout the assignment in India, I observed habitual violations of the aviation laws by Air India, which violations had an adverse impact on flight safety and potentially affected the lives of passengers. Those perpetual violations occurred at the behest of Air India's senior management and as a consequence of an autocratic and repressive management style which may accurately be described as a 'culture of lawlessness'.

The lack of any deterrent to violations of the Aviation Act, the Indian Aircraft Rules, or the criminal statutes led the 'culture of lawlessness' to thrive within the management of Air India and its fledgling subsidiary at that time, Air India Express.

CLIMATE OF UNSAFE AIRCRAFT OPERATIONS

The lawless milieu within Air India fostered disdain for the Indian Aviation Act of 1934 and the Indian Aircraft Rules of 1937, resulting in a climate of hazardous aircraft operations. That disdain had apparently been firmly established within Air India senior management over several years. The contemptuous attitude of management towards the governing laws and rules would not change unless addressed decisively in the courts.

The willingness and ease with which Air India management could and did violate the Aviation Act and the criminal statutes, and incite and coerce employees to do likewise, extended to a wide area of flight operations. A few representative examples are included below to highlight some but not all of those operational areas that were revealed. Credible and qualified witnesses can corroborate the examples presented below, of lawless and unsafe operations. Further examination will reveal to investigators many more pertinent examples representative of the climate of unsafe flight operations. It was this perilous climate of hazardous aircraft operations that contributed in great measure to the demise of Air India Express Flight IX-812 with the concomitant loss of 158 passengers and crew.

Some relevant aspects and examples of unsafe aircraft operations noticed at Air India are provided:

Maintenance Issues

There was coercion of flight crews and incitement to accept aircraft for flight with unsafe maintenance problems. For example, there were demands on flight crews to fly aircraft with tires worn below safe operating specifications. As a Boeing Instructor Pilot, I was one who experienced but resisted such a demand. There were demands to fly with unserviceable equipment, which was legally required by a 'minimum equipment list'; and so on.

Manipulation of ETOPS Flight Data

There was manipulation of flight data and weather forecasts relating to the rules governing 'Extended Range Twin Engine Operations' (ETOPS), by expediently but deceivingly changing actual weather data to fit the needs of the regulations. This aberration was documented and substantiated by four suppressed safety reports by another Boeing Company Instructor Pilot.

Flight and Duty Time Violations

For good reason, there has been careful consideration of human performance and limitations placed upon the 'time on duty' of pilots, as the demise of Flight IX-812 so acutely demonstrated. Yet, there were multiple examples of flight crews repeatedly exceeding flight and duty time limitations after pressure and incitement by Air India management. Those flight and duty time violations were not only common amongst pilots alone, but included cabin crews and dispatchers alike. Credible witnesses and flight logs corroborated the incidents of safety violations concerning legal limitations on flight time, duty time, and rest periods.

CAPTAIN'S SAFETY REPORT

A system for reporting safety issues within Air India was mandated by law through the Aviation Act of 1934 and the Indian Aircraft Rules of 1937. The Air India Charters Ltd Operations Manual (in compliance with Rule 140B of the Aircraft Rules of 1937) states in Section OM34-2 that Aircraft Commanders are required to report incidents and occurrences which are likely to endanger the safety of flight operations.

As a Boeing Company instructor pilot training Air India pilots, and as an aircraft commander flying on a temporary Indian license, I reported on specific incidents as well as the general climate within Air India to contravene the Indian Aviation Act as it pertained to flight safety. The intent was to help prevent aircraft accidents, which could potentially endanger the lives of Air India passengers, such as the crash of Air India Flight IX-812 at Mangalore on May 22, 2010. Corroborating safety reports were also filed by other Boeing Company instructor pilots who worked with me at Air India at that time. My own 'Captain's Safety Report' sternly warned Air India (and the Boeing Company as aircraft manufacturer and training company) some time before disaster struck, of the imminent dangers of pilot fatigue and of flagrant flight and duty time violations.

My safety report also warned of the dangers of *cumulative fatigue* from a schedule alternating between all-night flights and all-day flights, with minimum crew rest in between - all within the same work week. Such a schedule, rapidly alternating between long-duration day flights and long-duration night flights of maximum legal endurance, failed to allow the human body sufficient acclimatization time to changing circadian rhythms.

I was myself subjected to that alternating schedule and cumulative fatigue, and was aware of several safety incidents as a result of excessive fatigue. For example, there were several incidents not formerly reported, where both the captain and copilot of a two-person flight deck crew had simultaneously fallen asleep during flight, being physically unable to stay awake due to exhaustion. There was a further incident where a Boeing instructor pilot was unable to concentrate or (quote) 'keep his eyes open' during final approach to landing due to *cumulative fatigue*, whilst an inexperienced student co-pilot, still under training, landed the aircraft with a full load of passengers on board without close supervision.

These incidents highlight the threats to flight safety caused by flight and duty time exceedances and the cumulative fatigue of a two-person flight-deck crew during maximum endurance flights (nine hours maximum in India) without adequate rest periods and day/night acclimatization or re-orientation time.

SUPPRESSION OF CRUCIAL FLIGHT SAFETY WARNINGS

My Flight Safety Report was naturally embarrassing to Air India as it dealt with multiple contraventions of the Aviation Act and was thus suppressed by Air India officials acting in collaboration with Boeing Company officials. The safety warnings were never forwarded to safety departments within Air India or to the civil aviation authority, as was required by law. Instead of correcting the reported violations and lawless trend, Boeing Company and Air India officials acted in concert to firmly prevent dissemination of my damning report, through coercion and retaliation against me as eyewitness to those violations, and as author of the ominous safety warnings.

An urgent email from then Boeing Chief Pilot Training, concerning the required distribution of the report, tersely demanded: *"DO NOT, repeat DO NOT write any letters or initiate any other form of communication to anyone or any agency regarding flight operations involving any existing airline"*. The Boeing Company then wrongfully imposed disciplinary action upon me for issuing the professionally prepared, crucial, flight safety report to Air India. In the disciplinary action memo, Boeing further coerced me **not to** *(quote): "initiate written correspondence to any customers or outside entities [the India civil aviation authority] when such written correspondence relates to customer's policies and practices."* The 'practices' referred to, were unsafe and unlawful practices within Air India. Lawful duty to report such practices was thus unlawfully stifled. Boeing further threatened to terminate my employment, which threat effectively halted the onward distribution of the flight safety warnings to the relevant aviation authorities. The important and unsafe consequence was that crucial remedial actions were never instituted at Air India, and the peril to passengers remained.

With Air India's management up in arms about the report, Boeing's actions were no doubt motivated to protect its 11 billion US Dollar aircraft deal with Air India. Air India in turn, was motivated by its desire to protect its law-breaking senior officials from the legal consequences of their lawlessness and to save the company from public recriminations or fines for violating the Indian Aviation Act. The inappropriate (and criminal) behavior by Air India management in suppressing the safety warnings naturally set a precedent and sent a stern warning to all Air India aircraft commanders who dared submit unflattering flight safety reports. Air India aircraft commanders generally know what happens to those who dare report violations of the Aviation Act, which violations are enforced by management. Retaliation against those who spoke out ensured that Air India Management could quite literally 'get away with murder'. The suppression of the mandated feedback system led to a failure to correct deliberate and blatant errors and contributed to the general climate of unsafe aircraft operations.

As a result of the suppression of vital information regarding safety of flight issues and corrective action, the habitual safety violations in Air India and Air India Express continued, and concern for passenger safety remained. The unlawful course of action by Air India and Boeing officials to stifle further attempts to have the safety concerns addressed, entangled the two companies in the broader criminal conspiracy involving senior US Government officials and the Boeing Company. This criminal conduct of coercion and intimidation, by Boeing and Air India officials (in order to suppress my damaging but vital flight safety report), rapidly escalated beyond simple disciplinary action into the two previously mentioned abortive kidnap and murder attempts upon my person. As stated, those attempts were perpetrated by Boeing Company officials acting in concert with US Government agents under the direction of President George W. Bush. These attempts served the common purpose and benefit of the troika of Boeing, Air India, and President Bush acting via his government agents.

The trio of Boeing, Air India, and President Bush had illegally removed criminal complaints and other incriminating evidence from US Supreme Court records in case no. 05-140; they wrongfully terminated my employment; and they fraudulently revoked my flying license and prevented me from practicing my profession, thereby destroying my career and livelihood.

The motive of Air India officials to kill me was clearly to suppress and conceal the damaging flight safety warnings as well as evidence of their violations of the Aviation Act and the criminal statutes. The motive of US Government agents to assassinate me was, as stated, to suppress and conceal court evidence of criminal wrongdoing committed by President Bush in US Supreme Court case no. 05-140; and to cover up criminal wrongdoing by numerous other government officials who acted as his henchmen and co-conspirators.

Criminal complaints, which addressed the lawlessness of Air India management, were later filed in the India Supreme Court in Public Interest Litigation (Diary Number 5352/2006/SC/PIL). Charges were filed for the following serious criminal offences perpetrated by Air India officials: criminal intimidation, causing disappearance of evidence, conspiracy to obstruct lawful apprehension, criminal conspiracy to kidnap or abduct in order to murder, attempt to commit murder, and more. Criminal Complaints were also filed in the United States courts against Air India and Boeing officers for those and other violations. However, once again, because of the involvement of senior US Government officials in the crimes, all attempts to bring the perpetrators to justice have to date been quashed and all evidence suppressed – both in India and in the United States.

That lawless environment irrefutably impacted passenger safety in Air India, and the management of Boeing and Air India were warned of the risks to flight safety caused by such lawlessness. Air India and Boeing Company officials were specifically warned about the two primary risk areas, that of: (a) crew fatigue, and (b) ongoing violations of the applicable laws and rules for flight. Air India and Boeing Company officials had no excuse for willfully incurring risk to the flying public.

The dangerous circumstances would fester for four years before they produced the disaster warned about. The suppressed safety warnings and thwarted remedial actions were pertinent to the safety of Air India Express Flight IX-812. Both factors of crew fatigue and violations of the applicable laws played a crucial role in the death and injury of passengers and crew of Flight IX-812.

THE CRASH OF FLIGHT IX-812

Around 06:30 a.m. on the morning of May 22, 2010, Air India Express Flight IX-812, on a scheduled passenger flight from Dubai, overran the runway and crashed while landing at Mangalore International Airport, India. The flight was commanded by Captain Zlatko Glušica, who was assisted by First Officer H.S. Ahluwalia and four flight attendants. There were 160 passengers and six crew members on board the Boeing 737-800 aircraft. Among them, there were 158 fatalities and eight injured survivors.

The scheduled 3 hours 20 minutes flight of IX-812 from Dubai en route to Bangalore progressed without incident until just before top of descent. All was normal - *except for* the highly irregular and questionable occurrence of the captain being in a deep sleep in his seat at the controls, for some 100 or more minutes of the approximately 200-minute flight. The captain's fatigue was very likely a result of him being scheduled to fly the all-night flight - apparently at short notice - without preparatory rest and preparation time beforehand.

Having woken up (or having been woken up) only 21 minutes before landing, the captain was most likely not yet in full command of his senses or his aircraft during the descent from 37,000 feet, and possibly during the final approach and landing phases of flight. The Court of Inquiry Report on the accident refers to his *'sleep inertia'* (a sort of mental disorientation after suddenly being awoken from a deep sleep).

Due to the Mangalore Area Control Radar being unserviceable, the 'top of descent point' was delayed considerably by the young and less experienced co-pilot (while the captain slept), which put some encumbrance upon the flight crew to recalculate the descent profile and to re-examine the intended route to account for the delay of descent. As the impending events demonstrated, the flight crew failed to properly accomplish a revised descent plan.

Because of the late initiation of descent, combined with the lack of proper planning and curative action from the flight crew, the aircraft remained high in its descent profile, and high and fast in the approach procedure and final approach to landing. A whole series of violations of 'Standard Operating Procedures' and uncorrected errors led to a touchdown at 4,638 feet down the 8,038-foot runway - far beyond the aimed-for touchdown point at the 1,000-foot mark.

During an attempt to baulk the landing and to take off again, the Boeing 737-800 aircraft was unable to gain sufficient flying speed on the remaining runway. The aircraft overran the end of the runway and the safety area beyond, and crashed down a gorge, killing 158 of the 166 people on board and leaving the eight survivors gravely injured.

It is a widely accepted truism in the aviation industry that aircraft accidents are usually not caused by a single error alone, but by *a series* of events, incidents, and/or uncorrected errors, which combine to cause an accident. The fatal crash of Flight IX-812 was no exception to that well-established maxim. The series of events that led to the crash started before the top of descent with a non-compos-mentis aircraft captain. The cause of his state of mind was fatigue. The indirect, or more likely, direct cause of his fatigue was suppression of vital safety warnings concerning fatigue and its likely consequences. And ultimately, suppression and criminal neglect of proper remedial and preventative actions on those vital safety warnings.

FINDINGS OF THE COURT OF INQUIRY

The Court of Inquiry into the accident established that, inter alia, pilot fatigue and concomitant effects (sleep inertia), violations of Standard Operating Procedures, and a failure to initiate a timely go-around, played a dominant role in the chain of events that led to the accident of Flight IX-812 and the death of 158 passengers and crew.

Flight Crew Fatigue

Regarding crew fatigue, the Court of Inquiry identified an urgent need for, and independently the Bombay High Court mandated, a revision of Flight and Duty Time Limitations and related issues regarding fatigue, rest periods, and the effect of flying during the 'Window of Circadian Low' during the night. A need to take a fresh look at Duty Time Limitations for Cabin Crew, Air Traffic Controllers, and Aircraft Maintenance Engineers, was also identified by the Court of Inquiry. It was recommended that 'Fatigue Risk Management' training be incorporated and that a comprehensive view of the aspect of 'controlled rest in seat' be taken.

If the revision of Flight and Duty Time Limitations and related issues regarding fatigue were needed to be introduced *after* the accident, then much more so were they needed *beforehand*, because the impending dangers were known.

Yet, four years before the accident and before the Court of Inquiry, the problems of duty time and fatigue were raised in no uncertain manner in my safety warnings, which were suppressed with extreme indifference by Air India and Boeing Company officials. If those warnings were acted upon by Air India Express and the Indian civil aviation authority (DGCA), and were not concealed with help from Boeing, the same remedial actions recommended a posteriori by the Court of Inquiry and Bombay High Court could have been well-entrenched at the time of the accident of Flight IX-812. In all probability, the accident and loss of life would have been avoided.

My suppressed 'Captains Special Report' warned about:

> *"...habitual violations by Air India Express of the Aircraft Rules on Flight and Duty Time Limitations...... When the personnel in the operations and executive departments, who hold authority over the scheduling of flights and the duties of pilots, insist upon disregard of the Aircraft Rules it fosters a climate of unsafe aircraft operations.... It is self-evident that violation of flight time limitations, duty time limitations, and the neglect of required rest periods, endangers - or if not corrected would likely endanger - an aircraft flown by pilots subjected to such violation of limitations on a habitual basis, such as has occurred, without adequate rest".*

Violation of Standard Operating Procedures

Standard Operating Procedures (SOPs) are introduced not only to streamline flight operations, but are designed primarily to reduce error and enhance flight safety. The Court of Inquiry indicated in its accident report that violations of Standard Operating Procedures in the cockpit were a major contributory factor to the accident. During the last *21 minutes* of flight, alone, the Court of Inquiry identified some *28 violations* of Standard Operating Procedures by both pilots – more than one violation per minute on average.

The large number of deviations from safe flight procedures did not indicate a single flight anomaly or an incongruity in the last minutes of Flight IX-812 alone. Rather, it indicated 'disdain for the rules of flight' as a systemic problem in Air India Operations at the time. It must be remembered that the identified violations of the laws and flight rules only surfaced because of the tragic way the flight ended. If, on the other hand, the accident had been averted in the last minute, by a timely go-around, for instance, no one would be the wiser concerning the violations of the rules and the laws that most likely continued day after day at that time, in flight after flight.

Boeing and the Crash of Air India Flight IX-812

The crash of Flight IX-812 demonstrated unambiguously that the culture of lawlessness and disdain for flight rules, and the resultant climate of unsafe air operations, were as evident in Air India Express at the time of the accident as it was at the time my initial safety warnings were issued.

The Court of Inquiry stated in its report: *"It was, therefore, important that all crew followed standard and approved SOP of Air India Express. This would have enhanced the Situational Awareness and Communication Skills of the pilots to maintain a safer envelope of operations and better safety standards"*. There were further recommendations concerning this regard in the Court of Inquiry Accident Report. If those recommendations were needed *after* the accident, then more so were they needed *before*; again, because the impending dangers were known.

Yet, long before the Court of Inquiry Report, and long before the accident, Air India Directors and Boeing Company Directors, and other pertinent company officials, after being warned of a pending disaster, chose to violently suppress my warnings, which stated:

> *"There can be no expectation that flight crews will operate the aircraft in keeping with the law as laid down in the Rules of the Air when the example set by management is one of utter contempt for the laws that govern aircraft operations ...."* *"Failure to comply with the laws and rules governing aircraft operations give rise to ... occurrences affecting the safety of aircraft operations (and) are a prelude to accidents .... Decisive and effective corrective action and obedience to the laws governing safety will avert their recurrence".*

There *was no* obedience to the laws and *no* effective corrective action to the chronic problem of crew fatigue, thanks to the Boeing and Air India management suppressing my crucial safety warning.

As a consequence, the accident of Flight 812 *was not* averted. If those warnings were not suppressed and had instead been acted upon by the Boeing Company (as training organization), Air India Express, and the Indian aviation authorities (DGCA), the remedial actions I recommended, and those recommended a-posteriori by the Court of Inquiry, could have been well-entrenched at the time of the accident of Flight IX-812, and the loss of 158 lives and grave injury to 8 others would in all probability have been averted.

Sadly, flight crew fatigue and disobedience to the rules and laws governing flight operations proved to be *significant causes* in the horrific death of 158 people.

FUNDAMENTAL CAUSE OF THE CRASH

A *series of contributory causes* precipitated the succession of events which culminated in the aircraft crashing down a gorge and into the trees below. Breaking any one link in the chain of causes and events could likely have prevented the fatal crash. Some of the several contributory causes are briefly mentioned to illustrate this chain of events and to indicate *the fundamental cause at the start of the series.*

The 158 people on board Flight IX-812 were violently killed when the aircraft crashed down the gorge and into the trees, yet it would be naive to say that hitting the trees caused the accident. Rightly, it must be questioned what caused the aircraft to hit the trees. The aircraft crashed down the embankment and into the trees below because it overran the runway. Again, it should be asked, why did the aircraft overrun the runway? It did so because it touched down late, more than halfway down the available runway length, and the pilot failed to initiate timely 'go-around' procedures. Why then, did the aircraft touch down late? The reason was that it was too high and too fast on the 'final approach'.

Boeing and the Crash of Air India Flight IX-812

Continuing to build the chain of causes and succeeding events leading to the accident, the reason should be sought as to why the aircraft was high in speed and high in altitude on the final approach. The reason was that the flight crew overflew their top of descent point by 50 miles, failed to properly plan and fly their 'descent profile', and failed to properly monitor their 'descent and approach altitude' versus 'distance to go' to the landing.

Stepping back up the chain of events once more, one should ask: What then caused the overfly of the descent point and failure of the flight crew to properly plan and execute the descent and approach phases of flight? That pertinent failure was in turn caused by the captain being asleep for half the flight duration and until well past their normal descent and approach 'planning and briefing point'; and past their normal 'descent point' by some 50 miles. When the Captain awoke (or was awoken) from his deep sleep 21 minutes before touchdown, he was clearly suffering from impaired judgment, as the subsequent events so acutely demonstrate. In those 21 remaining minutes, he made numerous crucial mistakes and violated normal flight procedures on multiple occasions. The captain, being asleep at a time when he should have been in control and in command of his aircraft and his senses, was the *initiating event* (although not the initiating cause) of the impending accident.

Decisively, it should be questioned: What caused the captain to sleep at the controls for half the duration of the flight? The elementary and general answer, of course, is: *fatigue.* Once again, the cause must be sought: how could that dangerous abnormality happen? With certainty it can be said that Air India (Operations, Scheduling, and Dispatch Departments) and the flight crew of Flight IX-812 failed to respond to my dire safety warnings regarding crew fatigue as previously observed in Air India.

Why then, did Air India and the flight crew fail to respond to crucial warnings of an accident waiting to happen - warnings issued

101

A Dirty U.S. Government Secret

by an independent industry specialist tasked, amongst other, with the responsibility of flight safety? Resolutely it must be stated that they failed to respond because the safety warnings were suppressed and vital remedies never reached the relevant departments and flight crews. Air India, Boeing, and US Government officials silenced those warnings by forbidding their dissemination and instead retaliating against me as the author of those warnings, through terminating my employment and by attempting to kidnap and murder me.

CULPABILITY

The inquiry into the causes of the crash of Flight IX-812 verified the dire need for Air India to address pertinent safety issues raised in safety warnings prior to this accident. Timely corrective actions to the safety warnings, if instituted by Air India Express and the Indian aviation authority (DGCA), would have eliminated the chain of grievous events and prevented the accident from occurring. This point has painstakingly and unequivocally been made.

The Air India Chairman/Managing Director (CMD) and Board of Directors knew of those major factors affecting flight safety and knew of the suppressed safety warnings. Correspondence to the Air India Board of Directors, as well as documents filed in a 2009 court case against Air India Directors in the USA, substantiate that fact. (US District Court, Seattle, case no. 09cv825). Yet, no corrective action was taken upon the suppressed safety warnings, and they remained concealed.

Similarly, the Boeing Company CEO and Board of Directors knew about the safety concerns and suppression of the safety warnings - for indeed, it was Boeing officials who were responsible for their physical suppression. Correspondence to the Boeing Board of Directors and documents filed in a 2009 court case against Boeing

Directors in the US District Court, Seattle (case no. 09cv962), substantiate that fact.

Boeing and Air India were aware that suppressing crucial flight safety warnings was so imminently dangerous that it could significantly contribute to causing death or such bodily injury as is likely to cause death. Nevertheless, they suppressed the crucial flight safety warnings with extreme indifference and without any excuse for incurring the risk of causing death.

Standing rank and file behind the Boeing and Air India officials - and acting in concert with them - was a whole bevy of US Government officials who were involved in the assassination attempts upon me and the cover-up that ensured the safety warnings were kept suppressed. Or, who were knowingly involved in providing a safe haven and passage to the would-be assassins and their masters.

Air India and Boeing Company officials, and US Government officials who supported and enabled them, are responsible and culpable for the 'originating cause' of the accident, which initiated the series of events that led to the fatal crash of Air India flight IX-812.

MURDER CHARGES

In terms of the Indian Penal Code

The Indian Penal Code, Section 300 states that the act of causing death is considered murder if:

> **Section 300:** *"... the person committing the act knows that it is so imminently dangerous that it must, in all probability, cause death or such bodily injury as is likely to cause death, and commits such act without any excuse for incurring the risk of causing death or such injury as aforesaid.*

A Dirty U.S. Government Secret

Air India and Boeing Company officials knew of the dangers exposed in my flight safety warnings. They were cognizant of the strong possibility that suppressing those warnings and failing to correct a perilous situation warned about would very likely lead to an accident and death. Yet they chose to suppress the warnings and ignore the dangers without any excuse for incurring the risk of causing death. Air India and Boeing officials are thus *culpable, under Section 300, for the murder of the 158 people who perished.*

In addition, the Indian Penal Code, Section 301 describes culpable homicide (murder) by causing the death of persons other than the person whose death was intended: –

> **Section 301:** *"If a person, by doing anything which he intends or knows likely to cause death, commits culpable homicide by causing the death of any person whose death he neither intends nor knows himself to be likely to cause, the culpable homicide committed by the offender is of the same description of which it would have been if he had caused the death of the person whose death he intended or knew himself to be likely to cause".*

Whereas the deaths of the 158 passengers and crew *were not intended* by Air India, Boeing, and US Government officials implicated, *my death certainly was intended* by their abortive kidnap and murder attempts. The unintended culpable homicide committed by Air India and Boeing Company officials by suppressing safety information is of the same description as the *'kidnap and murder'* attempts made upon me; and my death *was intended* in their effort to suppress that safety information. Thus, the illegal acts of Air India officials, acting in concert with Boeing Company and US Government officials, also violate Section 301 of the Indian Penal Code and *constitute murder of the 158 people who perished.*

Murder Charges in terms of the United States Code

Simultaneous to the pressure exerted by Air India on the Boeing Company - in order to suppress the damning safety warnings and silence my testimony on violations of Air Law within Air India - President George W. Bush exerted pressure on Boeing to silence my testimony on criminal offenses the President committed in the United States Supreme Court. Included in the felonies was theft of incriminating evidence from the Court Record in Supreme Court case no. 05-140.

Consequently, the incitement by Air India upon the Boeing Company merged with the incitement by President Bush upon the Boeing Company. Their combined incitement resulted in a single series of malevolent responses by Boeing. The source of incitement of Boeing's actions is not distinguishable. Boeing responded to that simultaneous pressure from Air India and President Bush by unwarranted disciplinary action against me, followed respectively by threats against my employment, suspension without pay, termination of my employment, and abortive attempts to kidnap and murder me. Boeing officials attempted to inveigle me to an area away from my normal workplace, there to unlawfully seize me - kidnap me - in execution of the plot to murder me.

While the kidnap and murder attempts upon me were abortive, they were, however, entirely successful in suppressing the flight safety warnings issued by me, which in turn largely contributed to the disastrous end of Flight IX-812 and the concomitant loss of life.

Although the deaths of the 158 persons on board Air India Flight IX-812 were not caused with malice aforethought, their murder was perpetrated from a premeditated design unlawfully and maliciously to affect my death – and in that manner to suppress pertinent safety warnings and remedial actions, and suppress other crimes committed by Air India and Boeing Company officials, and by US President George W. Bush. The United States Code, statute 18USC1111, declares in relevant part:

> **18USC1111:** *In relevant part: "Every murder... perpetrated from a premeditated design unlawfully and maliciously to effect the death of any human being other than him who is killed, is murder in the first degree".*

The premeditated but foiled attempts by the troika of Air India officials, Boeing Company officials, and President George W. Bush and agents, to affect my death, suppressed my flight safety warnings, which led to 158 innocent people being killed instead. Those criminal acts violate the United States Code statute 18USC1111 and *constitute murder in the first degree.*

Murder Charges in terms of the RCW

Boeing Commercial Airplanes is based in Seattle, and Boeing's unlawful conduct to suppress the vital flight safety warnings was perpetrated in Seattle, Washington State. The Revised Code of Washington (RCW), statute RCW9A.32.030, states in relevant parts:

> **RCW9A.32.030:** *"(1) A person is guilty of murder in the first degree when: ... (b) Under circumstances manifesting an extreme indifference to human life, he or she engages in conduct which creates a grave risk of death to any person, and thereby causes the death of a person;"*

Boeing's unlawful acts of suppressing my vital flight safety warnings created a grave risk to flight operations at Air India in general and to Flight IX-812 in particular. The suppression and lack of remedial actions manifested an extreme indifference to human life, caused the death of 158 people, and pursuant to statute RCW9A.32.030 constitutes murder in the first degree.

Murder Charges against Accomplices and Accessories

Air India and Boeing Company officials, and President G.W. Bush and agents, do not carry sole culpability in the murder of 158 passengers and crew of Flight IX-812. There are many others who created the circumstances, offered the opportunity, furthered the commission of, or made it possible and enabled the offenders to commit murder. Still others assisted the offenders to escape justice, which served to perpetuate the concealment of the safety warnings.

They are the conspirators in the major criminal endeavor operating with impunity within the government and the courts of the United States, and further afield, as described in the earlier chapters of this book.

The conspirators acted to obstruct the administration of the laws upon those who attempted my murder and upon those who are culpable in the death of 158 people; they defeated the course of justice in the court cases; they provided protection from prosecution to the attempted murderers and they denied constitutional rights to due process and protection of the laws - to me as witness, and to the public at large. Knowing that heinous crimes were committed against the United States, the conspirators have to date prevented the apprehension, trial, and punishment of the murderers of 158 people. The United States Code, statute 18USC2, describes the criminal liability of *accomplices* as follows:

> ***18USC2:*** *(a) Whoever commits an offense against the United States or aids, abets, counsels, commands, induces or procures its commission, is punishable as a principal. (b) Whoever willfully causes an act to be done which, if directly performed by him or another, would be an offense against the United States, is punishable as a principal.*

The United States Code, statute 18USC3, describes the criminal liability of *accessories after the fact* as follows:

18USC3: "Whoever, knowing that an offense against the United States has been committed, receives, relieves, comforts or assists the offender in order to hinder or prevent his apprehension, trial or punishment, is an accessory after the fact".

Pursuant 18USC2 and 18USC3, every criminal conspirator from the United States Government (and further afield) who aided in any way in the commission of this murder or who assisted the Boeing and Air India murderers to escape arrest, trial, and punishment, is also liable in the murder of 158 passengers and crew of Air India Express Flight IX-812.

Where the Department of Justice willfully failed to prosecute, there I took up the responsibility to file criminal complaints and act as Prosecutor Qui Tam – meaning, a private prosecutor acting on behalf of himself and on behalf of the United States.

THE CULPABILITY OF PRESIDENT OBAMA

During his eight years and two terms in office, President Barack Obama was intensely petitioned to address the George W. Bush-Boeing seditious conspiracy and the escalating insurrection against the laws, sweeping through his Administration, the government, and the courts of the United States. He received details of those crimes in my 111 letters to him, in several filings of the Dossier of Crimes, and in quite a few court cases which involved him. (See Appendix 2). Instead of using his power and authority to terminate the ongoing criminal endeavor, President Obama protected from prosecution, former President George W. Bush, the Boeing Company, and the government officials implicated in the crimes. Obama not only failed his duty to take care of the faithful execution of the laws, where the laws were being violated en masse, but he also actively obstructed the due and proper course of justice in the court cases in which he was implicated. He enabled the criminal conspirators to continue the insurrection against the laws; and the seditious conspirators to escape justice. He enabled the Boeing Company's culpability in two air accidents and, by that deed, enabled the death and injury of 350 people. *Obama is therefore culpable in the murder of those who perished in the air accidents of Air India 812 and Asiana 214.*

FURTHER FLIGHT SAFETY WARNINGS ISSUED

After the accident of Air India Flight IX-812, when no action was taken by United States and Indian authorities to address Boeing and Air India's criminal violations, further flight safety warnings were issued by me to the Boeing Company and to President Obama and his Cabinet (including the Secretary for Transportation) concerning the lawlessness existing at the Boeing Company and the peril that it presented to the public safety, internationally. The new flight safety warning was also issued to Congress and to the Courts for their peremptory action, including the US District Court (Seattle) and the US Supreme Court. The flight safety warning bluntly stated that unless the lawlessness within the Boeing Company was addressed, the disastrous example of Flight IX-812 was going to be repeated with certainty, with further loss of innocent human life to the same causes.

Once again, the flight safety warnings were willfully and criminally ignored with extreme indifference to human life exhibited by the Boeing Company, by President Obama and his Cabinet, and by the US Congress and the US Courts. As a direct consequence of that failure to act upon and investigate and prosecute the lawlessness within Boeing, another avoidable accident would soon follow, with loss of life and grave injury to passengers and crew, namely, that of Asiana Flight 214 in San Francisco, as discussed in Chapter 9. The main cause turned out to be of a similar nature: suppression of crucial safety information that was vital to the safe conduct of that flight.

Yet, my many appeals to those in public office, to address the criminality within the Boeing Company and within the US Government, fell on deaf ears. As demonstrated in the next chapters, their roles in neglecting to deal with known criminality constituted an *'insurrection against the laws of the United States'*, with concomitant disastrous consequences.

Chapter 7
Insurrection against the Laws

"This is not an inconsequential case before you. On the contrary, failure to act against these offences will have profound implications that may well indicate the incipient but inevitable decay of the concept of 'Individual Rights'. Should this noble experiment by mankind fail in this country, it will fail in many other countries as well, where the embryonic ideals of human rights are less established. With these simple words, this nation is put to the test...."

Extract from Chapter 7.

PUBLIC OFFICE

Responsibility in Government

There are those in society who have the penchant to take on the weighty responsibility of public position – and that is a virtue. Assuming such a position, liability is taken on for the quality of life and the social well-being of the populace over whom they wield power - an onerous responsibility indeed. When that self-assumed responsibility is neglected in favor of their own personal self-interest or the personal interests of their colleagues, that misuse of their virtue becomes their vice. That vice can engender a violent impact upon society, as the sequence of events in this narrative, if carefully followed, will surely demonstrate.

Persons elected or appointed to an office of honor or profit in the civil service or uniformed services of the United States take an oath to serve to the highest good of the public, as follows:

Statute 5USC3331: "I do solemnly swear (or affirm) that I will support and defend the Constitution of the United States against all enemies, foreign and domestic; that I will bear true faith and allegiance to the same; that I take this obligation freely, without any mental reservation or purpose of evasion; and that I will well and faithfully discharge the duties of the office on which I am about to enter. So help me God."

Those men and women who dare to place themselves in a position of authority over their fellowman and who take an oath to serve their countrymen, proclaiming the welfare of their subjects at the center of their hearts, had better honor that oath and honor their subjects whilst acting in the name of the Deity of whom they/we know naught. For good measure, they should consider the immutable 'Laws of the Universe', perfect in their precision: error begets correction; ignorance begets learning; dastardliness leads to pain. Since one purpose of life's experiences, including justice and restitution, is to create the environment by which man can move closer to that Deity invoked in the United States 'Oath of Office.

Measure the acts and/or willful dereliction of duty of the public servants implicated in this case. Measure their acts or failure to act against their pact made with the nation and with the High One, ostensibly 'without any mental reservation or purpose of evasion'. Measure their malevolence in attempting to kill a citizen who has persistently sought justice and who has repeatedly reminded them of their oath and appealed to them to perform the duties they are only there for to perform. And measure their denial of justice and denial of protection of the laws to their quarry, in terms of immutable universal law. Sooner or later, there must be a correction of such error, learning from such ignorance, and experiencing the pain that such dastardliness unfailingly brings under universal law.

Yet, 'how weak are my words in comparison to the sublimity of this subject'.

Appeal to President Obama

Amongst my numerous letters to President Obama during the early build-up of this case regarding the matter of official misconduct, on May 1, 2009, shortly after he took office for his first term, I wrote:

"Dear President Obama,

Re: Anarchy within the Government and the Courts of the United States

I again bring your attention to a state of anarchy persisting within the government and the courts of the United States and the 50 States and entreat you as United States President to rectify this state of affairs. Numerous high-level government officials and politicians are conducting sedition and a virulent insurrection against the laws of the United States. The milieu in which this lawlessness has been allowed to proliferate is well known to you through my previous correspondence (see list of correspondence in Appendix 1); also, by means of a 'Dossier of Crimes' filed with you on several occasions, the latest being January 22, 2009; and through documents in the Supreme Court Case "United States of America vs. 14,164 Seditious Conspirators" filed with you, which case is currently and corruptly being stalled in the Supreme Court. (See proof of filing in Appendix 2). However, some pertinent examples of the sedition are herewith briefly reiterated for your aide memoire …….

The anarchy associated with this case is by no means isolated to this particular instance alone; it is merely symptomatic of the lawlessness that permeates the

113

entire United States government and judicial establishment. Your own insalubrious contributions thereto are considerable:

- *Criminally neglecting to address the criminal complaints presented to you for action pursuant to 18USC4 & 18USC2382.*
- *Callously protecting cold-blooded killers from prosecution whilst knowing that, in violation of 18USC1512, they continue their plot to murder me as a witness to crimes committed by government officers.*
- *Willfully acting in concert with malfeasant colleagues to obstruct justice and the administration of the laws in violation of 18USC3 & 18USC1505.*
- *Providing a safe haven and passage to common criminals with one paramount purpose in mind: to protect seditious officials from prosecution and public disgrace, knowing that they will do the same for you.*
- *Ignoring the US Constitution and the laws that debar you from holding an official position under the United States, pursuant to 18USC2381, 18USC2383, and the 14th Amendment, §3.*

The anarchy within the United States government stands deeply exposed in this matter. Your own failure to live up to your sacrosanct oath has fanned the fires of that anarchy. For the sake of present and future generations of Americans, this lawlessness must cease.

There is but one thing to do to mitigate past failures. You must come to recognize the cataclysmic condition facing the nation today, with its concomitant violent impact upon society, and you must take strong action to change it. That much you owe – not just to your fellow Americans, but also to yourself. Sincerely...."

No reply was received on this letter, and no action was forthcoming to this or any other appeals addressed to President Obama concerning the broad criminal conspiracy. What dishonor and disrespect does that show towards the American people who have bestowed upon the President their greatest honor and esteem? What integrity and what merit can there be in a leader who so unashamedly betrays the public trust?

Bush Plot Inherited

One hundred and eleven (111) appeals to Barack Obama as US Senator and/or President informed him of the seditious conspiracy and requested that he take care of the faithful execution of the laws. Evidence of the anarchy was presented to him on most of those occasions. Despite his first-hand knowledge of the ongoing murder plot (as reiterated in a White House meeting which he attended on January 7, 2009 before taking office); despite his obligations under the Constitution and his oath of office; notwithstanding his moral duties to society (and to himself), President Obama took no action to tend to the criminality and instead resolutely covered up the affair.

President Obama was directly responsible for the corrupt and summary dismissal of several criminal cases in the United States courts, which cases unsuccessfully attempted to address the crimes committed by US officials and their co-conspirators. President Obama was also implored to dismantle the trap set (by President George W. Bush) for my kidnapping at the Boeing Company and at the Federal Aviation Administration, and to repeal the government assassination plot. That he tacitly refused to do, leaving the murder plot inherited from President Bush menacingly intact and corroborating Obama's involvement – and culpability.

A Dirty U.S. Government Secret

Within the heart of the US Department of Justice, President Obama maintained an operational task force to manage various aspects of the criminal endeavor as well as the fallout from my efforts to instigate law, order, and justice upon the matter. That task force was also tasked to *'contend with me'* as principal witness to the crimes committed by US Government officers (including those committed by President Obama himself). That operational team, together with its predecessor under President Bush, was responsible for the tapping of my communications, slander of my good name, for destroying my career and livelihood, for preventing me from practicing my profession, for denying me justice in the courts, and for executing the attempts to kidnap and assassinate me. On that team were to be found the controllers of the assassins who had plotted my demise.

In direct response to my filing of a US Supreme Court case in re *'International Terrorism and Murder'* during December 2010, under President Obama, that team activated a third ploy to kill me – this time intending to operate through one of the Departments of the Washington State Government. Being timeously forewarned about that *third* assassination attempt and responding by immediately bringing the plot to light, it was apparently suspended.

As with President Bush, President Obama is a defendant in the criminal case *'United States of America vs. 14,164 Seditious Conspirators'* brought by the United States against the group of conspiring government officials. (Case number not assigned). The subversion case remains pending in the United States Supreme Court - although effectively and illegally obstructed. As a consequence of his criminal actions and adding to the insurrection against the laws, President Obama was legally debarred from holding office under the United States pursuant to the Constitution (14th Amendment, §3) and the statutes 18USC2381 & 18USC2383.

The United States Constitution, in the 14th Amendment, Section 3, states unequivocally:

> *"No person shall be a Senator or Representative in Congress, or elector of President and Vice President, or hold any office, civil or military, under the United States, or under any state, who, having previously taken an oath, as a member of Congress, or as an officer of the United States, or as a member of any state legislature, or as an executive or judicial officer of any state, to support the Constitution of the United States, **shall have engaged in insurrection or rebellion against the same,** or given aid or comfort to the enemies thereof. But Congress may, by a vote of two-thirds of each House, remove such disability".*

But in practice, the Constitution and the laws hold no influence on high officials. President Obama completed eight years in office without being affected in the slightest by the charges filed against him for enabling the seditious conspiracy in the government to continue, for leading the insurrection against the laws, and for willfully failing to take care of the faithful execution of the laws.

The Role of the President's Cabinet

The entire United States 'Executive' at that time, including every member of the Cabinets of Presidents George W Bush and Obama, had been informed of the seditious conspiracy against the United States of America. Every executive member had been provided with prima facie evidence thereof and was requested to take action against the subversion and crime. Every executive member under Presidents Bush and Obama had a duty to act and had taken an oath to perform that duty and to defend the nation against its enemies, *foreign or domestic*. And every executive member instead chose to provide aid and comfort and safe haven and passage to known insurgents against the laws – fellow government officers.

117

There are many other high-profile and politically powerful officials amongst the conspirators at the time of writing. Their propensity to malice and the absolute impunity with which they can and do violate the laws is amply demonstrated in the *'Dossier of Crimes'*. (See review of the dossier in *Appendix 3 – Overview of Evidence.*). When the extent of their legal predicament is considered and evidence of stalking is taken into account, further attempts to eliminate me as a witness are highly probable.

As a species, we take our cue from those in authority. As children, we mimic the ways of our parents; as school kids, we learn from our school teachers, and at university, from our professors and peers about life. At work, we involuntarily imitate the behavior and direction given by our supervisors and managers, and in turn, they take their cue from those above them. As a nation, we consciously or unconsciously follow the example and the norm set by our President, our Congress, our Courts, and our leaders in all spheres of civic life. What hope is there for this nation then, when that example is one of murder of any subject who crosses their path - and the protection from prosecution, of those who were sent to murder and those who sent them? Where, within the three branches of the United States Government today, does a moral and law-abiding spirit hold sway? Let us together take a look and truthfully answer this important self-addressed question.

INSURRECTION AGAINST THE LAWS OF THE UNITED STATES

The statute on ***Insurrection or Rebellion,*** 18USC2383, dictates that:

> *"Whoever incites, assists, or engages in any rebellion or insurrection against the authority of the United States, **or the laws thereof**, or gives aid and comfort thereto, is in violation of the statute on*

rebellion or insurrection and shall be incapable of holding any office under the United States".

The ongoing revolt *against the laws* of the United States is powerfully demonstrated by more than 15,000 US officials from all three branches of federal and state government who have become implicated in this matter. As time progresses, their numbers continue to rise. Their combined lawlessness constitutes a vituperative insurrection against the laws. Yet the perpetrators are protected and illegally remain in their positions of power from whence they persistently conspire against the United States and the rule of law. Unambiguous examples abound in the 'Dossier of Crimes' and in the proceedings of 62 court cases that fruitlessly attempted to address the burgeoning criminal endeavor within the United States government.

The Role of the Justice Department and the FBI

As far back as January 27, 2003, the United States Department of Justice, its Attorney Generals and US Attorneys, US Marshals, and FBI, have step by step been kept informed of the development of this pervasive 'insurrection against the laws' via more than *1000 letters* and 90 filings of the *'Dossier of Crimes'*. Thirty-eight letters of appeal were sent to FBI Director Mueller personally, four to Director Comey, and thirty-two to Director Wray. The noteworthy response of the Department of Justice and the FBI was to dispatch its FBI agents in February 2006, to coordinate my kidnapping and murder through surrogates at the Boeing Company and the FAA. When those attempts failed, the Department of Justice held meetings with all interested parties to plot their next malicious steps to thwart the administration of the laws.

Appeal to the Civil Rights Division

During the *very early stages* of the 'insurrection against the laws', I appealed to Assistant Attorney General Ralph Boyd from the Civil Rights Division of the United States Department of Justice:

> *"Dear Mr. Boyd,*
>
> > *Re: Oppression and Deprivation of Rights*
>
> *Civil Rights for individuals is a concept that has not been with us for very long in terms of human development. It took several hundred years from the time of the Magna Carta of 1215, for these avant-garde ideals on human freedom to mature sufficiently in the human psyche, to where the founding fathers of the emerging American nation could incorporate them into our Constitution. A further two hundred years were required for American society to learn to live up to the elevated principles in a bona fide way. Now a leading nation, America's triumphs are emulated by an increasing number of countries.*
>
> *Fledgling as these 'Rights' are, and treasured as they are today in American society, these forward-thinking ideas carry with them responsibilities for the individual to exercise these esteemed rights in such a way that they do not encroach upon the rights of another. When the balance is found in the practice of individual rights, a harmonious and benevolent society ensues.*
>
> *The government has been empowered by the people to ensure, protect, and maintain these 'rights of the individual'. This governmental function is written into the laws of the society.*

However, of late, this function of government has not been performed in Washington State. On the contrary, senior officers of that state have engaged in criminal acts against the public in general and an individual in particular, in an effort to protect a corrupt and lawless government. The custodians of the power intended to protect the 'rights of the individual' have turned that power upon the individual to repress and deny him his 'Civil Rights'.

Twelve hundred and thirty-nine (1,239) crimes have been committed against the basic rights of an individual by 195 Officers of Washington State, and two others. Every crime and every perpetrator had but one common goal, and that was to deprive a law-abiding citizen of his 'Rights'. The criminal acts are of a serious nature and include burglary, perjury, fraud, theft, removal of court evidence, denial of a fair trial, and rendering criminal assistance. All the crimes are directed at the oppression of the right to lawful possession of property, and at the oppression of the right to protection by the law.
... ...

This is not an inconsequential case before you. On the contrary, failure to act against these offences will have profound implications that may well indicate the incipient but inevitable decay of the concept of 'Individual Rights'. Should this noble experiment by mankind fail in this country, it will fail in many other countries as well, where the embryonic ideals of human rights are less established.

This landmark case puts America squarely at the crossroads of human development. This nation cannot hope to export forward-thinking views on human rights to less developed nations of the world, whilst practicing oppression of individual rights at home. Such insincerity will not reflect well upon the President and the leadership of this country, just as the case under consideration does not reflect well upon Governor Gary Locke and the Washington State Government.

The United States can deal decisively with the lawlessness of one of its rogue States and thereby eliminate the stain thus caused upon the nation. Or, where the rule of law and protection of individual property are concerned, this country can, in hypocrisy, join the likes of countries such as Zimbabwe under the shenanigans of President Mugabe.

This choice will be made in the Department of Justice by the Civil Rights Division. And that choice will not be irrelevant. I proffer that the choices made by this leading nation will not only be written into the records of this country, but will be recorded in the history of human development as well.

With these simple words, this nation is put to the test. Sincerely…"

Again, no reply was received on this letter, and no action was forthcoming from the Department of Justice regarding the extensive criminal conspiracy. To discover the accessory dealings, by criminal misconduct, of the very department of government tasked with law and order, is sufficient to shake one's confidence in humanity. Yet, I was determined to leave no stone unturned in my unrelenting pursuit of justice. But where else could I turn for help?

The Role of the Federal Courts

The revolt against the authority and the laws of the United States is also powerfully demonstrated by some 352 corrupt proceedings in the 62 court cases listed in *Appendix 2.* Of the 62 cases, sixty-one were conducted pro se. The patently lawless proceedings violate multiple statutes on innumerable counts in an effort to aid lawbreaking government officials to escape prosecution. That lawlessness undeniably contributes to the powerful 'insurrection against the laws' of the United States, perpetrated in most part by government officers.

From the earliest stages of the matter, the role of the federal judiciary has been one of considerable corruption. Amongst numerous other statutory obligations to act against malfeasant officials, the Federal Rules of Criminal Procedure (Rules 4 and 41) dictate that the courts *shall* arrest those defendants in a court action who are suspected of crimes and those crimes are filed with the court under affidavit. A judge has no choice in the matter; he *shall* obey the rules. Yet, not a single arrest has been made by the judges in the relevant cases. Not a single crime amongst a multitude committed by officials and filed under affidavit with the courts in the 62 cases has been investigated or prosecuted, despite overwhelming and unambiguous evidence presented under oath.

In every civil and criminal case filed against the seditious government conspirators, the federal courts simply swept all criminal charges against officials under the carpet, thereby impeding a critical function of government and nullifying their very own *raison d'être*. In that way, 1,252 fully informed federal judges aided and abetted known criminals to escape justice, with one paramount purpose in mind: to protect seditious officials from prosecution and public disgrace, knowing that those officials would do the same for them.

Three criminal cases against officials, *filed by the United States* in the US District Court of Colorado, were summarily and illegally dismissed by corrupt judges without addressing the underlying crimes. The three criminal cases were consolidated into a single subversion case titled *'United States of America vs. 14,164 Seditious*

Conspirators', filed in the US Supreme Court. The Supreme Court Justices, the supreme corruptors who are themselves defendants in that case, predictably obstructed the case in their court, thereby setting an abysmal paradigm for the entire federal court system on the matter.

The Role of State Governments and the Judiciary of the 50 States

The governments of the 50 States of the United States have each been fully informed of the insurrection and sedition through their governors, attorneys general, police chiefs, legislators, and the judges of three levels of state courts. The state governments and judiciary were provided with evidence of the crimes and the applicable laws, and were similarly requested to invoke their authority under law to take appropriate action against the subversion and the criminal conspirators within their State. No action has been forthcoming from any of the state governments or courts to address the torrent of crime. The states have instead provided safe haven and passage to the insurrectionists' resident in their own states.

Role of the United States Armed Forces

Given the extent of the insurrection within the government and considering the powerful obstruction to the administration and execution of the laws exercised by the insurgents, five Joint Chiefs of Staff and fifty-three other admirals and generals of the United States Armed Forces were informed of the sedition and were requested to address the insurrection against the laws.

The United States Armed Forces have a duty prescribed by law and its senior officers have taken an oath to defend the country against its enemies, *foreign or domestic*. Yet, amongst the nation's top military commanders, amongst 58 generals and admirals who are fully informed of the insurrection, no one has dared to break ranks and address the sedition; no one has shown the fortitude or rectitude to perform their clearly defined military duty; and not one has honored his oath to defend the nation against its domestic enemies in this case. *Not one.* Every one of the 58 generals and admirals has actively assisted and engaged in rebellion or insurrection against the authority of the United States, *and the laws thereof*, and has given aid and comfort thereto.

The Role of the US Congress

Amongst some 14,000 written appeals for protection of the laws are numerous appeals to every one of the 535 Members of Congress, individually and collectively, to address the criminal conspiracy within the government. In addition, the Senate and House Judiciary Committees, the Senate Committee on Government Affairs, the House Committee on Government Reform, the Senate President, and the Speaker of the House have all been requested through multiple letters to take action pursuant to congressional oversight jurisdiction over the executive and judiciary. *To no avail.*

Instead of addressing the crimes detailed in the 'Dossier of Crimes' and tackling the corruption in the Courts and Administrations, the committees and Congressmen shunned the requests and willfully failed to perform their critical oversight duties. With callous indifference, they sanctioned the criminal activities of their government peers.

Incestuous Relationship between the Three Branches of Government

The criminality stretches from top to bottom of all three branches of the United States Government. The insurgents and traitors are found in Congress, in the Supreme Court of the United States, and in the White House and Administration.

The courts illegally protected consecutive Presidents Bush and Obama and their co-conspirators from culpability for crimes committed - including the crime of conspiracy to kidnap and murder, party to Boeing mass murder, seditious conspiracy, insurrection against the laws, and treason against the United States. Congress consecutively protected the Presidents and corrupt judges from impeachment, removal, and prosecution. In their turn, the Congressmen enjoyed the protection of the Presidents and the courts from culpability for *their* failure of crucial duty to the people and to the state. One dirty hand washes the other.

The evidence to hand vividly exposes the incestuous relationship between the three branches of the United States Government. This undesirable closed loop association, which saturates all levels of the establishment, has fostered mutual assistance and incitement to engage in rebellion and insurrection against the laws of the United States and has provided aid and comfort, safe haven and passage, and impunity to known insurgents and traitors against the Constitution.

The Constitution and the laws forbid the insurgents and traitors from holding office under the United States - yet they do so in blatant defiance of the United States Constitution and statutes.

The Role of a 'Free' United States Press

In the strongly polarized political climate of the present era, the country's news media have become mere gossip columns and propaganda apparatus for one or the other political party. Not even the damage and cleanup following a major hurricane, for example, is free from political mudslinging against 'the extreme incompetence of the other side'. Nor were 1.2 million American deaths from COVID-19 free from partisan profanity upon the other party, where both catastrophes were clearly acts of nature that were dealt with as best as one can under prevailing circumstances

Since the case under scrutiny in this story is apolitical and involves wrongdoing in both Republican *and* Democratic parties and their leadership, the news media have for years chosen to keep their vociferous and untrustworthy tongues at bay lest reporting stain their particular side's name and reputation. The point of view is held that the American media has a moral duty, if not a legal duty, to inform the American nation of the known lawlessness within the government establishment.

Periodic press releases to the main American news media (166 releases to date), informed correspondents during two and a half decades of the proliferation of the seditious conspiracy and insurrection against the laws. Throughout the propagation of the criminal endeavor described herewith, the American press – monopolized, manipulated, and controlled, though fully informed – has remained silent and has thereby ensured that the American nation slumbers on, blissfully unaware.

Somewhere in the corrective process, this nation (and many others besides) will be forced to reorient its media, which so pulverizes the population.

COLORADO CRIMINAL CASES RE INSURRECTION

Responding to criminal complaints that I filed with the United States District Court in Colorado, the Clerk of the Court appropriately opened three criminal cases on February 21, 2008. Those complaints addressed the insurrection against the laws and seditious conspiracy against the United States.

On the same day on which the court cases were filed, a District Court Judge hurriedly, corruptly, and illegally (in violation of 18USC3041 and 3060) dismissed those cases from court without addressing the crimes or arresting the criminals as per due process. In each of the three cases, appeals were filed in the United States 10th Circuit Court of Appeals. The cases are:

United States vs. Bush, Roberts, Gonzales, Mueller
1. U.S. District Court, District of Colorado, Case # 08-cr-00085-ZLW

2. U.S. Court of Appeals, 10th Circuit, Case # 08-1064

United States vs. 443 Known Insurgents

3. U.S. District Court, District of Colorado, Case # 08-cr-00086-ZLW
4. U.S. Court of Appeals, 10th Circuit, Case # 08-1063

United States vs. 535 Members of the 110th Congress

5. U.S. District Court, District of Colorado, Case # 08-cr-00087-ZLW
6. U.S. Court of Appeals, 10th Circuit, Case # 08-1061

United States vs. 14,164 Seditious Conspirators

7. U.S. Supreme Court, case number not assigned.

It became apparent that the wave of criminality amongst government and judicial officers, aimed at protecting law-breaking officials from prosecution, inundated these six criminal cases as well. Attorney General Michael B. Mukasey and the United States Attorney for Colorado failed to put in an appearance as attorneys on behalf of the United States Government. The Department of Justice willfully failed to summons and/or arrest the defendants; and deliberately failed to convene an independent counsel to address the crimes of the senior officials implicated, as the statutes dictate. The Department of Justice further failed to prosecute the defendants who stand accused of the serious crimes of insurrection, seditious conspiracy, and conspiracy to kidnap and murder a witness (or cover up of that conspiracy), and more.

The numerous crimes committed by the District Court Judge in her hasty dismissal of the cases were presented as integral parts of the three Appeal Briefs to the 10th Circuit. In their turn, the 10th Circuit Appeals Court judges collectively and willfully failed to arrest and/or summons the defendants, and failed to address their crimes – in violation of 18USC3041 and 3060. The Circuit judges also failed to request or appoint a prosecutor. An urgent ex parte motion calling for the court to appoint a prosecutor, as was the court's duty, was perversely denied as being 'moot'.

The three appeal cases were dismissed on the fraudulent grounds that the witness who reported the crimes had no standing to 'prosecute'. Incidentally, there is no law that forbids a witness or victim from filing a criminal case. More importantly, the legal standing of the witness was irrelevant in the case since it was *the United States* and not the *witness* that brought the criminal cases and had the duty to prosecute the cases. A 'Motion for Joinder' of additional conspirators was granted by the 10th Circuit Court before dismissal, and the three criminal cases were appealed to the US Supreme Court as a single consolidated case, titled: *United States of America vs 14,164 Seditious Conspirators* (no case number was assigned by the Supreme Court).

However, the virulent criminal ring operating in the US Supreme Court embroiling the Supreme Court Police, the Court Clerk and his personnel, and the nine Justices, has been allowed to continue its criminal activities with impunity. The subversive activities of this group of seditious conspirators were well described in the Petition for Writ of Certiorari filed in the combined case against the 14,164 seditious conspirators, and in the *'Dossier of Crimes'* accompanying the certiorari petition.

The Supreme Court Justices, who are named defendants in the consolidated criminal case, were requested to recuse themselves. They were requested to appoint judges who are not involved in the insurrection to hear that important case. The serious felonies, committed by 14,535 malfeasant government officials and 54 others (as of that time), have yet to be investigated and prosecuted, including the crimes of: theft of court record, tampering with a witness, intimidation and retaliation against a litigant, attempted kidnap and murder of a Supreme Court litigant, obstruction of justice, insurrection against the laws, and seditious conspiracy against the United States, and many more severe crimes.

Thus far, protection from prosecution has been *absolute* for the law-breaking government officials implicated. The government officers, who continue to violate the laws at the expense of the common man, *remain unassailable.* At the time of writing these facts, the combined appeal case, as with 13 other associated cases, effectively obstructed and remains pending, but illegally obstructed and suppressed for years, in that venue of supreme corruption: the United States Supreme Court.

However, it is not the US Supreme Court alone, but many other courts and government agencies acting in concert in the pervasive official misconduct, that has broken down the institutions of law and order.

Chapter 8
Pervasive Official Misconduct

"All tyranny needs to gain a foothold is for people of good conscience to remain silent" - *Thomas Jefferson.*

THE MODUS OPERANDI

The lawlessness within the United States Government exposed in this matter has persisted over an extended period of two and a half decades after the first criminal charges were filed in the matter and left unattended. The seditious conspirators have enjoyed the full cooperation of all state and federal government institutions tasked with law and order, to enable them to so persistently obstruct and defeat the normal course of justice. It necessitated the sanction and collaboration of multiple agencies, who willingly colluded without restraint, and with zest, to assist the law-breaking officials to escape punishment.

In an endeavor to highlight the scourge of impunity, some random examples of the *modus operandi* of those government agencies and officials are illustrated in this chapter. For more serious investigators, a thorough picture will only emerge through familiarity with the incriminating evidence in the court cases, in the Dossier of Crimes, and in the correspondence (see Appendix 3: An Overview of Evidence). Nevertheless, the reprehensible examples presented herewith should provide the interested reader with sufficient insight into the methods used by government officials to obstruct justice on law-breaking colleagues in every conceivable and inconceivable way possible – and then to veil those methods from public scrutiny by deceit and dishonesty.

Failure of any one agency within the chain of agencies in the legal process is sufficient to defeat the normal course of justice. However, in this matter, law enforcement agencies, prosecutors, judges, congressmen, the 50 State Governments, the US Executive, and the armed forces, *all* demonstrated a tacit refusal to perform their lawful duties; or to obey their oath of office; or to protect the American public against the onslaught of seditious officials. Or, to investigate grave criminal offenses against the public, including Boeing Company mass murder, insurrection against the laws, seditious conspiracy, and treason against the nation. A combination of institutions acting in concert is what has defeated justice so absolutely in this matter. The criminal dereliction of duty *by every agency* in the chain of the legal process (the due process of law) is best illustrated by specific examples, which are provided below.

LAW ENFORCEMENT AGENCIES

Federal Bureau of Investigation

As a national security organization, the stated mission of the FBI is to protect and defend the United States against terrorist and foreign intelligence threats, to uphold and enforce the criminal laws of the United States, and to provide leadership and criminal justice services to federal, state, municipal, and international agencies and partners.

The affirmed *priorities* of the FBI focus on "threats that challenge the foundations of American society or involve dangers too large or complex for any local or state authority to handle alone". Would a major seditious conspiracy and insurrection against the laws, domestically, not perhaps qualify? The FBI further declares that the agency will "produce and use intelligence to protect the nation from threats and to bring to justice those who violate the law". The noble stated priorities of the FBI aim to:

- o Protect the United States from terrorists;
- o Combat public corruption at all levels;
- o Protect civil rights;
- o Combat national/transnational criminal organizations and enterprises;
- o Combat significant violent crime;
- o Support federal, state, local, and international partners.

The FBI *motto* is: "Fidelity, Bravery, and Integrity", whilst their *core values,* as expressed in their own words, are:

- o Rigorous obedience to the Constitution of the United States;
- o Respect for the dignity of all those we protect;
- o Compassion;
- o Fairness;
- o Uncompromising personal integrity and institutional integrity;
- o Accountability by accepting responsibility for our actions and decisions and the consequences of our actions and decisions;
- o Leadership, both personal and professional.

Measured against this mouthful, the FBI has fouled itself. How hollow these words do echo when compared to the realities exhibited in the practical application of their law-enforcement duties:

a) *Not one* of the myriads of serious offenses presented to the FBI in this case has been investigated or presented for prosecution – despite thousands of pages of evidence provided and a plethora of additional evidence available to investigators;

b) *Not one* of 15,000-plus malfeasant and lawbreaking government officers has been questioned, investigated, or arrested, as dictated by Rule 4 of the Federal Rules of Criminal Procedures;

    c) *Not one* complaint by the United States of America with respect to murder, misprision, sedition, insurrection, and treason being perpetrated against the United States by government officials has been pursued by the FBI;

    d) *Not one* of 121 requests to the FBI to date, for protection of the laws against a conspiracy to kidnap and murder, or to investigate crimes, have been acquiesced to.

Nowhere in the actions or omissions of the FBI in this case can there be found a trace of protection of the United States or of individuals against public corruption, crimes including murder, or conspiracy against civil rights, etc. Nowhere in the actions or omissions of the FBI in this case can a rigorous obedience to the Constitution and laws of the United States be found, or can respect for the dignity of citizens, or compassion towards or fairness to all those the FBI purportedly protects be found. Nor can there be found personal or institutional integrity, accountability, or courage and fortitude in their leadership. Only insincere, hollow words - in profusion. Dishonesty in its liaison with the American people. And a central role in the attempts to kidnap and murder a US Supreme Court witness and litigant. Some micro examples of the FBI's deficiencies are provided below.

On January 17, 2003, the Federal Bureau of Investigation was first informed of the criminality within the government of the United States and was presented with prima facie evidence thereof by way of the 'Dossier of Crimes'. On 38 occasions since that date, the FBI Field Office in Seattle was kept informed of the escalating sedition and violent suppression of justice. The Seattle FBI Office was informed of the mass murder of 507 people and of the attempted kidnapping and murder of a key witness, and was requested to act in terms of its mandate. The only response from the FBI Office in Seattle was to categorically, but falsely, maintain that such crimes did not fall "within their investigative and prosecutive guidelines".

Pervasive Official Misconduct

On 38 subsequent occasions, a former Director of the FBI, Robert Mueller, was informed of the growing criminal endeavor within government (and the FBI). Additionally, on the latter eighteen of those occasions, another seven of Director Mueller's top aids in the FBI were simultaneously informed and were presented with updated evidence of the criminal activity by way of the 'Dossier of Crimes'. On four occasions, former FBI Director James Comey was informed; on one occasion, Acting Director Andrew McCabe was informed; and on thirty occasions, Director Christopher Wray was informed of the escalating insurrection against the laws. An additional thirty-seven appeals for protection against physical violence were made to the agents in charge of a further thirty-seven FBI Field Offices in different States. For the most part, there were no responses to the multiple requests to investigate. However, seven replies *were* received to 121 communications and filings over a 25-year period. Bear in mind that the criminal activities included serious allegations of murder, theft of court records, retaliation against a witness, attempted kidnapping and murder, seditious conspiracy, insurrection against the laws, and treason against the United States.

The FBI replies declared in part:

a. "Your recent communication to the Federal Bureau of Investigation (FBI) has been received, and based on the information you provided, no violation within the investigative jurisdiction of the FBI could be identified".

b. "Based on information you provided, we are unable to identify any violation of federal law within the investigative jurisdiction of the FBI".

c. "In the above-referenced letter, you allege the 'willful failure of duty' by the FBI for being unwilling to initiate a formal investigation based upon your allegations of criminal misconduct by senior officials of the United States Government, including President George W. Bush. You also refer to your April 2005 request for a criminal investigation into this matter and the FBI's response that no federal violations were identified that were within the FBI's jurisdiction. Inasmuch as the information you provided in your current communication reflects no additional information and contains no specific allegations of misconduct by an FBI employee, the Inspection Division has determined that this matter does not warrant the initiation of an investigation. We consider this matter closed".

d. "The information you have provided in your correspondence has been reviewed; however, based on the information you provided, we are unable to determine if a federal violation exists".

e. "The Public Corruption Unit has not reviewed your materials. However, we have promptly forwarded your information to the Seattle Field Office for Review". (The Public Corruption Unit was at the time fully informed of the criminal misconduct within the Seattle branch. No reply or investigation ensued from the Seattle Field Office).

f. "Since FBI investigations are conducted by our local field offices, your communication has been forwarded to the FBI Seattle Field Office for appropriate handling." (Having again complied with their request, once more, no reply or investigation ensued from the Seattle Field Office).

g. On and on through the years …….

Pervasive Official Misconduct

The FBI's actions and lack of action where investigation was due, although inexcusable, can be explained in terms of their direct involvement in the criminal endeavor. Why would they investigate criminal activities in which their own organization was so deeply implicated and had full knowledge of? The FBI's lack of formal investigation into grave and obvious crimes has, by itself, indicted the very organization.

The FBI shamefully directed the abortive assassination attempts upon me early in 2006, as President Geroge W Bush's opponent in US Supreme Court case No. 05-140. As mentioned, those actions were commanded by President Bush in order to silence my testimony on official misconduct. The plot to murder, initiated in the US Supreme Court under Chief Justice Roberts via the Chief of Supreme Court Police, was coordinated and led by the FBI, and was executed firstly by the Boeing Company (acting simultaneously at the behest of Air India), and secondly by the Federal Aviation Administration.

On September 22, 2010, the FBI Director and Agents in Charge of 37 FBI Field Offices were requested to investigate the murder of 158 people (at that time, after the Air India accident), and three attempts upon my life as a witness to that mass murder. Although fully informed, over that period of more than a decade and a half, not a single crime associated with this major criminal endeavor (as detailed in the *Dossier of Crimes*) had been investigated by the FBI.

By virtue of the FBI's actions and inaction where action was due, and in terms of statute 18USC1961, the FBI, as an entity, falls under the legal definition in the United States Code of a *corrupt organization*.

Secret Service, US Marshals, CIA

The Secret Service was kept informed throughout the proliferation of the criminal endeavor within the government by a series of 27 letters and several filings of the 'Dossier of Crimes'. Similarly, the US Marshal Service was kept informed, via their headquarters *and* their field offices in every State, through a series of 33 letters and filings of the dossier. Likewise, was the CIA informed, provided with prima facie evidence of the intensifying criminal endeavor, and requested to ensure protection of the laws. *All without any investigation or other effect.*

No investigations have been initiated by these law-enforcement agencies into any of the offenses reported to them, including the murder of 507 people and injury to another 189, the ongoing attempts to kidnap and murder me as a witness / Prosecutor Qui Tam, and the multitude of crimes detailed in the Dossier of Crimes.

PROSECUTORS

The federal duty of the Attorney General and United States Attorneys - to prosecute for all offenses against the United States - is promulgated by statutes 28USC509 and 28USC547:

> **Statute 28USC509 states in relevant part:** *"All functions of other offices of the Department of Justice and all functions of agencies and employees of the Department of Justice are vested in the Attorney General ..."*

> **Statute 28USC547 states in relevant part:** *"Except as otherwise provided by law, each United States Attorney, within his district, shall (1) prosecute for all offenses against the United States..."*

Offenses committed by the common man against the United States will, in general, be rigorously pursued without hesitation and without delay. On the other hand, in this matter under discussion, where it is the other way around, every attempt has been made by bureaucrats to conceal criminal offenses committed by malfeasant government officials against a citizen, including the heinous crime of attempted murder. Eight consecutive United States Attorneys General (at the time of writing) have been involved in that obstruction of justice and suppression of evidence of crimes committed by government officials. They are Attorney Generals Ashcroft, Gonzales, Mukasey, Holder, Lynch, Sessions, Barr, and Garland. Eight, and counting....

Federal prosecutors (United States Attorneys) from every one of the 50 States, and State prosecutors (Attorney Generals) from each of the 50 States, were informed and kept abreast of the proliferation of the offenses of seditious conspiracy and murder. Despite copious correspondence to all, *none* of the United States prosecutors called for an investigation of the prima facie evidence supplied, or for prosecution of the matter. If 25 years of history is the measure to go by, then it is reasonable to conclude that bureaucrats of the United States Department of Justice have no intention of performing their vital duties of prosecuting the law-breaking officials implicated.

In addition, in many of the court cases associated with the criminal endeavor (for example, *'Keyter v. President Bush'; 'Keyter v. 230 Government Officers'; and 'Keyter v. Senator McCain et al'*), public prosecutors were compelled by law to prosecute the defendants for crimes committed. Instead, United States Attorneys acted as Defense Counsel for the malfeasant officers in the civil suits, which were based on those very same crimes, in conflict with the law.

Anarchy within a government starts and ends with its judicial system. To date, no investigations have been initiated by any law enforcement agency into any of the multitude of offenses reported to them in the 'Dossier of Crimes'. Where State and Federal

Prosecutors have willfully refused to prosecute, I have taken up the task as a Qui Tam prosecutor on behalf of myself and on behalf of the United States.

THE 50 STATES

State governors, legislators, attorneys general, police chiefs, prosecutors and judges, from the 50 states, were approached via a series of 23 letters over several years *to each of those institutions in each state*, together with prima facie evidence of the seditious conspiracy against the United States and the proliferating insurrection against its laws. State officials have the same responsibilities as federal officials, under statutes 18USC4 and 18USC2382, to deal with or to report (further up the chain of authority) felonies reported to them which were committed by the offenders who are resident in their States. State officials have taken an oath of fidelity to support the Constitution of the United States.

Officials from the governments and courts of the 50 States, who were informed of the sedition against the United States and insurrection against its laws, willfully failed in their positions of authority under law to take appropriate action against the subversion. Instead, the state officials continued to provide safe haven and passage to insurgents in their states and elsewhere in the United States, and dealt with the correspondence in much the same manner as federal officials did - that is to say, by obfuscation, prevarication, sidestepping, and by unashamed dishonesty concerning jurisdiction and responsibility. A small sample taken over the 25-year proliferation, of the irrelevant, non-sensical, and deceitful responses to the initial reporting of *criminal activity in their state*, are presented below. Though some may have occurred several years ago, the modus operandi of delinquent government officials remained the same through the years.

Pervasive Official Misconduct

a. Virginia Governor – "… Unfortunately, the Governor does not have the authority to provide legal advice or intervene in a judicial matter". (No advice was requested, and he had a duty to address criminal offenses in his State.)

b. Michigan Attorney General – "…We sincerely regret our inability to provide assistance at this time and hope that this matter is resolved to your satisfaction. (No assistance was requested; the AG had a duty to address the criminal charges presented).

c. California Attorney General – "… We appreciate hearing from citizens on matters of public concern. However, we are prohibited by law from representing private individuals or providing legal advice, legal research, or legal analysis to private individuals under any circumstances". (No representation or legal advice was requested - criminal offenses were reported on which they were duty-bound to react to).

d. Kentucky Governor – "… I urge you to contact your Congressional representatives as well as the US Attorney General since these assertions pertain to wrongdoing at the federal level of government". (False and misleading statement, as the assertions also pertained to wrongdoing at the state level in Kentucky State, which they had a duty to deal with).

e. Sixth Judicial Circuit Court, MI – "…the issues presented in your letter and 'Dossier of Crimes' are beyond the jurisdiction of this Court… consequently, I consider this matter closed". (In fact, the court had very clear and concise jurisdiction).

f. Ohio Dept Public Safety – "The issues you bring forth in your letter(s) will not be addressed by this agency. As such, we will take no action and request that you refrain from further writing".

g. North Carolina Administrative Office of the Courts – "… Furthermore, we do not have the authority to analyze the rights, responsibilities, or remedies of private citizens, or give them legal advice. (No advice was requested; criminal offenses were reported on which they were duty-bound to act).

h. Montana Governor – "Thank you for contacting my office. I appreciate you taking the time to share your thoughts". (Criminal offenses were reported).

i. Kentucky Court of Appeals – "… the Kentucky Code of Judicial Conduct prohibits Judges from responding directly to your charges of criminal conspiracy involving government officials … Accordingly, the Kentucky Court of Appeals can take no action whatsoever regarding the charges you allege in your correspondence to the Judges of the Court of Appeals". (In truth, the judges had a well-defined legal duty to act under statutes 18USC4 and 18USC2382).

j. Lieutenant Governor of Texas – "As Lieutenant Governor of Texas, I take any allegation of terrorism, foreign or domestic, very seriously. As a result, I directed my policy staff to ensure your information is sent to the Texas Department of Public Safety". (Nothing was heard since or issued forth from the Texas Department of Public Safety. No investigations took place, and the matter was quashed.

k. Supreme Court of Tennessee – "…Because Chief Justice Holder cannot review or discuss the information contained in the documents on the electronic disk you enclosed with your letter, I am returning them to you unread with this letter".

l. House Speaker, State of Connecticut – "… Investigating allegations of this magnitude is beyond the purview of my office". (The House had a well-defined legal duty to act under statutes 18USC4 and 18USC2382).

m. Et cetera.

From north to south, from east to west, across the United States, and across the 25 years, the fabrications and dishonesty remain the same.

THE UNITED STATES CONGRESS

United States Congressmen have taken an oath (individually) to support and defend the Constitution of the United States against all enemies, foreign and domestic, to bear true faith and allegiance to the same, and to well and faithfully discharge the duties of their office. (*See* Appendix 4, statute 5USC3331, for Oath of office). Congressmen have unambiguous oversight duties over the executive and judicial branches of government. (See, for example, House Rule X). Congressmen carry that responsibility collectively as a body and as individual Senators and Representatives who constitute that body.

To date, 128 letters have appealed to each and every one of the 535 Senators and Representatives individually, to perform those oversight duties and to see to the defense of the nation against our enemies (the seditious conspirators, insurrectionists, and those involved in the criminal activities described in this case); and to address the subversive conspiracy within the government and the courts. In addition to the letters and evidence addressed to Congressmen individually, 48 letters have been sent to members of the House Committee on the Judiciary; 54 appeals to the Senate

Committee on the Judiciary; 31 to the Senate Committee on Homeland Security & Government Affairs; 35 letters to the House Committee on Oversight and Government Reform; and scores more to the Senate President and the Speaker of the House, requesting action on the criminal enterprise pursuant congressional oversight jurisdiction. *To no avail.* A full set of those letters is filed with Senate Legal Counsel and House General Counsel, in their positions as legal representatives of all Congressmen.

With callous indifference, Congressmen shunned the requests and willfully failed to perform their critical oversight duties regarding the criminal activities of government officials as reported to them in the *'Dossier of Crimes'* and in my many communications. I can come to no other conclusion than that the United States Congress has demonstrated no intention of addressing the lawlessness within the government in any way or form. Of the very few replies from Congressmen, received in response to information on the extensive *criminal endeavor* and early appeals for protection of the laws, the following extracts provide clear insight as to where the attention of Congressmen is focused:

a) Rep. Timothy Bishop – "I share your belief that this country is heading in the wrong direction … I want to make clear that I did not vote to renew the Patriot Act …. I am also opposed to this Administration's continued use of signing statements …. I will remain vigilant regarding this and other initiatives that threaten our civil liberties … If I can be of further assistance, please do not hesitate to contact me".

b) Rep. Eleanor Norton – "I always appreciate hearing from my constituents. I shall take this information under advisement and refer to it in making future decisions".

c) Rep. Brian Baird – "… I appreciate hearing from you … I share your concerns …. I am a strong supporter of Congress asserting its right to conduct oversight of the executive branch actions that are not in our nations best interests … I take my responsibility to represent the people who live in Southwest Washington very seriously … I will keep your thoughts in mind as I continue to represent Southwest Washington … please visit my website at… if you wish to sign up for periodic email updates about my work in Congress".

d) Sen. Joe Lieberman – "… My official Senate website is an excellent source of information about my work here…." Again: "… I hope you will continue to visit my website at … Please contact me if you have any additional questions or comments about our work in Congress".

e) John Cornyn – "I have received your letter and regret the problem you describe appears not to be one over which I have jurisdiction as a United States Senator …. I appreciate having the opportunity to represent you in the United States Senate. If I can be of assistance to you with other matters, please contact me".

f) Hillary Clinton – "… Although I would very much like to help, the matter you discuss involves another state".

g) Ad nauseam.

These examples have been taken throughout the proliferation, but there has been no *meaningful response* from Congressmen concerning the broad criminal conspiracy within the United States Government, bar for similar silly, irrelevant replies.

A Dirty U.S. Government Secret

THE ARMED FORCES

As a last line of defense of the Constitution, the United States Armed Forces may be called into federal service to enforce the laws or to suppress an insurrection against the laws, *"where unlawful obstructions, combinations, or assemblages, or rebellion against the authority of the United States, make it impracticable to enforce the laws of the United States in any State or Territory by the ordinary course of judicial proceedings".* (Statute 10USC332).

In addition, the United States Armed Forces may be called into federal service where a seditious conspiracy *"so hinders the execution of the laws of any State, and of the United States within any State, that any part or class of its people are deprived of a right, privilege, immunity, or protection named in the Constitution and secured by law, and the constituted authorities of any State are unable, fail, or refuse to protect that right, privilege, or immunity, or to give that protection; or where such conspiracy opposes or obstructs the execution of the laws of the United States or impedes the course of justice under those laws".* (Statute 10USC333). In any such situation, the State shall be considered to have denied the equal protection of the laws secured by the Constitution.

With these laws and Constitutional protections in mind, 58 generals and admirals of the armed forces were approached to perform the duty they took an oath to perform: to protect and defend the Constitution of the United States against all enemies, foreign and domestic. Fifty-eight (58) generals and admirals of the armed forces willfully failed to perform those duties, willfully failed to obey their oath of office, gave aid and comfort to the seditious conspirators (who are considered domestic enemies of the United States) by assisting them to evade punishment, and thereby committed an unmitigated act of treason against the United States.

In a further twist of irony, *the President* must consider it necessary to suppress any insurrection, domestic violence, unlawful combination, or conspiracy to be able to justify the use of the armed forces in a rebellion. When it is the President himself who is leading the insurrection against the laws, he will clearly not be motivated to sanction his own investigation and prosecution. With the United States President(s) involved in the offenses or their cover-up, it becomes a closed loop cauldron of crime and subversion for which there is no practical remedy under the current practice of protection of malfeasant officials.

Amongst the 34 appeals addressed to the Joint Chiefs and Combat Generals over several years, on February 1, 2010, I wrote:

> *The Joint Chiefs of Staff and Combat Generals*
> *Office of the Chairman of the Joint Chiefs of Staff*
> *400 Joint Staff Pentagon*
> *Washington, D.C. 20318-0400*
>
> ***Attention:***
> *Incumbent Joint Chiefs of Staff, including:- Admiral Mullen; General James Cartwright; General Peter Pace; Admiral Gary Roughead;* General T. Michael Moseley; *General Casey; General James T. Conway; Incumbent Combat Commanders, including:- Admiral William J. Fallon; Vice Admiral David C. Nichols Jr.; Major General Timothy F. Ghorley; General Bantz J. Craddock; General William E. Ward; General William D. Catto; General Lance Smith; General John R. Wood; Admiral Miles B. Wachendorf; Gen. Gene Renuart; Gen. William G. Webster Jr.; Gen. Paul J. Sullivan; Admiral Timothy J. Keating; Lt General Daniel P. Leaf; Rear Admiral William Van Meter Alford, Jr.; Admiral James G. Stavridis; General Glenn F. Spears; General Nolen V. Bivens; Admiral Olson; General Brown; General Waldhauser; Gen. K.P.*

Chilton; Gen. J W Ramsaur II; Gen. C R Kehler; Gen. M R Musick; Gen. H B Bromberg; Admiral D McClain; Gen. B L Bash; Gen. R Mercer Jr.; Gen. R J Elder, Jr.; Admiral D L Philman; Gen. W L Shelton; Gen. K Alexander; Gen. J M Davis; Gen. K T Campbell; Gen. M Maples; Gen. M A Welsh III; Admiral W P Loeffler; Gen.C E Croom; Gen. J C Koziol; Gen. Norton Schwartz; Admiral Ann Rondeau; Gen. William H. Johnson; Gen. Duncan J. McNabb; Gen. Kathleen M. Gainey; Admiral Robert D. Reilly; Gen. Charles Fletcher; Admiral Mark Harnitcheck; Gen. Daniel Dinkins Jr.; Gen Harold L. Mitchell; Gen. David Patreaus.

Dear Generals and Admirals,

Officials Legally Debarred from Holding Office

Certain State and Federal Government Officials are legally debarred from holding office under the United States, or under any State, as a consequence of subversive acts committed against the United States in contravention of statutes 18USC2381 and 18USC2383, and the 14ᵗʰ Amendment of the Constitution. They are nonetheless still holding office in contravention of the laws and the Constitution. As a person in authority, you are obligated and herewith requested to ensure that the US Constitution is adhered to and that the aforementioned laws are faithfully executed against the law-breaking officials.

Details of the subversive offenses committed by the debarred officials were presented to you on January 10, 2010, in a 2000-page 'Dossier of Crimes'. The dossier provides prima facie evidence and describes acts of domestic terrorism, an insurrection against the laws, a seditious conspiracy, treason against the

United States, and a conspiracy to kidnap and murder a witness to these crimes. The names of the debarred officials were also provided to you in Chapter 3 of Volume I of the 'Dossier of Crimes'.

The debarred officials all had knowledge of widespread sedition against the United States and had an individual and collective duty to address the subversion. Despite their peremptory duties to the United States and to the public - and notwithstanding their oath of office to perform those duties - the debarred officials took no meaningful action to terminate the subversion or to bring the enemies of the United States to justice. Instead, the debarred officials provided safe haven and passage to the domestic enemies of the United States. They aided and abetted known criminals to escape justice. They provided domestic terrorists with aid and comfort by retaining those terrorists in the pay of the government and in positions of authority from whence they continue to commit subversive acts against the United States. These and other offenses exclude the debarred officials named in the dossier from holding government office.

This rendering of criminal assistance by disqualified officials to law-breaking colleagues is succinctly demonstrated in the proceedings of three recent court cases that in vain attempted to address the seditious conspiracy within the government and the courts. {See US District Court (Maine) case nos.. 09-516, 09-517, and 09-518; First Circuit Appeals Court case nos.. 09-2617, 09-2618, and 09-2619; and their respective appeals in the US Supreme Court (case numbers not assigned)}. The full documentation on these cases, including copies of documents stolen from the court records, will be made available to investigators. Thousands of additional pages of evidence against the debarred officials await investigation.

Yet, these high-level and debarred officials have illicitly seen to it that no investigation takes place and that the abovementioned felonies against the United States are not prosecuted. They have pursued selfish ambition and self-interest to the exclusion of those whom they are there for to serve. Despite their oath of responsibility to the state and to the public, the debarred officials believe that they are beyond the authority of the Constitution and the reach of the laws that govern the civility of this society, and which govern the lives of ordinary, well-intentioned citizens.

As a person in authority, you cannot allow this iniquity and impunity to continue day after day, in court after court, and in administration upon administration. You are obligated to address the malevolent and unjust system of justice that permits government assassins in your ranks the freedom to ply their trade upon a hapless populace. You are compelled to deal with the imperfect system of government that has fostered and encouraged this deluge of lawlessness within the courts and the government, as presented to you in the 'Dossier of Crimes'. You are duty-bound to halt the domestic terrorism, insurrection, sedition, and treason against the United States, as well as the criminal conspiracy to kidnap and murder a witness to these crimes. In addition, you are duty-bound to commence by removing the debarred government officials from their positions of power, as the US Constitution and laws demand.

Yes, your duties and obligations to restrain this iniquity arise from the nation's laws and

Constitution – the very Constitution you swore to uphold with your invocation: "So help me God". When you took office, you mustered the courage to take this oath, and once made in hallowed presence, should you not remain true? Should you not honor the peremptory duties you vowed to perform with His assistance? For, doubt not for one moment that a Greater Hand than yours or mine guides the destiny of man and of nations.

Kindly inform me of any meaningful action you may have taken to deal with the domestic terrorism plot and the other criminal complaints presented to you, and to debar the felonious officials from positions of authority under the United States or under any State. Sincerely....

No reply and no positive action was forthcoming from the 58 generals and admirals.

US PRESIDENTS AND THEIR CABINETS

With a failure of state and federal government institutions tasked with law and order to address the anarchy within the government, it becomes the responsibility of the President to *"take care of the faithful execution of the laws"* pursuant to Article II, Section 3, of the Constitution. But therein lies the paradox in this matter.

President George W. Bush

Eighty-seven (87) letters to President George W. Bush, plus numerous filings of the 'Dossier of Crimes', and 16 letters to his cabinet, kept the Bush Administration fully informed of the proliferation of the international criminal endeavor and appealed for judicial action. The only action forthcoming from George W. Bush, his cabinet, and his Administration, of course, was the two attempts

151

to kidnap and murder his Supreme Court opponent and prime witness to the criminality within the United States Government.

President Barack Obama

One hundred and eleven (111) letters dispatched to President Obama, and 38 to his cabinet, kept the Obama Administration fully informed of the ongoing criminal endeavor and appealed for judicial action. No action was forthcoming from President Obama or from members of his cabinet or Administration, including his Attorney General. At the behest of and under the command of President Barack Obama, a third attempt was made to kidnap and murder me via a department of the Washington State Government and by utilizing the same plot held over from President Bush.

President Joe Biden

Coming into office after President Trump's first term, President Joe Biden was kept fully informed of the criminality within the U.S. government. First as US Senator, then as Vice President, and later as US President, Biden received 125 letters of appeal to address that criminality. President Biden and his cabinet's choice was to ignore all of those requests and to continue the cover-up of the criminal endeavor.

Former Presidents Jimmy Carter, Bill Clinton, and George H. W. Bush (Senior)

In addition to the sitting Presidents, former Presidents Jimmy Carter, Bill Clinton, and George H. W. Bush (Senior) were informed of the criminal endeavor in government through eight letters, three updated copies of the Dossier of Crimes, plus a series of evidence. They were further informed through their attendance at a meeting at the White House on January 7, 2009, where this extensive case of anarchy within the United States government was discussed. Thus, three former United States Presidents, prior to GW Bush, were fully informed of the subversive activities against the United States and had done nothing to terminate the sedition and insurrection against the laws, even pursuant to their citizens' duty demanded by statute 18USC4.

This case convincingly demonstrates that when a President is involved or instigates criminal acts, he can also very effectively prevent any investigation or prosecution of his own wrongdoing, and prosecution of that of his henchmen. As it stands in the United States of America today, a President can kidnap and murder and can enjoy protection against any prosecution from the entire government establishment. In return, the President will protect malfeasant officials from the consequences of *their* wrongdoing - even promote them or bestow favors upon them, as in the case of GW Bush promoting John Roberts to Chief Justice of the United States, for the favor of assisting him to escape justice in the DC Circuit Court of Appeals.

President Donald Trump

Amongst 27 letters that went to President Trump and his Cabinet in his first term, shortly after his inauguration in January 2017, I appealed to President Trump on February 3, 2017, for his constitutionally required action:

> *Dear President Trump,*
>
> > *Re: Your Action Required to Terminate*
> > *A US Government Assassination Plot*
>
> *Your peremptory action is requested to terminate an active government assassination plot against me, a US Citizen, as an opponent of former President George W. Bush in US Supreme Court Case No. 05-140. The Federal Aviation Administration (which has also been implicated) recently confirmed that the government assassination plot is still current and*

ongoing. Four recent attempts upon my life (and/or that of my twin brother, Barry) may have conclusively verified that fact. Without investigation, we will not know for sure.

During 2005, I was an opponent of President George W. Bush in a civil case that found its way to the US Supreme Court. Some 41 documents (out of 47 filed in the case) incriminated President George W. Bush in criminal offenses and were unlawfully thieved from Supreme Court records. Criminal charges were filed against President Bush in Supreme Court Case No. 05-140 for theft of court records.

That legally required report immediately precipitated three (foiled) attempts to kidnap and murder me in an effort to silence my testimony and caused a seemingly endless cycle of criminal offenses and cover-up, in order to protect lawbreaking government officials from prosecution. That seditious conspiracy, involving many senior government and Boeing Company officials acting in concert, escalated into a full-blown insurrection against the laws and treason against the United States. The crimes and cover-up also led directly to the death and/or grave injury of 350 people in two separate and avoidable air accidents.

None of the multiple and serious criminal offenses have been investigated or prosecuted. Obstruction of justice at every level of government during the Administrations of Presidents GW Bush and Obama led to further criminal charges being filed against a growing number of government and court officials who actively assisted in defeating the course of justice. Presidents Bush and Obama were fully involved in protecting law-breaking officials from prosecution and in denying the American public, including me, protection of the laws.

The extensive seditious conspiracy within the government is well documented, and three sources of evidence corroborate the facts. The first is a 2400-page 'Dossier of Crimes' which details the countless criminal offenses over more than a decade. The dossier is herewith filed with you for your imperative action. The dossier has also been filed with, but has been suppressed by the DOJ and the FBI, and suppressed by Supreme Court Chief Justice Roberts in the 'Consolidated Boeing Company Murder Case'. The large number of criminal conspirators is listed in Volume I, Chapter 3, of the Dossier of Crimes. A 'Synopsis of the Case' is included herewith as essential reading for you to fully appreciate the ruthlessness and extent of the ongoing criminality within the US Government.

The second source of evidence consists of thousands of letters to government officials over more than a decade, insisting on action and protection of the laws, which have never been forthcoming. Copies of that correspondence are available to investigators. The third source of evidence is some 330 corrupt proceedings in 59 related and quashed court cases, which in vain attempted to bring the criminal conspirators to justice, only to be illegally suppressed and dismissed by co-conspiring judges who acted to protect the law-breaking officials from prosecution.

The laws have not been faithfully enforced and administered concerning this matter (referred to as the 'Boeing Company Murder Case'). Officials from both the Administrations of GW Bush and Obama have deliberately been delinquent in their government functions so as to defeat the ends of justice. The blatant lawlessness can without difficulty be demonstrated to serious investigators who would instead choose to obey the Constitution and the law.

On January 20, 2017, you took an oath before God and the nation to uphold the tenets of the Constitution. The United States Constitution clearly states in Article II, Section 3, that: "The President... shall take care that the laws are faithfully executed". You are thus requested - and pursuant to your Oath of Office, you are legally obligated - to take care that the laws are faithfully executed upon the seditious conspirators and murderers.

Kindly advise me of your willingness to address and terminate the government assassination plot and the state-supported tyranny upon the populace, as detailed in the Dossier of Crimes. I will be of assistance to the extent that I can.
Sincerely,

Enclosures:
1. *Synopsis of the Case*
2. *The Dossier of Crimes, dated 1.27.25*

As with the Presidents before him who were informed and who were requested to deal with the matter, in his first term President Trump and his Cabinet and Administration simply turned a blind eye and ignored 26 further appeals to address the seditious conspiracy and insurrection against the laws, and continued to cover up the United States Government's dirty secret. Now in his second term in office, at the time of publishing, President Trump and his Administration have a second opportunity to do the right thing – to obey the Constitution and to "take care of the faithful execution of the laws" upon the 240 criminal complaints filed with them in the 'Dossier of Crimes'.

OFFICIAL IMMUNITY

In several court cases against law-breaking government officials, it was fraudulently claimed by the courts that government officials who failed to perform their official duty or who committed crimes, acted in their 'official capacity' and are therefore immune from suit. That supposed immunity was then falsely invoked to dismiss and prevent *both civil and criminal* prosecution in the court cases.

For example, in the case Keyter vs Bush, the judge dismissed the case sans addressing the criminal offenses filed therein, partially on the grounds of immunity, quote: *"Neither the Complaint or plaintiff's subsequent pleadings make clear whether plaintiff seeks to hold the president liable in his personal capacity or in his official capacity. Under either theory, however, the president is immune from the instant suit. It is well recognized that some government officials, including the President, are absolutely immune from suits for damages".*

The District Court, the DC Appeals Court, and the US Supreme Court not only dismissed any damages suits but they dismissed all criminal complaints against President GW Bush (and other officials) under the same statement and guise, without addressing the criminal charges.

However, in reply to the learned judge, it is an elementary truth that committing a crime is forbidden by law. It is an elementary deduction to conclude that government officers are not authorized to commit crimes against the United States in their official capacity. Government officers, like any other citizen, are also not authorized to commit crimes against the United States (or any person) in their personal capacity. If they do commit crimes, they are not acting in their official capacity, *since they possess no such capacity or duty.*

Failure of duty implies that government officers are *not acting* in their official capacity when they do not perform their duty – they cannot be *acting* in an official capacity whilst they are *not acting* in an official capacity. Furthermore, willful failure of official duty to secure protection of the laws where those laws are being violated is a crime. (See, for example, statutes on 'Denial of Rights, 18USC241'; and 'Conspiracy against Rights', 18USC242, in *Appendix 4: Extract of Statutes*). Government officials committing such crimes do not commit those crimes in their official capacity, *for they possess no such capacity.*

Government officers are not and should not be immune from criminal or civil prosecution *for criminal offenses, or criminal neglect, or for harm and loss inflicted by those criminal offenses or neglect.* Government officers committing crimes in their personal capacity should be treated the same under the law as any other denizen of the United States. To treat them differently under law, to bestow immunity upon them for criminal deeds committed, is to invite tyranny upon the populace. This case unambiguously demonstrates that verity.

The governing principle behind these statements is easily discerned by some simple examples. If a policeman on duty goes on a rampage and randomly kills a number of people, is he immune from prosecution for murder? Of course not. In such an example, he did not commit murder in his official capacity, as he has no such capacity, has no such duty, and has no immunity for criminal wrongdoing.

In a further example: if the policeman on duty had willfully stood by and watched someone else commit murder; that is, if he failed to prevent that murder whilst having the capacity, the authority, and the duty as law enforcement officer to stop such an odious act, does he have official immunity or is he guilty as an accomplice? Of course, he is guilty of failing to do his duty and of failing to act in his official capacity. 'Failing to act' in an official capacity *is the opposite* of acting in an official capacity. And there can be no official immunity for *not acting* where action is due; for not doing the duty one is there for to do. This principle applies to all the government conspirators dealt with in this narrative.

A similar question can be asked about a US President: "Does the President of the United States have immunity against prosecution for the crime of murder or attempted murder while in office? If the answer to this question is yes, the President indeed has protection from prosecution, then the inevitable conclusion must be that the President is exempt from all the laws of the United States. Consequently, he can murder at will, and such tyranny upon the populace would then in fact be sanctioned by this false application of law. In such a case, any Constitutional protections bestowed upon the public are meaningless - in theory and in practice.

Conversely, if the answer to the above question is *no*; if the President and officials in general do not have immunity for the crime of murder; if government officials are as guilty as any other citizen for transgressing the laws - as common-sense dictates - then, the President(s) and all the Presidents' men implicated in the case presented in this saga must be punished for mass murder - by theory of law. Clearly, the concept of 'immunity', falsely invoked by the courts, will need to be revisited and demarcated in order to protect against government tyranny for future generations.

However, this case demonstrates that, *in practice,* the Constitution and the laws of the United States are de facto transgressed by government officials on a daily basis with astounding frequency, with grave consequences to public safety, and with impunity.

APPLICATION OF THE LAWS IN PRACTICE

Thus, it has come to be that within the United States federal and state governments, the laws that would imprison the common man for life if transgressed are violated by government officials day after day, in court after court, and in Administration after Administration. State and federal government officials engaged in that lawlessness have done so, and continue to do so, with complete immunity to prosecution.

In theory, the Constitution and the laws of the United States ought to guard against such lawlessness. However, the evidence unmistakably demonstrates by harsh personal experience (the experience of the author) that *in practice,* the laws of the United States are most arbitrarily applied. That evidence includes some 14,000 letters to officials, appealing for protection of the laws, only to be sent to the waste paper basket. The evidence also includes a series of 62 related court cases, 61 of them illegally dismissed without trial, sans tending to the criminal charges filed against officials in those cases, as mandated by law. The evidence further includes every one of more than 352 proceedings in those court cases, corruptly and dishonestly denied or dismissed. The evidence also consists of a bottomless number of criminal offenses, meticulously documented in the 'Dossier of Crimes', which are, to date, yet to be investigated and prosecuted.

In general, the laws are rarely applied to law-breaking government officials. In particular, through the methods described in this chapter and the next, the laws have not been administered upon some 15,000-plus lawless state and federal officials, and their co-conspirators, who have literally gotten away with:

- o Cover-up of the murder of 507 people and attempted murder of another 189;
- o Three foiled attempts to kidnap and murder a witness to their crimes;

- o Sedition against the United States;
- o A major insurrection against the laws of the United States;
- o Treason against the United States;
- o Cover-up of $1.42 trillion international stock exchange fraud;
- o As well as an untold number of other serious criminal offences against the United States.

There is more than sufficient evidence to confirm the veracity of these facts.

In the next chapter, we will further look into the excruciating price paid by the flying public as a result of allowing lawlessness to prevail within the United States Government and within their partner in crime, the Boeing Company. The crash of Asiana Flight 214 is discussed in order to show the continuing criminal tendency of the Boeing Company, to demonstrate the culpability of the U.S. government therein, and to reveal the arbitrary nature with which the government dispenses justice.

Chapter 9
Boeing and the Crash of Asiana Flight 214

The extreme indifference to human life demonstrated by Boeing Commercial Airplanes - and by those US Government officials who assisted and made it possible for Boeing officials to commit further crimes - violates the Revised Code of Washington, RCW 9A.32.030(1)(b) and constitutes murder on three other counts.

Extract From Chapter 9.

United States government officials had provided impunity for the Boeing Company against prosecution for the heinous criminal acts described in earlier chapters. That impunity assured that Boeing's criminal corporate culture would endure and that further crimes would follow in the same pattern. Boeing faced no deterrent, and its modus operandi of doing business and looking after its finances at the expense of flight safety remained intact.

On Saturday, July 6, 2013, Asiana Flight 214, a Boeing 777 on a scheduled passenger flight from Seoul, South Korea, crashed while attempting to land at San Francisco International Airport. Two people were killed as a direct result of the accident, and a third died of injuries right after the accident. In addition, 181 people were gravely injured. Criminal misconduct on the part of the Boeing Company prior to the events of July 6, 2013, played a significant role in the accident and is in large part to blame for the crash of Asiana Flight 214 and the concomitant injuries and death.

Murder charges were filed with the Obama Administration and with the US District Court in Seattle, case no. 2:13cv982, against the Boeing Company, its senior executives, and its government co-conspirators, in the death of the three passengers who perished. The charges supplemented the existing murder charges filed against the Boeing Company in the death of the 158 passengers and crew who died on Air India Flight IX-812. The Obama Administration and the US District Court feloniously ignored the charges and swept them under the carpet.

Both sets of criminal charges arise from similar and ongoing criminal misconduct within Boeing that underlies both the Asiana Flight 214 and Air India Flight IX-812 accidents. That criminal misconduct common to both air accidents is Boeing's suppression of known flight safety issues, in favor of commercial profits, which in each case led to the deaths of passengers and crew as a consequence of that suppression. The extreme indifference to human life demonstrated by Boeing Commercial Airplanes and by those US Government officials who assisted, made it possible, and enabled Boeing officials to commit further crimes violates the Revised Code of Washington, RCW 9A.32.030(1)(b), and constitutes murder on three additional counts.

CAUSES OF THE ACCIDENT OF ASIANA 214

From the Accident Report made public by the National Transportation Safety Board (NTSB) on June 24, 2014, the following facts about the accident of Asiana Flight 214, and the role of the Boeing Company in that accident, are known:

The NTSB found that during the *initial part* of the 14-mile-long final approach to landing on runway 28L at San Francisco International Airport on July 6, 2013, Asiana Flight 214 (a Boeing 777) was too high and too fast in the approach. The NTSB also found that in the *final part* of that unstable approach, below an altitude of 500 feet, Asiana 214 became too low on the 3-degree glideslope, and too slow in airspeed, and hit the seawall prior to reaching the runway. The impact broke off the tail section behind the aft bulkhead and spun the aircraft around 330 degrees before the final impact, which brought the aircraft to rest some distance down the runway and off to the left side of the paved surface. The airplane was destroyed by impact forces and a post-crash fire. Miraculously, only three passengers were killed, but 181 passengers and crew were badly injured in the crash.

NTSB Probable Cause

The National Transportation Safety Board (NTSB) determined that the *probable cause* of this accident was pilot error, quote:

> *"...the flight crew's mismanagement of the airplane's descent during the visual approach, the pilot flying's unintended deactivation of automatic airspeed control, the flight crew's inadequate monitoring of airspeed, and the flight crew's delayed execution of a go-around after they became aware that the airplane was below acceptable glidepath and airspeed tolerances". (NTSB Accident Report, P129, Para 3.2).*

NTSB Contributing Causes

Besides these obvious pilot errors, the NTSB identified several other *contributing causes* to the accident, of which the most important contributing causes were: (a) the lack of low-speed protection (called 'autothrottle wake-up') covering all phases of flight; and (b) the complexities of the auto flight system that were not sufficiently addressed in Boeing training or documentation, quote:

> *"...the complexities of the autothrottle and autopilot flight director systems that were inadequately described in Boeing's documentation and Asiana's pilot training, which increased the likelihood of*

mode error; ... " (NTSB Accident Report, P129, Para 3.2).

Dissenting Opinion on 'Pilot Error'

At least one of the four Board Members on the accident panel (Mr. Robert L. Sumwalt) strongly dissented with the Board's finding that the probable cause of the accident was *pilot error.* Mr. Sumwalt appropriately gave equal weight to the two most important contributory causes and instead described the accident as a *systems error* accident:

> *"Contrary to what some may believe, this accident is not just another 'pilot error' accident. Like most accidents, the causation of this accident is complex and involves the interaction of several elements of the system". (Accident Report, P136) .... "In my opinion, this accident was a systems accident". (NTSB Accident Report, P139).*

Implicated in that *'system'* referred to is the manufacturer, the Boeing Company, and its criminal neglect relating to pertinent safety aspects concerning the B777 aircraft. Whether the probable cause of the accident was mainly pilot error or mainly systemic errors is merely a matter of semantics. The essence of the matter is: several pilot errors combined with several system errors to produce the accident. It was thus an inseparable compendium of factors that caused the dreadful crash.

Each error interacted with and was an important link in the unbroken chain of events and errors, without which the accident would in all likelihood have been prevented. Each uncorrected error held an *equal measure of consequence* in the final outcome of the crash and held as much responsibility as the preceding or succeeding error. That includes (a) the aircrew's mismanagement of the airplane's descent, *and* (b) the inadequacy/failure of Boeing's documentation and training to describe the unique scenario encountered by the aircrew, which caused them to mismanage the descent and approach. That dangerous and unique scenario was known to Boeing. Yet, Boeing took no action to fix the anomaly or to inform and train aircrews on the anomaly.

DISCUSSION OF CAUSES AND BOEING'S ROLE

The three major and obvious causes mentioned above as to why Asiana 214 was flying too low and too slow below 500 feet on the final approach to landing in San Francisco are complex and not easily integrated by a layman unfamiliar with the terminology and equipment in a modern jet-liner cockpit. Nevertheless, the causes are herewith simplified and explained in more detail in order to delineate and clarify the Boeing Company's role and criminal culpability in the crash.

The First Cause

The first reason why Asiana 214 was too low and too slow on the final part of the approach was that the flight crew failed to sufficiently monitor and timely correct altitude and airspeed deviations from the desired flight path. The reason for that was that the pilots mistakenly relied on the Boeing 777 autothrottle system to maintain the commanded airspeed - without cross-checking whether their autothrottles in fact operated as commanded. (The 'commanded airspeed' means the airspeed which the pilots programmed into the flight computer – thereby commanding the auto-flight system to automatically secure that speed by thrust changes on the engines). The NTSB Report, in Finding No. 3, described the consequences:

> *"The flight crew mismanaged the airplane's vertical profile during the initial approach, which resulted in the airplane being well above the desired glidepath when it reached the five nautical mile point, and this*

increased the difficulty of achieving a stabilized approach". (NTSB Accident Report, Para 3.1).

The first cause in the series of three primary causes of the accident (namely, insufficient monitoring of altitude and airspeed) is unquestionably ascribed to the flight crew. However, it should be noted that the Boeing 777 Flight Crew Training Manual recommends that 777 pilots fly with *autothrottles* controlling airspeed even when manually manipulating the flight controls. As seen by the pilots, Boeing's recommendation imparts a certain degree of reliance upon the autothrottle system to control the airspeed – and that's what the aircrew of Asiana 214 did during the final approach.

But sadly, in this specific case, that reliance by the aircrew upon the autothrottle to maintain airspeed proved *not* to be dependable. Two inconsistencies (anomalies, or discontinuities) appeared back-to-back in the autothrottle system, which were equally responsible for the slow airspeed and low altitude that followed on the final approach. Those two pertinent causes of the accident (explained below as the second and third causes) are ascribed to the Boeing Company, not the aircrew! Without those two causes, the accident would most likely have been avoided. Sufficient thrust on the engines would have alleviated the deficiency in the interrelated flight parameters of altitude and airspeed.

The Second Cause

The *second major reason* why Asiana 214 was too low in height and too slow in airspeed was that the autothrottles, in reality, *did not* maintain the airspeed the pilots had commanded. The NTSB found in its investigations that, despite the airspeed commanded on the 'Mode Control Panel' being 137 knots, the actual 'automatically controlled' airspeed decreased down to 103 knots. How could that happen?

The reason why the autothrottles did not maintain the commanded airspeed was that, unexpectedly and unnoticed by the pilots, the autothrottles reverted to the 'HOLD' mode. In the 'HOLD' mode, the autothrottles maintain the last given power setting on the engines. Practically, this happened when the autopilot was disconnected in the 'Flight Level Change' mode and the pilot flying manually moved the thrust to idle, where it then stayed in 'HOLD' mode – despite being armed and commanded to maintain a higher speed and therefore higher power setting. The autothrottles never re-engaged.

Though the explanation might sound a bit technical, suffice it to say that the pilots found themselves in a situation (a) not trained for, (b) likely not previously encountered in the aircraft (c) not recognized, and (d) not described or alternatively *not adequately described* in the Flight Crew Training Manual or Operating Manual of the Boeing 777 aircraft.

The condition is sometimes described by those very few in the industry who have encountered this rare situation before as a 'trap' for unsuspecting pilots. It is obvious that the pilots of Asiana 214 were not familiar with that so-called 'trap'. It is referred to by those who have encountered the unusual scenario as the *'Flight Level Change trap'*. (The full explanation of this so-called trap for B777 pilots is of a technical nature and is elucidated in the NTSB Accident Report). The NTSB Accident Report provides details of the situation:

> *"As a result of complexities in the 777 automatic flight control system and inadequacies in related training and documentation, the pilot flying had an inaccurate understanding of how the autopilot flight director system and autothrottle interacted to control airspeed, which led to his inadvertent deactivation of automatic airspeed control. (NTSB Accident Report, Para 3.1, Finding No. 10).*

The inadequacies in related Boeing training and documentation to properly describe the effect of the complexities in the 777 automatic flight control system constituted willful neglect by the Boeing Company, since the problems and the dangers were known to Boeing. The insufficiency in describing the known flight safety issues to the Asiana pilots contributed in a major way to the accident, is attributable to the Boeing Company, and led directly to the associated third cause.

The Third Cause

The *third major reason* for Asiana Flight 214 being too low and too slow on the final approach was that the autothrottles failed to provide *'slow speed protection'* as it was *expected by the aircrew to do,* despite being armed to provide that protection. The aircrew expected 'slow speed protection' to be operable because it was briefed and demonstrated (during simulator training) to do so – as part of the Boeing training. The 777 Flight Crew Training Manual (FCTM), issued by Boeing, described the details of that demonstration. However, Boeing deliberately never mentioned the inconsistencies, anomalies, and discontinuities in the 'slow speed protection system'. As a Boeing Company B777 instructor, I myself never knew of the anomalies. Boeing training, in fact, demonstrated that the system operated as advertised, yet willfully neglected to provide information on the rare scenario where the system *did not operate.* The NTSB Accident Report on page 137 referred to the training demonstrations:

> *"While these demonstrations showed how and when the airplane will protect against critically slow speed, they did not demonstrate when the airplane would not intervene when speed got too slow - precisely the situation experienced by the crew of Asiana flight 214".*

A Dirty U.S. Government Secret

NTSB Accident Report, Para 2.4.1: "Further, the Boeing 777 FCTM, upon which Asiana based much of its training, did not explain the conditions under which the A/T would not automatically engage. The FCTM recommended A/T use during all phases of flight, including manual flight, and presented a stall protection demonstration that did not include situations when the A/T would not automatically activate".

The autothrottle low speed protection system is designed (as a last resort back-up) to automatically drive the speed up and away from the aerodynamic stall speed (where an aircraft ceases to fly), back to the minimum maneuvering airspeed, any time the airspeed decreases halfway down into the amber band (a caution zone on the speed indicator). From the low speed of 103 knots reached by Asiana 214, it is evident that the autothrottle stall protection system (also called autothrottle wake-up) *did not operate* in the auto-throttle 'HOLD' mode which Asiana 214 was flying in – another inconsistency, anomaly, or discontinuity, in the system not expected or known to the aircrew - and not known by me as an experienced Boeing Company B777 instructor pilot. I had demonstrated 'autothrottle wake-up' to all my students as per the Boeing training syllabus, but the lack of autothrottle wake-up in the 'hold' mode was not in the syllabus, not in the Flight Crew Training Manual, was not known, and therefore not demonstrated. The NTSB Accident Report, in 'Finding No. 11', described the consequence of the inconsistency or discontinuity:

> *"If the autothrottle automatic engagement function ("wakeup"), or a system with similar functionality, had been available during the final approach, it would likely have activated and increased power about 20 seconds before impact, which may have prevented the accident. (NTSB Accident Report, Para 3.1).*

170

Thus, notwithstanding the failure of the pilots to sufficiently monitor and correct their altitude and airspeed, if the autothrottle system had operated to provide slow speed protection in all its modes instead of only some, the disaster could have and most likely would have been averted. In addition, if the B777 manuals and Boeing training had described the lack of protection in certain modes, the aircrew would likely not have relied on that protection during a critical phase of flight. This was another willful failure attributable to the Boeing Company, which contributed in a major way to the accident.

BOEING COMPANY CRIMINAL CULPABILITY

Consequently, two very obvious anomalies or inconsistencies appeared one after the other in the autothrottle system of Asiana Flight 214. Those anomalies were major contributors to the unstable approach path and resulting accident, without which the accident would very likely have been avoided. The question of Boeing's criminal culpability in the accident rests upon: (a) whether Boeing knew of the inconsistencies and anomalies in its auto flight system; (b) whether Boeing knew of the dangers posed to life and limb by those anomalies; (c) whether Boeing and its officials had a legal and a moral duty to fix them, and/or, a duty to unambiguously warn aircrews of the problem areas and train them to cope with those areas; and, (d) whether Boeing in fact did or did not perform its legal and moral duty.

Boeing's Knowledge of Safety Issues

As a result of the National Transportation Safety Board investigation into the accident, the NTSB made the following new safety recommendations (Accident Report, Para 4):

(A) To the Federal Aviation Administration:

"Require Boeing to develop enhanced 777 training that will improve flight crew understanding of autothrottle modes and automatic activation system logic through improved documentation, courseware, and instructor training"; and "require operators and training providers to provide this training to 777 pilots.

"Require Boeing to revise its 777 Flight Crew Training Manual stall protection demonstration to include an explanation and demonstration of the circumstances in which the autothrottle does not provide low speed protection;" and "Require operators and training providers to incorporate the revised stall protection demonstration in their training".

(B) To Boeing:

"Revise the Boeing 777 Flight Crew Operating Manual to include a specific statement that when the autopilot is off and both flight director switches are turned off, the autothrottle mode goes to speed (SPD) mode and maintains the mode control panel-selected speed".

"Develop and evaluate a modification to Boeing wide-body automatic flight control systems to help ensure that the aircraft energy state remains at or above the minimum desired energy condition during any portion of the flight".

If these recommendations were necessary after the accident of Asiana Flight 214, in order to prevent future accidents caused by the same scenarios, then more so were they necessary ***before*** the accident, *since the Boeing Company was very much aware of the problem areas, but nothing was done about them.* The NTSB

Accident Report describes similar problems in the auto flight system of the Boeing 787, which were raised and fixed on the new aircraft, but the same fix was not made for those same problems existing in the Boeing 777:

> *"He [an FAA Test Pilot] raised his concern throughout the FAA certification chain. Officials with EASA also became concerned. As a result, Boeing added additional and clearer guidance in the Boeing 787 manuals regarding this system logic. **But for the Boeing 777—an airplane with the same basic system - nothing was done".** (Accident Report, P136, second last Para).*

Boeing's Suppression of Known Safety Issues

Prior to the accident of Asiana 214, the Boeing Company was fully aware of the anomalies/ inconsistencies in the auto flight system and their potential effects, and as the manufacturer, had a definite responsibility to act upon the anomalies/inconsistencies.

(Just in the same way as the company 'General Motors' had a responsibility to act upon a faulty ignition switch in its motor vehicles a while ago).

Usually, when an aircraft displays such quirks or anomalies, the manufacturer would design a fix for it. Alternatively, if not a serious anomaly, the pilots would be informed through their flight crew training manuals and would be trained to deal with the incongruities or peculiarities. The Accident Report affirms this procedure in a Safety Board Member Statement on page 138:

> *"In making safety improvements, the well-known system safety order of precedence should be followed: the largest potential for safety improvements comes from design and engineering enhancements, while the lowest form of safety improvement comes from training and procedures".*

For reasons of their own, most likely favoring their own commercial interests (as in the Air India accident), Boeing officials masked their knowledge of the autothrottle anomalies prior to the accident and did not address the shortcomings in a positive and remedial way. The dire effects of the inconsistencies were not taught, or expressly and adequately mentioned, in the Boeing 777 Manuals. This hush-up by Boeing is taken as deliberate suppression of vital flight safety information by the Boeing Company that could otherwise have prevented the fatal crash of Asiana 214. The NTSB Accident Report refers to those inadequacies in the Boeing documentation:

> *"The NTSB Board members unanimously determined that "the complexities of the autothrottle and autopilot flight director systems that were inadequately described in Boeing's documentation and Asiana's pilot training, which increased the likelihood of mode error." This concurring and dissenting statement enumerates some of those complexities and inadequacies. (Accident Report, page. 137).*

Notwithstanding the Asiana flight crew's 'mismanagement of the airplane's descent' and their failure to 'sufficiently monitor and manage their airspeed', the suppression of two known flight safety issues relating to the B777 autothrottle system contributed greatly to the accident of Asiana 214 - *in equal measure* as the flight crew failures. Boeing's willful suppression of vital safety issues demonstrated an *extreme indifference to human life,* those safety issues being: (a) the failure of the autothrottle to maintain speed in the 'flight level change' mode which Asiana 214 was flying in; and (b) its failure to provide low speed protection and autothrottle wake-up in that mode.

Boeing's Disregard of FAA Safety Concerns

Prior to the accident of Asiana 214, the Boeing Company received flight safety warnings that cautioned Boeing on the potential disastrous consequences of the anomalies/ inconsistencies in the Boeing 777 autothrottle system. The warnings came from a Federal Aviation Administration (FAA) Test Pilot, Mr. Eugene Arnold, who had unexpectedly encountered the very same two back-to-back scenarios during flight testing of the B787 aircraft (which aircraft had a near-identical autothrottle system as the B777).

Thus, not only were the *Asiana aircrew* caught by the autothrottles' unexpected behavior, but so was a seasoned FAA test pilot caught unawares by the very same inconsistencies in the system. If a seasoned FAA Test Pilot - who was acutely focused upon the aircraft and systems he was busy testing - could unexpectedly fall into the so-called 'Flight Level Change trap' during a moment's distraction by a traffic advisory, then so much more could the average line pilot be caught unaware – as the Asiana crew inadvertently and disastrously confirmed.

FAA Test Pilot Arnold felt that *"even though the [B777] system had been certified previously and had met the requirements of Federal Aviation Regulations, it was a less-than-desirable feature and it could be improved upon".* (NTSB Accident Report, Para 1.18.2). In response, Boeing callously replied that the Boeing 777 autothrottle had been certified and had no problems in service, and had "met the requirements for what was intended for the system". Although a note was added to the B787 Airplane Flight Manual, no such note was added to the B777 Airplane Flight Manual.

The hazardous autothrottle scenario, which caught the FAA Test Pilot unaware, later caught the Asiana 214 aircrew by surprise and led to the accident of Asiana 214. That sadly demonstrated that the anomalies/ inconsistencies in the B777 autothrottle were indeed a problem in service – despite Boeing's assertion to the contrary. The NTSB recommended in their Accident Report Summary that a 'special certification design review' be convened to evaluate the potentially unsafe design features on the previously approved B777 aircraft.

Boeing's Disregard of EASA Safety Warnings

The discussions on the B777 and B787 autothrottle inconsistencies/ anomalies reached the European Aviation Safety Agency (EASA) who warned Boeing prior to the Asiana accident that inconsistencies in flight automation had in the past been a strong contributor to aviation accidents. The NTSB Accident Report describes the EASA concerns and recommendations:

> *The European Aviation Safety Agency (EASA) also voiced a concern about A/T automatic engagement on the 787 in a document titled "EASA Debrief Note on Boeing 787-8 RR EASA Validation Familiarization Flight Test Visit," dated May 22, 2011. In an item titled "Major Recommendation for Improvement #3," the debrief note pointed out that A/T automatic engagement (wake up) was not available in a FLCH or VNAV SPD descent with the A/T in HOLD mode and stated that "although the certification team accepts that this 'Autothrottle wake up' feature is not required per certification requirements, these two exceptions look from a pilot's perspective as an inconsistency in the automation behavior of the airplane." According to the note, a major recommendation for improvement is "an item which meets the required standard but where considerable improvement is recommended." The debrief note further stated that "the manufacturer [Boeing] would enhance the safety of the product by avoiding exceptions in the 'Autothrottle wake up' mode condition." (NTSB Accident Report, Para 1.18.2).*

Boeing similarly and callously disregarded the European Aviation Safety Agency's warnings and recommendations. For the B777 autothrottle anomalies, no remedial action was taken.

Boeing's Unrepentant Response to NTSB Safety Recommendations

The NTSB found in its Accident Report on the crash of Asiana 214 that, quote "A review of the design of the 777 automatic flight control system, with special attention given to the issues identified in this accident investigation and the issues identified by the Federal Aviation Administration and European Aviation Safety Agency during the 787 certification program, could yield insights about how to improve the intuitiveness of the 777 and 787 flight crew interfaces as well as those incorporated into future designs". The NTSB thus recommended that the FAA:

> *Convene a special certification design review of how the Boeing 777 automatic flight control system controls airspeed and use the results of that evaluation to develop guidance that will help manufacturers improve the intuitiveness of existing and future interfaces between flight crews and autoflight systems. (A-14-42). (NTSB Accident Report, page 130).*

> *Task a panel of human factors, aviation operations, and aircraft design specialists, such as the Avionics Systems Harmonization Working Group, to develop design requirements for context-dependent low-energy alerting systems for airplanes engaged in commercial operations. (A-14-43). (NTSB Accident Report, page 130).*

In a strong response to these NTSB safety recommendations, Boeing issued an unrepentant statement saying that the company respectfully disagreed with the NTSB's findings that the 777's auto-flight system contributed to the Asiana 214 accident, and that it did not believe that the NTSB's findings were supported by the evidence. Boeing's reply to the NTSB safety recommendations further demonstrated their unresponsiveness to correct pertinent flight safety issues and revealed their indifference to human life when their company profits were at stake.

Boeing's Systematic Pattern of Suppressing Safety Warnings

The disregard for air safety demonstrated by Boeing in the Asiana case does not stand in isolation and was not the only incident showing the company's extreme apathy to human life. Boeing already had 'blood on its hands' (to use a phrase) by their violent suppression of vital flight safety warnings, which in turn led to the death or injury of 166 people in the accident of Air India Flight IX-812. That suppression of critical safety information is fully described in the murder charges filed against Boeing in Washington State Superior Court Case No. 13-2-19597-6KNT (transferred to US District Court, Seattle, as case no. 13cv982, and irregularly and corruptly dismissed).

Boeing was further warned by me personally, as a former seasoned B777 instructor for the company, that their lawless corporate culture would lead to more deaths in preventable aircraft accidents caused by their unimpeded lawlessness and reduced safety considerations when it affected their bottom line.

Boeing callously failed to heed the warnings of the European Aviation Safety Agency; failed to heed the warnings of FAA Test Pilot Eugene Arnold; and coldly disregarded my own warnings as (retired) Senior Boeing Instructor Pilot. Boeing suppressed the warnings and vital information on the B777 autothrottle anomalies and inconsistencies. Boeing's cruel indifference created grave risk of death and injury to all who flew on its B777 aircraft and, in equal measure to 'Asiana pilot error', that lack of concern led directly to the death of three passengers and grave injury to another 181 on Asiana 214.

Boeing's extreme indifference to human life violated the Revised Code of Washington, statute RCW 9A.32.030, and, concerning the three passengers who perished, constitutes murder in the first degree. Boeing's lawless behavior also violated the United States Code 18USC1111 (and/or 18USC1112) and constitutes murder or manslaughter under those statutes. Concerning the 181 injured passengers, Boeing's culpability in the accident of Asiana Flight 214 constitutes attempted murder pursuant to statute 18USC1113.

The US Department of Justice, the FBI, and the Courts failed to investigate, prosecute, and administer the laws, instead giving Boeing a free pass. Thus, acting as Prosecutor Qui Tam, I filed the criminal charges with those and several other institutions tasked with law and order: The White House and Cabinet, the Congress, and the US Supreme Court, et al.

OBAMA AND THE US GOVERNMENT'S SHARED CULPABILITY

Here, at this juncture in the story, we connect back to the link between Boeing's criminality and delinquent government officials, as described earlier in these pages. Exacerbating and fostering the lawlessness of the Boeing Company is the impunity with which Boeing has been able to violate the laws. That impunity was provided with the full knowledge of the United States Courts and the White House and other government institutions tasked with law and order – and led by Obama. For several years, Boeing has enjoyed the protection from civil and criminal prosecution afforded by the United States authorities.

On June 13, 2013, some three weeks *prior to* the accident of Asiana 214, I issued a flight safety warning to President Obama and his Cabinet (including the Attorney General and Secretary of Transportation); to the US District Court judges in Seattle; to the Justices of the United States Supreme Court; and to every member of the United States Congress, warning of further imminent air accidents if the lawlessness within the Boeing Company was not arrested.

Each of those institutions and their high officials was fully informed and aware of that lawlessness; each had a duty to address and arrest the lawlessness and the Boeing officials involved; and each institution and official once more chose to ignore the warnings and instead to protect the Boeing Company from prosecution. Each US Government institution approached could have addressed and terminated the lawlessness within Boeing and thereby helped to avert the accident of Asiana 214, but willfully failed to do so. Instead, those institutions assisted the Boeing Company in its lawlessness and enabled and made it possible for Boeing to commit further crimes in the form of criminal culpability in the Asiana accident and deaths.

Statute 18USC3 demands that whoever, knowing that offenses have been committed against the United States, assists the offenders in order to hinder or prevent their apprehension, trial, or punishment, is an *accessory after the fact*. Statute 18USC2 demands that anyone who aids or abets an offense against the United States is punishable as a principal. Each US Government officer, who had the ability to take action and who failed to heed the flight safety warning, is as culpable in the resultant deaths and injuries on Asiana 214 as is the Boeing Company, its Board of Directors, and its executive officers.

Boeing thus shares criminal culpability with US Government officials who took no action on Boeing's lawlessness, despite having a duty to do so. Those US officials who failed to act created the circumstances for Boeing's misconduct; offered the opportunity;

perpetuated the concealment of the safety warnings; prevented remedial actions; and furthered the commission of or enabled Boeing to yet again commit murder. Still others assisted the Boeing offenders to escape justice, and are culpable as accessories after the fact in the murder of the three who died and attempted murder of the 181 who were injured in the accident. The guilty include the Boeing Board of Directors, President Obama and his Cabinet, the Congress, judges of the US District Court (Seattle), justices of the US Supreme Court, and their co-conspirators – together constituting the 15,000-strong criminal conspiracy within the United States Government.

CONSIDER YOUR VERDICT

Having carefully considered the prima facie evidence at hand regarding the two aforementioned air accidents, and having measured that evidence against the laws prohibiting murder, *what is your verdict?* At the time of writing, none of the crimes have been investigated, and none of the criminals have been apprehended - neither in the United States nor in India. That fact alone is sufficient to indict delinquent government officials as co-perpetrators and/or as accessories.

Sadly, where there is no deterrent to wrongdoing by Boeing, there is bound to be more deaths caused by that same continuing criminal conduct. Many more, in fact. And the President, the US Courts, and the US Congress were once more warned of that strong potential – again to no avail. With an extreme lack of sympathy for the loss of human life, corrupt government officials, together with callous Boeing Company officials, continued to ignore the flight safety warnings regarding Boeing's quest for profits at the expense of flight safety. That created a grave risk of death to passengers and crews. That conduct by Boeing was soon to cause the avoidable deaths of another 346 people in two separate crashes of the new Boeing 737 MAX aircraft, as well as another close call when a door plug blew off in flight, as we shall see in a later chapter.

However, in the next chapters, we shall examine more closely the role of crime in the courts, that aberration in the intensifying criminal endeavor, and the impact upon the American nation.

Chapter 10
Crime in the Courts and the Defeat of Justice

Every court and every judge involved in those 62 cases had the ability, the authority, and the legal and moral duty to terminate the lawlessness. Yet, in vituperative mockery, every court and every judge chose to protect the malfeasant judicial and government officials from prosecution, and thereby joined with and augmented the travesty of justice. There were no exceptions.

Extract From Chapter 10.

INCENTIVE FOR THE COURT CASES

Protection against the criminal acts of malfeasant officials and redress for the harm and loss caused by their malevolent actions (or their failure to act where action was due) were sought in both civil claims for damage and in criminal cases. Sixty-two court cases were assembled in all, in the quest for due process and protection of the laws. Each court case addressed different aspects of the insurrection and different groupings amongst the seditious conspirators. (Cases are listed in *Appendix 2)*. Every court and every judge involved in those 62 cases had the ability, the authority, and the legal and moral duty to terminate the lawlessness. Yet, in vituperative mockery, every court and every judge instead chose to protect the malfeasant judicial and government officials from prosecution, and thereby joined with and augmented the travesty of justice. There were no exceptions.

The court cases were fought 'pro se' without the benefit of a lawyer. Because, amongst some 22 lawyers initially approached, not one could be found who had the courage or was willing to tackle the delinquency in the courts or the deluge of criminal offenses committed by government officials in the broader case.

Philosophy Behind the Civil Suits

As a general principle, every act or omission negligently or willfully perpetrated that harms another person constitutes a cause of action in a tort law claim for damages. The criminal statutes indicate the more serious breaches of societal norms, common law principles, and responsibilities. It follows, then, that every criminal act or omission that harms another also gives rise to a civil claim for damages. The US Constitution, 14th Amendment, and the statutes 42USC1983 and 42USC1985 make provision for civil restitution for conspiracy against and denial of an individual's rights. In this particular case, redress was sought for the denial of the unambiguous constitutional rights to due process of law, protection of the laws, and ownership of 'de jure' property.

Consequently, as a result of the failure of the criminal justice system to act against law-breaking government officials or to provide that protection of the laws, civil suits for damages were filed against malfeasant government and industry officials who, through their acts or omissions, breached common law protections and the criminal statutes and thereby caused me harm and loss. A number of civil actions were pursued through various courts via state superior courts, a state appeals court, and a state supreme court; federal district courts, federal appeal courts, and the US Supreme Court. The courts ruled on more than 352 proceedings in the 62 cases, that is, motions, injunctions, appeals, mandamus petitions, certiorari petitions, etc.

Criminal Cases

As mentioned in Chapter 7, the United States of America, on its own volition, opened three criminal cases to address, in part, some of the crimes of only some of the conspirators. All three criminal cases were summarily and illegally dismissed from the United States District Court by a corrupt judge. That illegality in the US District Court of Colorado was, in turn, wrongfully upheld by the United States Court of Appeals, in order to further relieve the government offenders and prevent their trial. Subsequent appeals to the United States Supreme Court were obstructed by the US Supreme Court Justices. All evidence of those criminal cases was either removed from the Supreme Court Record or simply not filed under whatever false pretext. Due process of law was thus denied to the American public by the US District Court, the 10th Circuit Appeals Court, and the US Supreme Court. Although still effectively obstructed at the time of writing, the criminal cases remain pending in the US Supreme Court because of judicial fraud.

Judicial Obligations of Judges

Judges receiving criminal complaints under affidavit are bound by law to act upon the reports. Title 18USC3041 empowers a judge to act where a Complaint or an Affidavit (such as the 'Dossier of Crimes') provides probable cause of criminal offenses. In truth, the affidavits filed with the courts in this case provided *strong evidence* of multiple offenses. Under such circumstances, statutes 18USC3046 and 18USC3060 demand that judges arrest the offenders and hold a preliminary hearing (or grand jury) into the offenses.

> **Statute 18USC3041** *states in relevant part: "for any offense against the United States, the offender may, by any justice or judge of the United States ... be arrested and imprisoned".*

185

Statute 18USC3046, regarding warrant or summons, states in relevant part: "Issuance upon complaint, Rule 4: "If the complaint or one or more affidavits filed with the complaint establishes probable cause to believe an offense has been committed and that the defendant committed it, the judge must issue an arrest warrant to an officer authorized to execute it." Rule 4 (c) states: Such warrant must "command that the defendant be arrested and brought without unnecessary delay before a judge".

18USC3060 states in relevant part: (a) Except as otherwise provided by this section, a preliminary examination shall be held within the time set by the judge or magistrate judge pursuant to subsection (b) of this section, to determine whether there is probable cause to believe that an offense has been committed and that the arrested person has committed it.

This case demonstrates that, *in practice,* when those felonies are committed by government officials, such reports are not welcome in the courts and are suppressed by judges or by court clerks and their assistants who act on behalf of the judges. No action was forthcoming from judicial officials to whom the criminal offenses were reported. Every one of the judges criminally neglected the abovementioned statutory duties to impartially administer justice and instead prevented the arrest of the conspirators, concealed their crimes, and assisted the offenders to escape justice.

CORRUPT PRACTICES IN THE COURTS

Legal System Milieu

Cursory observations into the workings of our courts demonstrate that the greater milieu of the United States legal system is totally fetid. It is a legal system that is imploding upon itself from nonsensical and incomprehensible conventions, conflicting case law and judgments, dissections, and cross threads. All of that entangled into such complexity that it is not even fully understood by the practitioners, but is generally to the detriment of the basic and pure principles of justice, which can hardly survive in a system such as that.

The administration of this system of entangled case law and conflicting judgments allows for a completely arbitrary interpretation of the law. The judicial system does not provide clear, concise parameters or guidance to judges. Hence, there is almost zero percent possibility of securing 'justice' in such a system. And not just in the broader case under discussion in this book - for if that is my personal experience, what of the other 340 million Americans, less those in authority?

It is this flawed system that breeds the formidable deceit, carelessness, callousness, and insensitivity that so characterizes the United States legal system today and which is responsible for the breakdown of law and order in general. The corruption of the laws, the debauchery of the administration, and a system that produces crooked officials, crooked legal men, and crooked judges; these are the obstacles that deny access to due process of law. It is these crooked judges and legal men and women who are directly blocking justice - the ones who pounce to take advantage of the disarray in the system so as to prevent the apprehension, trial, and punishment of lawbreaking colleagues and officials.

Lawlessness of Government Defendants

In this matter, once the law-breaking officials were brought to court (on paper at least, for there is yet to be a trial), they did everything in their power to counteract and nullify the court cases and to escape prosecution, by fair means or foul – and mostly foul.

The officials /defendants embarked upon tampering with and theft of court records and incriminating evidence, conspiracy with judges to manipulate court judgments, and a path of malicious intimidation and retaliation against me as the primary witness to the crimes committed by the various groups of officials. The 'Dossier of Crimes', which provides prima facie evidence of the criminal offenses of some 15,000 officials/defendants - was illegally removed from several court records and from all associated cases filed in the US Supreme Court. The collaboration of judges in the crimes of the defendants can readily be traced through correspondence and through the various court rulings.

Lawlessness of Judges

In all 62 court cases, not one judicial decision showed a semblance of justice or followed the law. Except for the initial civil case, which gave rise to the criminal endeavor, in every other court case, crooked and politically motivated judges joined forces with the seditious conspirators to dismiss the cases before trial in flagrant violation of the laws, without tending to the volume of criminal charges filed in the cases. Every one of the 352 motions or proceedings filed to date was denied or dismissed in order to assist the lawbreaking government officials to escape justice. Judges simply acted as if they were part of the defense team of the malfeasant officials. They acted as if the laws did not apply to them. *Because, in practice, they don't.*

Over and over again, judges ignored the statutes and simply failed to address the criminal offenses underlying the cases or the multiple offenses committed in their courts. Judges who became personally implicated through such blatant dereliction of duty failed to recuse themselves when circumstances dictated that they do so, thereby violating the statutes 28USC144[11] and 28USC455[12].

The lawlessness shown in the courts was demonstrated across all 352 proceedings in the 62 associated cases. Protection of the laws was sought over the two and a half decades, via 23 separate requests to every one of 1,252 federal judges and 2,689 state judges individually and in groups – *3,954 judges in all.* Those judges were on the bench of 208 different courts: 140 State Courts, plus 54 Federal District Courts (out of a total of 89), plus all 13 Federal Circuit Appeals Courts, and disgracefully, the United States Supreme Court. Under the dictates of statute 18USC4, protection of the laws was sought over the years from, amongst others, US Supreme Court Justices individually and collectively. Those Justices were: Roberts, Breyer, Ginsburg, Kennedy, Scalia, Souter, Stevens, Thomas, Alito, Sotomayor, Kagan, Gorsuch, Kavanaugh, Coney Barrett, Brown Jackson, O'Connor, and Rehnquist. Fourteen Supreme Court cases and 163 letters in total informed the Justices of the subversive criminal conspiracy.

Thus, well-nigh *4000 state and federal judges, who had explicit jurisdiction, who had an unambiguous duty, and who had taken an oath before God and the nation to perform that duty,* criminally neglected their judicial duties concerning the reports of offenses committed by government officials. Those offenses were reported

---

[11] 28USC144 (Recusal of Judges)
"Whenever a party to a proceeding in a court makes and files a timely and sufficient affidavit that the judge before whom the matter is pending has a personal bias or prejudice either against him or in favor of any adverse party, such judge shall proceed no further therein, but another judge shall be assigned to hear such proceeding."

[12] 28USC455 – Disqualification of a Judge
"(a) Any justice, judge, or magistrate of the United States shall disqualify himself in any proceeding in which his impartiality might reasonably be questioned."

to the judges on repeated occasions through the 'Dossier of Crimes'; and/or, in affidavits/criminal complaints filed in the 62 cases. Not a single criminal offense was brought to trial. Not a single judge appointed a prosecutor, ordered an investigation, issued an arrest warrant, or held a preliminary hearing. *All cases* (except the originating case) were *corruptly* dismissed. *All 352 or more proceedings* in those cases were corruptly denied, dismissed, or simply ignored and not ruled upon, as if they didn't exist.

To illustrate that lawless modus operandi in the courts, a sample of the offenses committed *by the judges* is listed below:

a. Theft of Record
Removing or concealing unwanted motions from the court records, motions that opposed or did not benefit the premeditated and preconceived judgments of the judges. This type of obstruction occurred frequently throughout the 62 cases.

b. Removing or concealing criminal charges
Removing or concealing unwanted criminal complaints from the court records; alternatively, simply ignoring criminal complaints as if they were never filed. This type of obstruction also occurred very frequently throughout the 62 cases. (For example, early in the two decades-long process, the removal of criminal charges of March 4, 2006, from Supreme Court case no. 05-140 against President Bush; or the removal of the 'Dossier of Crimes' from the Supreme Court Record on 34 separate occasions).

c. Tampering with (threatening) a Witness
As litigant and witness, judges threatened me with contempt of court or other unwarranted censure if I continued to (lawfully) pursue criminal allegations against judicial and government officers. (For example, in the case *Keyter vs. 230 Government Officials*). I have no doubt in my mind that the threats of censure meant imprisonment on some fabricated pretext, perhaps made-up contempt charges.

d. <u>Criminal conspiracy between the courts to quash unwanted cases</u>
There was collusion between the courts to get rid of cases against malfeasant government officials. For example, a criminal conspiracy between the US District Court of Western Washington and the US District Courts of Delaware, Northern Texas, and Oregon, to get rid of several unwanted criminal cases related to insurrection and sedition.

e. <u>Criminal conspiracy between judges and court clerks</u>
Judges colluded with court clerks and assistants to frustrate, obfuscate, prevaricate, delay, and obstruct important (but unwelcome) criminal cases against government officials by means of dishonesty or by invoking petty rules or format requirements such as wrong font and wrong typesetting, etc. Such techniques of harassment and obstruction are limitless in number and were demonstrated throughout the 62 cases. Such obstructions can keep unwanted cases (against government officials) out of the courts for years and years until the complainant finally fatigues, runs out of money, time, or patience to pursue the case. A supreme example of this type of abuse and obstruction of justice hails from the US Supreme Court, where the court failed to file 11 criminal appeal cases (including the case filed concerning mass murder) with the following simple, misleading statement, *irrelevant* to the facts concerning those 11 cases:

> *"Under Article III of the Constitution, the jurisdiction of this Court extends only to the consideration of cases or controversies properly brought before it from lower courts in accordance with federal law and filed pursuant to the Rules of this Court. The Court does not give advice or assistance or answer legal questions on the basis of correspondence. Your papers are returned herewith".*

As with the first three associated cases involving government officials engaged in crime (which were summarily dismissed from the US Supreme Court), the latter 11 appeal cases *were properly brought before the Supreme Court* from the lower courts, in full accordance with federal law and the court's rules of procedure.

f. Denial of Mandamus Petitions
    Thirteen separate petitions for writ of mandamus were filed in the court cases. Those petitions requested one thing: to command government and judicial officials to obey the Constitution and the laws that they were in breach of. All thirteen petitions to compel government and judicial officials to abide by the laws were denied or simply ignored, essentially giving those officials free rein to continue to violate the laws *with the sanction and protection of the courts*. Ponder the effect of this last statement.

    A petition for a writ of mandamus was also filed in the US Supreme Court (in Keyter vs Bush) requesting the Supreme Court to compel President Bush to see to his constitutional duties *"to take care of the faithful execution of the laws"* where the judicial process had broken down with respect to the offenses of this conspiracy. However, that petition was illegally removed from the court record before the Justices could deliberate thereon. It was re-filed on six occasions, but illegally removed from the Supreme Court Record on each and every occasion. Thus, the US Supreme Court and lower courts, which denied the petitions for a writ to command the malfeasant officials to obey the laws, in effect legitimized the criminality within the government (in violation of statutes 18USC2, 18USC3, and 18USC242).

g. Campaign contributions to judges' election campaigns, by lawyers
    Contributions given by lawyers to judges' election campaigns leave judges indebted to lawyers and present

lawyers with an opening to exert undue influence over judges. Such contributions, when cashed in for favors at a later stage, are nothing less than bribe money to be collected upon at some future date. Such a *bribe* is most likely the root cause of the clearly pre-determined and patently unjust outcome of the originating Washington State case of *'Keyter vs. Keyter'*.

Examples of the lawlessness abound in the 62 court cases, and multiple criminal acts were perpetrated by judges with complete impunity. In the case of *'Keyter vs 230 Government Officers'*, for instance, presiding judge Charles Lovell breached 21 laws. The statutes violated are enumerated herewith as illustration and are detailed in **Appendix 4** for interested readers:

> *Contempt of Court - 18USC401; Tampering with a Witness - 18USC1512; Tampering with Evidence - 18USC1506; Misprision of Felony - 18USC4; Obstruction of Justice - 18USC1505; Accessory after the fact, to the crimes in the dossier - 18USC3; Conspiracy to commit offense - 18USC371; Investigation of Crimes involving Government Officers - 28USC535(b)(1); Conspiracy against Rights – 18USC241; Deprivation of Rights – 18USC242; Personal Bias or Prejudice - 28USC144; Recusal of Judge - 28USC455; Oath of Office - 28USC453; Rendering Criminal Assistance - RCW 9A.76.080; Official Misconduct - RCW 9A.80.010; Failure of Duty by Public Official - RCW 42.20.100; Federal Rules on Criminal Procedure, Rule 4; Perjury -18USC1621; Fraud; Washington State Constitution & US Constitution - Due process and Protection of the Laws.*

The US Constitution demands in Article III, Section 1, that judges shall only hold their offices during good behavior. Under this dictate, a single crime committed by any judge against the United States ought to be sufficient to debar a judge from the bench.

But, again, *in practice, the laws or the Constitution do not apply to judges.* A litany of crimes, such as is presented above, is simply tolerated and ignored by the court system, by judicial conduct commissions, and by bar associations, thereby fostering the perpetuation and escalation of the profound lawlessness over time.

Dereliction of Judicial Duties

United States judges have all taken an Oath of Office to 'administer justice without respect to persons and to do equal right to the poor and to the rich, and to faithfully and impartially discharge and perform all the duties incumbent upon them under the Constitution and laws of the United States'. They have all avowed those duties with the invocation: "So help me God". (Statute 28USC453).

Some 4000 state and federal judges involved in the criminal matter at hand willfully failed to perform their legal duties to administer justice upon malfeasant government officials. The dereliction of their judicial duty was malevolently aimed at obstructing and defeating the due and proper course of justice and the administration of the laws; and aimed at assisting their government colleagues to escape punishment for criminal wrongdoing. In doing so, the judges joined with and furthered the aims of the broad insurrection against the laws of the United States. Nearly 4000 state and federal judges combined, colluded, acted in unison, and:

- o Willfully failed to provide 'due process of law' in the courts, in this matter, as prescribed by the Constitution and the laws, in violation of the 5th and 14th Amendments.
- o Willfully failed to provide 'protection of the laws' against the ongoing international criminal endeavor and assassination plot, in violation of the 5th and 14th Amendments.

- o Willfully failed to return stolen property, in violation of the 14th Amendment.
- o Willfully failed to protect Constitutional rights where those rights had been quashed.
- o Willfully failed to properly docket criminal cases based on criminal complaints and to obey the rules of criminal procedure.
- o Willfully failed to apprehend known criminals and murderers, in violation of 18USC3046.
- o Willfully failed to appoint a prosecutor to investigate and prosecute the crimes committed by government officers, pursuant to 28USC535 (b), and 28USC591 & 592; and/or failed to request the government to prosecute.
- o Willfully failed to hold a preliminary examination, in violation of 18USC3060, to determine whether there was probable cause to believe that offenses had been committed.
- o Willfully failed to administer the laws upon the criminals and their offenses.
- o Willfully failed to prohibit the ongoing breaches of law by malfeasant officials by way of writ of mandamus or command from the court.
- o Willfully failed to provide protection and relief requested in urgent motions for injunction to secure the personal safety of a litigant.
- o Willfully failed to address or prevent known tampering with a witness.
- o Willfully failed to address or prevent known tampering with court evidence.
- o Willfully failed to address or prohibit illegal interception of communications, in violation of the tenets of the Patriot Act.

- ○ Willfully failed to address and terminate the ongoing criminal endeavor as detailed in the 'Dossier of Crimes'; that is, the ongoing seditious conspiracy and insurrection against the laws.
- ○ In short, judges willfully failed to honor their 'Oath of Office', to faithfully and impartially discharge and perform the duties incumbent upon them.

Fraud, murder, obstruction of justice, misprision, conspiracy against rights, seditious conspiracy, and insurrection against the laws – these are but some of the innumerable criminal offenses some 4000 state and federal judges deliberately failed to address. That willful dereliction of duty was without doubt aimed at providing aid to a large group of government officials - seditious conspirators/ insurrectionists against the laws, domestic enemies of the United States – assisting them to escape apprehension, trial, and punishment. That unrestrained aid and comfort to our domestic enemies constitutes treason in terms of the law (18USC2381).

Profound Dishonesty in the Courts

Some of the deceitful methods used by judges to corruptly obstruct and then dismiss the cases are described below. These are common schemes used by judges, court clerks, and clerk's assistants, all operating in unison as a team to defeat the course of justice when that is what they desire in any of the cases. False statements by the judges, clerks, and their assistants generally violate statutes 18USC1621 and/or 18USC1001. Examples of dishonesty are found throughout the 352 proceedings of the 62 court cases. Some random illustrations are presented below:

a) *False representation as to the nature of the cases*

Judges frequently misrepresented the classification of the cases, treating *criminal cases* (based on criminal complaints addressing criminal offenses) as *civil cases* seeking damages. Judges then dismissed the cases based upon arguments that applied to civil cases, not criminal cases, without addressing the crimes or the criminal complaints; and without following the rules of criminal procedure.

b) *False representation of the gravamen of the cases*

Judges frequently misrepresented the gravamen, the essence or most serious part of the cases, thereby deceitfully shifting the emphasis to something trivial so as to facilitate easy and respectable dismissal of the cases. For example: misrepresenting 'criminal acts' as trivial matters, concerned with the originating divorce case. Additionally, judges dismissed cases with trite and deceitful excuses, for instance, that the cases were 'frivolous' or had 'no cause of action', when indeed there was strong substance to the matter. For example, the 'kidnap and murder attempts' were referred to as a 'frivolous matter', and the criminal complaints were dismissed accordingly. (I refer to judgments in US District Court Delaware, case nos. 08-97, 10-36, and 10-802). Conspiracy to kidnap and murder a Supreme Court litigant ought not to be treated as a *'frivolous matter'* by the courts, since these crimes shall be punished by imprisonment for any term of years or for life.

c) *False representation of jurisdiction in the cases*

Judges and court clerks often falsely misrepresented the court's true jurisdiction in cases and dismissed those cases for ostensibly lacking jurisdiction when, in fact and in truth, those courts *did have* jurisdiction concerning persons under their geographical area of responsibility.

d) *False representation of the facts in the cases*

Judges frequently misrepresented the facts in the case or fraudulently *reconstructed* the facts in order to deliver ostensibly respectable judgments. They then constructed fallacious arguments in their ruling and decided the case on the fallacious arguments relating to the false facts which the judges themselves had conjured up. During the appeal, the false statements of lower court judges were given further credence and respectability when appeals court judges quoted the same glaringly false statements as if they indeed were facts, even after having been provided with the proper set of facts. That travesty was then carried forward to the very loose and inadequate system of case law, where the false statements fabricated by judges end up as *'case law'*.

e) *Quoting 'case law', which is irrelevant to the case*

Judges frequently quoted case law which was irrelevant to the case under consideration, but often relevant to their false statements, false classification of the case, or conjured facts which the judges themselves had fabricated to motivate and reinforce their deceitful arguments and orders.

f) *Quoting statutory law irrelevant to the facts*

Judges frequently quoted statutory law irrelevant to the facts of the case under consideration, but only relevant to their own false and misleading statements, which were fabricated to reinforce their deceitful rulings.

g) *Repeating false statements frequently*

Judges tended to repeat their own false statements often so as to reinforce their deceitful reconstruction of the facts. In the case *'Keyter vs. 230 Government Officers'*, for instance, Judge Lovell repeated two such false statements no less than 26 times in his judgment of the case.

On most occasions, the deceitful and perjurious statements made by the judges were attacked and the correct set of facts provided to the courts, but, predictably, those corrections were simply discarded.

Truth is an essential pillar of justice. In its essence, justice is founded upon the strict and truthful weighing of the facts. Without truth, there can be no justice. And judges are called upon to be just and to do right – a call they must answer under oath. No man, whether he be a judge or otherwise, does right by another with false representations that harm that other person. Such an injury breaches the oath of a judge to do justice. Manipulation of the facts to one's own ends and deception employed in a judgment are not righteous acts but a perversion that amounts to malevolence and perjury.

The presiding judges in the court cases had but one objective in mind, and that was to dismiss the cases against government officers (and the Boeing Company) – whether by right or not. In that way, they could assist malfeasant government officers or Boeing officials in order to prevent their apprehension, trial, and punishment - thereby to save the federal and state governments the acute embarrassment of public exposure of the criminal acts committed by their senior officers. In almost all cases, dismissal was 'justified' by profound dishonesty, by judges and court clerks alike. Such dishonesty in the court system renders 'justice' wholly unattainable.

It is strange to me. From the voices of some emanate harmonious and uplifting sounds, virtuous and melodious sufficient to rival the sweet song of the birds. From the foaming mouths of others come unbridled dishonesty and maliciousness, so repugnant as to rival the growl found deep in the bowls of the earth. It all depends on the content of the heart of the speaker.

All Relief Denied

The courts were explicitly requested to ensure *'protection of the laws'* against the deluge of criminal offenses detailed in the 2,400 pages of the Dossier of Crimes, including against the ongoing attempts to kidnap and murder the petitioner (the writer). Judges had the ability, the authority, and the duty to provide that protection. Without exception, all such requests were denied – some 352 in all - in their bias towards protecting the malfeasant government officials from the consequences of their crimes. Details relating to such callous denial of constitutional rights (in violation of 18USC241 and 18USC 242) appear in all 62 court cases. Some random examples are presented below:

a) *Keyter vs. the Boeing Company:* (1) Case no. 09cv962: Despite a succinct 'affidavit of prejudice', Judge Jones found no merit to the allegations against him and declined to recuse himself from the action. Affidavit/criminal complaint against Judge Jones was ignored; motion to compel compliance with the law was ignored; motion to appoint a prosecutor was ignored; motion for arrest of criminal conspirators was ignored; the Dossier of Crimes was ignored. (2) Case no.12cv474: 8 motions were disregarded; 8 criminal complaints plus Dossier of Crimes were disregarded; case dismissed by Judge Lasnik, who was himself a named defendant in the case.

b) *International Terrorism and Murder case,* Delaware case no. 10-802: Motion for clarification of memorandum order denied as moot; affidavit/criminal charges against Delaware judicial personnel denied as moot; the Dossier of Crimes was ignored.

c) *Keyter vs McCain et al – US District Court:* All pending motions were denied as moot when the case was dismissed (motion to terminate ongoing crimes; motion for joinder, etc). *Appeals Court:* motions for injunction (to secure personal safety) - denied; motion for default - denied; criminal complaint re defendants – ignored; criminal complaints in the Dossier of Crimes - ignored. *US*

Supreme Court: Petition for writ of certiorari – denied; motion for rehearing – denied; affidavit/criminal complaint re justices – ignored; writ of mandamus re justices – deceitfully returned; motion for due process of law – ignored; motion for preliminary injunction re defendants – deceitfully returned; motion to disqualify justices – ignored; affidavit of prejudice re justices – ignored; motion for preliminary injunction re justices – ignored; affidavit/criminal complaint on 5/19/07 re seditious conspiracy – ignored; affidavit/criminal complaint re defendants – ignored; the Dossier of Crimes - ignored.

d) On and on, to include more than 352 proceedings.

Fraudulent Judge's Rulings

Throughout the 62 court cases, *judges simply did not speak the truth in their rulings.* Judges fraudulently and deviously constructed their judgments to serve a predetermined outcome and cleverly masked their true motives with lies. The predetermined outcome was aimed at the circumvention of criminal charges filed against government officials and thereby protecting those officials from punishment. Some illustrations of the deceitful and fraudulent rulings are presented herewith as examples:

a) In the case *'Keyter vs. 230 Government Officers'*, presiding US District Court Judge Charles Lovell, under oath himself, made 47 fraudulent misrepresentations in his ruling to justify dismissing the case. The case was dismissed with prejudice for, amongst other reasons: the complaint being defective; being frivolous; being an abuse of the court system; the defendants possessing immunity; the court lacking subject matter jurisdiction, etc. The judge found the motion for his own disqualification to be without merit.

b) In the marital dissolution case *'Keyter vs Keyter'*, Judge Van Deren, being under oath herself, made 64 perjurous statements to motivate and cloak her fraudulent judgment, in which, effectively, the entire estate was illegally awarded to the wife.

c) In the Delaware US District Court case no. 08-97, Judge Sue Robinson based her dismissal on eight blatantly perjurious statements.

d) In Washington State, US District case no. 08-5235, Court Judge Ronald Leighton based his dismissal on nine blatantly perjurious statements.

e) In the Arizona US District Court case no. 05-01923, in *Keyter vs. McCain et al.*, Judge Campbell based his dismissal on eight false statements.

f) International Terrorism and Murder case, US District Court Delaware, case no. 10-802 - summarily dismissed with the words: "The court concludes that plaintiff is attempting to use this court to pursue abusive and vexatious litigation .... All pending motions are denied as moot and the complaint is dismissed".

g) The case *Keyter vs McCain, et al.* was dismissed from the District Court ostensibly for lack of subject matter jurisdiction. The case was dismissed by the Appeals Court, because [amongst other] the district court "made substantive findings of frivolousness and the order was narrowly tailored to curb the abuses of this particular litigant". Certiorari, Rehearing, and all motions in the case were denied in the Supreme Court.

h) The Massachusetts 'criminal' case no. 09-11700, based on the reporting of a seditious conspiracy and other criminal offenses committed by President Obama and his Cabinet, Congress, and US Supreme Court Justices, was summarily dismissed from the District Court under the fraudulent ruling that: the complaints were insufficient; the witness was "attempting to use this court to pursue abusive and vexatious litigation"; the witness was continuing to engage in a pattern of filing lawsuits that attempt to bring criminal charges against hundreds of government officials". The witness, who reported the crimes to the court under the demands of statutes 18USC4 and 18USC2382, was warned that "he could be enjoined from filing further reports and that he could be subject to monetary sanctions should he make any additional frivolous and/or unreasonable submissions to this court".

i) The affidavit/ criminal complaint in re 'Domestic Terrorism Plot', reported to the US District Court of Eastern Virginia and filed as 1:01mc5 (AJT/IDD), was placed in a miscellaneous file and closed "to avoid possible infection of the court's computer system", stating it was from an *unknown origin*, whilst the name and address of the complainant who sent it was included and was used by the court in return mail.

j) The civil claims against the companies Boeing, Ford and Air India, for criminal acts including attempted murder, and subsequent harm and loss, were summarily dismissed (without addressing the criminal offenses filed in the Dossier of Crimes) for, amongst other: continued abuse of legal process by the complainant; and because "the court does not effectuate arrests except in narrow circumstances that are not present in any of these cases"; and by authority of a Bar Order: "The plaintiff is hereby prohibited from filing in this court any action which arises from his previous divorce and plaintiff's resulting actions to remedy the alleged injustices".

k) Colorado criminal cases [a) USA vs. Pres. Bush, et al, case no. 08-85; b) USA vs 443 Known Insurgents, case no. 08-86, and c) USA vs 110th Congress, case no. 08-87] were dismissed for lack of standing of the complaining witness, implying that the witness *could not legally prosecute*. On the other hand, in direct opposition to the afore-going opinion, the 'terrorism case' in the 3rd Circuit Appeals Court, case no. 10-4296, was dismissed for 'failure of the witness to prosecute', meaning: the case was dismissed because *the witness should have, but did not prosecute*. In truth, in both cases, the 'standing' of the witness who reported the crimes to the court was irrelevant to the prosecution. It was the *United States,* not the witness, who was obligated to prosecute, but who willfully and illegally failed to do so.

l) The criminal complaint in the case *'In Re International Terrorism and Murder'* was dismissed from the US Supreme Court, for, amongst other reasons: "The Court does not give advice or assistance or answer legal questions on the basis of correspondence".

Dishonesty in Court Correspondence

Reports of criminal offenses committed by malfeasant government officers, furnished under the demands of 18USC4, were filed with the relevant authorities tasked with law and order in the geographical area or state where the malfeasant officers worked. This law unambiguously *dictated* that I make the offenses known to some judge or other person in authority. (See quote in paragraph on

'Judicial Obligations of Judges', above). The reports filed contained information of malfeasant government officers engaged in subversion against the United States, murder, and attempted murder of a witness to those crimes, etc.

Reaction of governmental institutions (including the courts) to the reports of those serious felonies loosely fell into the following categories, viz., (a) no reaction; or no reply to the reports, letters, or criminal complaints; (b) non-sensical, obfuscating, and evading responses, oft unrelated to the reports; (c) false and misleading statements concerning jurisdiction or their ability or authority to respond; or (d) various other random prevaricating misrepresentations and excuses. Deceitful replies generally violated statute 18USC1001[13].

Some examples of the sheer nonsense and inane babble disseminated in the replies *by judicial officials* are presented herewith. Those judicial officials had the ability, the authority, and the legal duty to act, had the machinery of state to support them in their task, and had taken an oath to perform their duty and to serve the public good.

   a) Court of Appeals, Arkansas: *"We are in receipt of your application re law clerk position. The law clerk positions are presently filled".* [Fact: I did not apply for a law clerk position. I submitted three criminal complaints to the court

---

[13] 18USC1001 – Fraud and False Statements or entries generally
(a) Except as otherwise provided in this section, whoever, in any matter within the jurisdiction of the executive, legislative, or judicial branch of the Government of the United States, knowingly and willfully -- (1) falsifies, conceals, or covers up by any trick, scheme, or device a material fact; (2) makes any materially false, fictitious, or fraudulent statement or representation; or (3) makes or uses any false writing or document knowing the same to contain any materially false, fictitious, or fraudulent statement or entry; shall be fined under this title, imprisoned not more than 5 years or, if the offense involves international or domestic terrorism (as defined in section 2331), imprisoned not more than 8 years, or both.

titled: i) Conspiracy to kidnap and murder, ii) Insurrection and seditious conspiracy, and iii) Charges of treason].

b) Supreme Court of Alabama: *"We regret that it is not possible for the personnel of this office to advise or counsel you about the questions you raise in your letters, or perform legal research for you.* [Fact: No advice was sought from the court; no questions were raised; the court was not requested to perform legal research for me. The matter titled 'USA vs 14,264 Seditious Conspirators' and the 'Dossier of Crimes' was filed with the court for their action pursuant to statutes 18USC3041, 18USC3046, and 18USC3060].

c) US District Court, Alaska: *"The court cannot address any of your claims or appeals without a case being filed".* [Fact: It was the duty of the *Court Clerk* to file a case to address the criminal allegations reported to the court under the dictates of statute 18USC4].

d) Court of Appeals, 2nd District, California: *"There is no appropriate or permissible action for the court to respond; the matter is closed. Do not contact the court again with this matter".* [Fact: Three criminal complaints were filed with the court regarding attempted kidnapping and murder, insurrection, seditious conspiracy, and treason.] Then again later: *"There is no record of pending action. The Court is unclear of the nature of the relief you seek".* [Fact: The Dossier of Crimes was filed with the court, which described multiple criminal offenses against the United States. The nature of relief sought from the court was clear, and I quote: "Your immediate action is required to investigate and enforce the laws pertaining to the crimes presented herewith and heretofore and to re-establish the rule of law within state and federal government and the courts"].

e) US District Court, Central California: *"The documents are not in proper format"*. [Fact: No specific format is required in which to report criminal offenses to a federal court. Even if hypothetically, there was such a requirement, the substance of the matter (insurrection, treason, and a murder plot) took preference over the format of the documents].

f) Supreme Court of California: *"This office is prohibited by law from giving legal advice"*. [Fact: No legal advice was sought from the court. A criminal complaint was filed with the court, which should have been dealt with according to the Federal Rules of Criminal Procedure.

g) Supreme Court of Colorado: *"It is not appropriate to write to justices"*. [Fact: This is a false statement by a public official in violation of 18USC1001. Statutes 18USC4 and 18USC2382 demand that I report known crimes to a judge or other person in authority without delay. Failing to do so can mean incarceration for 7 years.

h) US District Court, Southern Florida: *"We are having a difficult time telling from your submission exactly what you want the court to do, if anything"*. [Fact: In a letter titled 'In Re: Further request to act against insurrection, treason, and murder plot', the court was supplied with the 'Dossier of Crimes' and expressly asked, and I quote: "Once more I request that you honor your legal obligations to the American people and take care of the arrest of the seditious conspirators, and terminate this powerful insurrection against the laws of the United States of America. There can be no further delay. Urgent action is not only prudent but essential under the prevailing circumstances"].

i) Supreme Court of Georgia: *"The justices cannot advise you as to how to go about trying to solve the problem you describe"*. [Fact: No advice was sought from the court. Action was demanded regarding reported criminal offenses, in terms of their peremptory duties under statutes 18USC3046 and 18USC3060 to issue a warrant for arrest and to convene a preliminary hearing].

j) US District Court, Maine: *"While there is no statutory prohibition against the filing of a criminal complaint by a private citizen, there is a decisional law to the effect that citizens have no right to present complaints directly to the magistrate....The court is not taking any action in response to your filing"*. [Fact: Statute 18USC4 demands that citizens report known criminal offenses to a judge or other person in authority].

k) US District Court, Western District, Missouri: (Clerk's letter and Judge's ruling): *"The document does not properly identify this court. The document appears to be a criminal complaint from a person not authorized to institute such proceedings. The document states no complaint cognizable by law. As such, the document is without legal effect and is unsuitable for filing. Strike the document from the record and return it to the author ... So Ordered"*. [Fact: The documents precisely identified the court. It was not the reporter but the court that was obligated to institute the criminal proceedings, and that failed to do so. The complaint tabled numerous unmistakable violations of the United States Code]. Again, on a later date, the court prevaricated: *"Order: I have reviewed the most recent communication ... I assume he is not requesting that it be filed. For that reason and for the reason that it is not in proper form to be filed, you are directed to return the correspondence…"*[Fact: The court was supplied with an affidavit reporting criminal offenses committed by government officials, together with a request, quote: "You are requested to promptly deal with the criminal charges filed with you herewith and heretofore, and to have the courtesy to advise me of what action, if any, you have taken to address the insurrection, seditious conspiracy, and treason against the United States].

The list goes on ad infinitum; however, the above examples are quite likely sufficient to indicate to the reader the general trend of the deceit and dishonesty employed in the courts, and their methods of obfuscating and misleading the public. These examples display a profound dishonesty and relentless resistance to addressing the serious criminal allegations against government officials, submitted to the courts in terms of my statutory obligations, as sketched above. The excuses provided for not acting were just that – fraudulent excuses. In many instances, preference was given to 'form' over the 'substance' of the matter - a serious legal anomaly. As if the incorrect 'form' of a filed pleading or report significantly outweighed the grave 'substance' of the matter, namely: *sedition, insurrection, treason, and mass murder*.

JUDGE'S MOTIVES

Protecting Their Own

One may well ask how so many of our judges could participate in this corrupt endeavor and coordinated criminal conspiracy. Firstly, there exists a powerful 'primordial' instinct amongst judges to protect their own; that is, to protect malfeasant colleagues and fellow officials who, in turn, will protect them from the consequences of any wrongdoing. This is a trait of human nature, which failing is responsible for a large portion of the crimes committed in this matter.

In addition, 'the system' in which judges in the United States operate today is absolutely intolerant of 'betrayal' in their ranks, such as the prosecution of members of their own 'family', no matter what the offenses. As demonstrated in these pages, even the serious offenses of subversion, mass murder, and attempted kidnapping and murder of a court litigant and witness have been illegally swept under the carpet and concealed by judges.

There is clearly no moral perfection in a man or woman merely because he/she has assumed the cloak of a 'judge'. It can also not be said that our judges are good, moral, and pure, and that in their 'untainted' minds will be found neither corruption nor defilement nor malignant bent. No, our judges merely reflect the prevailing consciousness of today's society - its scruples and its ills, which ills are so acutely, yet sadly, demonstrated in this case.

Lawbreaking Officials Remain Unassailable

The paradigm presented herewith demonstrates that *in practice* the protection of law-breaking government officials by their colleagues and by the courts is absolute; that government officers who break the law at the expense of the common man are for the most part unassailable; that America's 'Constitutional Rights' and protections which are so proudly touted to a cynical world, are in fact most arbitrarily applied by our courts - the United States Supreme Court included. The abuse of the common man by those who hold positions of power and authority can, without any fear of contradiction, be termed a definite brand of 'tyranny' upon the populace of the United States. The facts irrefutably attest thereto. These assertions are amply demonstrated in the discussion of this matter in terms of the statutes, as follows in Chapter 13.

From an assessment of the facts of the broader case, a reasonable mind can come to no other conclusion than that the corruption demonstrated in this case is not unique, but merely a reflection of endemic corruption throughout all levels of government and the courts across the United States. Without exception, each one of the government officials who were approached to provide protection of the laws and who had the authority and the legal duty to do so, instead, illegally protected lawbreaking officials and rendered assistance to them to escape criminal culpability. Without exception, each one of the nearly 4000 judges who were approached moved to shield those government officials from criminal investigation and prosecution - in flagrant violation of their oaths and the laws on subversion. The judges thus became co-conspirators in the broad criminal conspiracy and culpable of, amongst other crimes, *treason and murder.* Yet, despite these serious offenses against the authority of the United States, the conspirators have remained unassailable.

BRINGING A JUDGE TO JUSTICE

In light of the aforementioned practical examples of judicial misconduct, I ask the rhetorical question: *How do you bring a lawless judge to justice?* How do you address and correct the willful and exceedingly harmful delinquency of even one wayward judge? Remember again, this massive rebellion against the laws started with the criminal offenses of a single judge - and look what it has turned into. Clearly, my personal odyssey in pursuit of justice demonstrates that, in the United States of America today, you cannot bring even one malfeasant judge to book - unless you can simultaneously apprehend another 4000 judges together with the first one. That is because they will do everything in their power, legal and illegal, to assist an errant colleague to escape apprehension, trial, and punishment.

Well then, the question should fairly be asked: *what does it take to bring, not one, but 4000 lawless judges* who are just as guilty (as accessories after the fact) to the crimes of the first offending judge whom they are hell-bent to protect? Once again, in my experience, it's impossible to do, because the 4000 judges are in turn protected by another 11,000 government officials who will assist those judges to escape prosecution. Furthermore, you can't apprehend the combined criminal gang of 15,000 lawless government and judicial officials, for they are sequentially provided safe haven and passage by the chief protector of lawless government officials: the Commander in Chief himself - the President of the United States of America. All right then, the solution to the dilemma seems to have been found: in order to bring a judge to justice, you will also have to bring to book the whole conspiring horde - plus the President, for protecting his lawless henchmen from punishment.

That is how difficult it is in the United States today to find justice for a simple legal wrong perpetrated by a single state judge. After 25 years of exhaustive labor in the unrelenting pursuit of justice, and after much intimidation and being targeted for murder along the way for doing so, I unpretentiously deem myself well qualified to make the aforementioned assertion.

Still, when the law finally catches up with the mob of lawless judges and their fellow malfeasant government officials - as inevitably it must if this country is to survive as a civilized nation - they could face the ultimate sentence for their transgressions. That is, provided the courts indeed operated as they were designed to under the Constitution and are obligated to do so under the laws. My illustration is rooted in stern reality. The potential punishment facing judicial and other malevolent government officials is based on the cold, hard facts of the law. The United States Code, statutes 18USC2381 and 18USC1111, which they are in breach of, sternly dictate that the death sentence is a potential penalty for their crimes.

Crime in the Courts and the Defeat of Justice

The lawlessness in the US Courts and their defeat of justice affect the lives of people across the globe. For example, the consequences of their delinquency and willful failure to bring Boeing Company perpetrators to justice, is reflected in the subsequent Boeing 737 Max accidents and the death of 346 people, as discussed in the next chapter.

Chapter 11
Boeing and the 737 Max Crashes

That cancer of which I speak .... has not been exorcized .... and, without some strong medicine, that cancer will continue to spread within Boeing until either the corporate culture of extreme indifference to human life is eradicated for good; or until the 100-plus year-old Boeing Company succumbs from terminal cancer. Both eventualities are equally possible.

Extract From Chapter 11.

THE CONSEQUENCES OF CRIMINALITY WITH IMPUNITY

The Boeing Company is a large and powerful international corporation that has grossly abused its power and status in society. Boeing has time and again demonstrated its callous disregard for the well-being and safety of individuals and of the international flying public, in favor of its commercial profits. That absence of virtue continues to cause injury, harm, loss, and death, and is of an *ongoing* nature.

In the decade from 1999 to 2009, the Boeing Company's stock price slowly climbed from $42 to $49 per share. In 2013, Dennis Muilenburg became President of Boeing, and when he took over as CEO in July 2015, it stood at $140 per share. Under his leadership style of 'profits before safety', fueled by a culture of greed, in the next four years, the stock price tripled from $140 to $422 per share (on the last trading day before the Ethiopian Airlines 737 Max crash). Between 2015 and 2018, Muilenburg personally benefited over $95 million from that increase, almost $2 million per month. His relentless focus on the stock price and profits, and the unhealthy and undue pressure upon employees to perform, had a profoundly negative impact on the building of safe Boeing aircraft, as is shown in the details below. The company's culture of greed, at the Executive and Board level, compromised flight safety to a perilous degree.

The Boeing Company delivered 806 commercial jet aircraft by year's end in 2018, up from the previous record of 763 jets. Production of Boeing's best-selling Boeing 737 topped an amazing 52 aircraft per month. That figure included the Boeing 737 MAX model, with an astonishing order book for 4,700 aircraft of the new model.

The Boeing 737 MAX was born from Boeing's fierce competition for aircraft sales with the world's other major aircraft manufacturer, the European consortium, Airbus. In 2011, Airbus was ahead of Boeing in its rivalry for single-aisle jets (the likes of the Airbus A320 and Boeing 737). Airbus was in the development of the A320 Neo, a fuel-efficient plane with stronger and more efficient engines and better performance than its own previous models, and also with better performance than Boeing 737 models. Boeing was at that time still considering whether to build an entirely new aircraft that would be ready ten years hence, or whether to upgrade its trusted workhorse, the Boeing 737. The potential loss of a sale of hundreds of new aircraft to American Airlines, an exclusive Boeing customer for some time, but who was ready to sign a large order for the Airbus Neo, compelled Boeing to decide on the 737 upgrade with a shorter development phase of six years. Thus, the fierce competition with Airbus began and pervaded the design and development of the Boeing 737 MAX. Production and certification of the 737 MAX was rushed in order for Boeing to stay in the strong commercial competition.

For the most part, it can be said that the Boeing Company has an efficiently run factory and has an impressive bevy of employees who keep the wheels turning. Over the previous decades, we have come to accept that the Boeing Company builds fine and reputable aircraft. As one who has had the privilege to fly a number of types and models of Boeing aircraft, I will be the first to admit that. I loved to fly a Boeing, and of the types and models that I have flown, the Boeing 777 handles exceptionally well and remains my favorite jetliner to fly.

Still, no aircraft manufacturer can make a flawless aircraft, just as no motor car manufacturer can make a faultless motor vehicle. The same holds true for manufacturers of vehicles such as boats, trains, and spacecraft, and the like. Sometimes, inadvertent problems creep in during design or building, and those anomalies, once discovered, need to be fixed with honesty, efficiency, and speed so as to prevent loss of life. In addition, no pilot of an aircraft, or driver of a motor car, or sea captain, or train driver, has a perfect operating record without blemish, without momentary lapses or error. We are human, after all. Yet, problems caused by deliberate shortcuts and unworthy acts of willfully cutting into safety margins, or ignoring and concealing potential danger areas for the sake of profits, fall into an entirely different category of behavior.

A definite pattern of *criminal wrongdoing* by the Boeing Company has emerged over the past two decades. The two air accidents described in the previous chapters, and two more air accidents involving the new 737 MAX, plus Boeing's attempts to murder one of its own Senior Instructor Pilots, provide prima facie evidence of a clear *pattern* of Boeing's extreme indifference, abhorrent misconduct, and its culpability in what must surely be termed 'crimes against humanity'.

Sadly, Boeing's criminal conduct has for years been allowed to continue with impunity by high United States Government officials who have, for reasons of their own, protected the Boeing Company and its officials from criminal accountability. Boeing, like many other large United States corporations, is just too large and too influential to prosecute or to bring down. The collusion in the top echelons of the US Government, in Boeing's criminality, includes theft of court records, corrupt quashing of court cases, and suppression and concealment of numerous criminal complaints against the Boeing Company. That lawlessness by the US Government includes suppression of a pending US Supreme Court case, namely: the "Consolidated Boeing Company Mass Murder Case". None of the criminal charges filed against the Boeing Company in the US Supreme Court, and detailed in the 2,400-page 'Dossier of Crimes', have to date been investigated or prosecuted. Not one. The 'Dossier of Crimes' meticulously documents that perilous state of affairs. (At the time of writing, that dossier remains suppressed and concealed in the US Supreme Court).

Thus, a potent combination of factors has made it possible for Boeing to quash vital safety and technical issues in favor of its commercial profits. The impunity provided by top US Government officials has led Boeing to develop a criminal corporate culture and an insatiable drive for profits, regardless of flight safety concerns.

For a number of years, as Senior Boeing Company Instructor Pilot (and later as a Boeing retiree), I have on numerous occasions sternly warned the Boeing Board of Directors and its Executive Council, and warned Boeing's co-conspirators in the US Government, of the likely consequences of Boeing's lawlessness in this safety-sensitive industry. My warnings were simply swept aside and went unheeded. This state of affairs did not bode well for flight safety and for the well-being of the international flying public. These factors combined to form a deadly cocktail which has manifested itself in a systematic pattern of crimes against humanity of mass murder and other inhumane acts in which 507 people have died and 189 have been gravely injured.

At the present time, there exists a dark stain upon the very heart of this otherwise vibrant and impressive aerospace company – a stain which has over time steadily been growing without rectification. The cancer of which I speak, are the acts of extreme indifference to human life, performed in favor of its commercial interests, which have led to the preventable deaths discussed in previous chapters. That cancer has not been exorcized, and as a result, it has spread to the vulnerable organs of the company. That potentially terminal cancer, symbolically speaking, has been allowed to grow and to engender a violent impact upon the international flying public, as demonstrated in two 'avoidable air accidents' on the Boeing 737 MAX aircraft. That is: the fatal crash of Lion Air 610 and the fatal crash of Ethiopian Airlines 302. A third incident in the same category was the in-flight blow-out of a door plug on Alaska Airlines Flight 1282. To continue my metaphor, without some strong medicine, that cancer will continue to spread within Boeing until either the corporate culture of extreme indifference to human life is eradicated for good, or until the 100-plus year-old Boeing Company succumbs to terminal cancer. Today, both eventualities are equally possible.

THE CRASH OF LION AIR 610

On Monday, October 29, 2018, at 6:20 am local time, Lion Air Flight 610, a new Boeing 737 MAX 8, took off from Jakarta, Indonesia, on a one-hour local flight to Pangkalpinang with 181 passengers, six cabin crew, and two pilots on board. Some thirteen minutes after take-off, the pilots lost control and the aircraft plunged headlong into the Java Sea, killing all 189 people on board.

The new Boeing 737 MAX type of aircraft had been in international service for just 17 months, since May 22, 2017. The specific Lion Air aircraft, registration PK-LQP, was put into service on August 13, 2018, and had only operated for two months until the crash. At the time of the accident, it had about 800 flying hours in service. The crash of Lion Air 610 constituted the first accident of the new B737 MAX type.

After take-off from Jakarta, the aircraft had circled around onto its north-easterly course, which it more or less held until the accident. A few minutes after take-off, the flight deck crew had requested a turn back to the airport because of control problems. That return to base did not occur in actuality, and the flight path of the aircraft showed abnormal variations in airspeed and in altitude while the pilots fought for control of their aircraft.

By 06:33 am on October 29, 2018, thirteen minutes into the flight, all communications with the control tower had ceased. The aircraft had entered a steep dive from which the pilots did not recover. Flight 610 crashed into the Java Sea northeast of Jakarta, some 18 nautical miles offshore. Observers on an oil platform a few miles from the crash site observed the aircraft hit the water at high speed in a steep dive angle. The debris came to rest on the ocean floor in water approximately 115 feet deep. After the accident, on November 1, 2018, the so-called 'black box' flight recorder was located and recovered from the seabed.

From analysis of the recorded flight data, the Indonesian National Transportation Safety Committee found that the aircraft experienced erroneous inputs from one of its angle-of-attack sensors. Two angle-of-attack vanes on the side of the aircraft's nose measure the in-flight angle between the aircraft's longitudinal (fuselage) axis and the relative airflow and then feed that information to the air data computers. Maintenance records showed that previous flights had been having problems with instrument readings and the angle of attack sensor as well.

It was conditionally concluded that the new enhancement to the B737 flight control system (the Maneuvering Characteristics Augmentation System, or MCAS) reacted to the faulty angle-of-attack sensor input with commands that automatically pushed the nose of the aircraft down. With 'MCAS' activated the system does not allow further pullback of the control yoke by the pilots to counter that system's automatic action. That MCAS action is to hold the nose down. Thus, the pilots of Lion Air 610 did not and could not recover from that situation via the normal method of control through the control yoke.

Through a conscious and deliberate decision by Boeing, pilots on the B737 MAX 8 worldwide had intentionally not been informed of the addition of the Maneuvering Characteristics Augmentation System to the flight control system of the new B737 MAX. Boeing had willfully not informed pilots of potential failure modes of that undisclosed system. Concealment of that technical and malfunction information prevented emergency procedures from being formulated, promulgated, and trained for by the Lion Air 610 pilots.

Boeing's deliberate withholding from airline pilots flying the B737 MAX 8 of pertinent technical, operating, and emergency procedures created a grave risk of death to passengers and crew, in general. That grave risk acutely demonstrated an existing corporate culture within the top echelons of Boeing – a culture of extreme indifference to human life - and constitutes criminal misconduct on the part of the Boeing Company. The risk specifically manifested itself in the situation faced by Lion Air flight 610 pilots and is in large part to blame for the concomitant death of 189 people. That conduct, which created a grave risk of death and which subsequently caused death, violates the Revised Code of Washington State (where Boeing Commercial Aircraft is headquartered) and constitutes *murder in the first degree.*

New Flight Control System of the 737 MAX

The Maneuvering Characteristics Augmentation System (MCAS) on the B737 MAX 8 was a new addition to the B737 flight control system and was designed to provide stall protection. This system does not exist on earlier Boeing 737 models. With more efficient though bigger and heavier engines on the Boeing 737

MAX, as compared to older Boeing 737 aircraft, the engine position on the wing was changed to a position more forward and higher relative to that on earlier models of 737. That change in placement of the engines in turn changed the center of gravity and made the new MAX 8 model less stable in certain flight regimes of high angle of attack. The maneuvering augmentation system was intended to compensate automatically for those changes in stability and control of the aircraft.

The augmentation system was designed to operate during conditions of high angles of attack between the airflow and the wings (that is, in 'high G' situations), and in steep turns, as well as in slow flight approaching aerodynamic stall angles. The high-angle-of-attack conditions are measured and signaled to MCAS through the angle of attack sensors.

In the circumstances where the Maneuvering Characteristics Augmentation System would activate, at angles of attack of 10 to 12 degrees, the system would automatically provide input to the flight control system to pitch the nose of the aircraft down. In a situation where the angle of attack remained too high, the new MCAS would repeat its pitch-down commands every 10 seconds.

The Boeing Company *deliberately* did not include any mention or technical description of the system in its flight crew technical or operations manuals for pilots. The reason was to keep the time and cost low that was spent on 'conversion training' for the new model. This decision, in turn, was driven by the need to stay on par in the competition with the Airbus Neo. It was not a decision based on safety considerations but on the sale of aircraft and profits. Thus, B737 MAX 8 pilots were unaware of the existence of the Maneuvering Characteristics Augmentation System until the accident of Lion Air 610. More importantly, B737 MAX pilots were not trained on any failure modes of the new system, of whose existence they were uninformed. No emergency or non-normal checklist was provided by Boeing for this type of failure. These factors played a major role in the Lion Air 610 accident.

Technical Description of the Malfunction

The Maneuvering Characteristics Augmentation System (MCAS), which was designed to enhance flight safety, in this case and in reality, decreased safety, and in the final analysis, caused the horrific accident. The initiating malfunction was a faulty angle of attack sensor on the captain's side (the left side of the aircraft). Data retrieved from the aircraft's 'black box' showed that even in the taxi-out before take-off, the left angle of attack vane was substantially offset from the right vane, showing a higher angle. The right vane remained constant while the left vane continued to migrate towards higher and higher angle of attack readings.

Because of the erroneous *high* angle of attack that was signaled by the left vane, on lift-off the left stick shaker activated, giving a false warning to the pilots of a stall, and stayed on for most of the rest of the flight. Wrongly sensing that the aircraft was dangerously close to the aerodynamic stall angle, the flight control computer automatically engaged MCAS. When the flaps were retracted after take-off, the augmentation system did what it was designed to do, and that was to automatically trim the nose of the aircraft down to reduce the angle of attack, using the stabilizer trim to accomplish that task. Since the signal was false in any event, the nose-down pitch of the aircraft did not change the wrongfully sensed angle of attack (which it would have if the input was true and correct).

The aircraft briefly descended and then resumed its climb. The pilot stopped the MCAS movement of the stabilizer by electrically trimming the stabilizer nose up, only to have the MCAS start up again five seconds later in an attempt to trim forward and push the nose of the aircraft down again, ostensibly reducing the angle of attack. There followed 26 alternating repetitions of that sequence:

the pilot trimming the nose of the aircraft up (with the electric trim), and MCAS following five seconds later by trimming the nose down again. In each excursion, the pilot managed to hold the stabilizer roughly in trim, even though the stick shaker was going off continuously, erroneously warning of an impending stall.

At a certain stage in the short flight, the captain transferred control to the first officer. At the time of that transfer, the MCAS was able to trim nose down in two successive cycles without opposition from the first officer, ensuring a steep nose down attitude of the aircraft. The captain resumed control of the aircraft and pulled back hard on the control yoke. MCAS was able to increase the nose down trim even further before the captain was able to stop the trim movement, but the stabilizer trim had gotten away from the pilots, beyond anything that they could do to regain control of the aircraft. The captain's hard pull-back on the yoke to pull the nose up and out of the dive to reclaim control proved futile. The hard pull-back did not stop the nose down trim from MCAS – as it would have done in a 'trim runaway' emergency.

The MCAS was designed not to *allow the pilots* any pull-back response to counter its own actions of keeping the nose down until the high angle of attack was resolved. Again, in this case, the angle of attack signal was never resolved because it was a faulty signal in the first instance. So, the pilots could not stop the downward pull of the nose with their own control yoke inputs in opposition to the operation of the Maneuvering Characteristics Augmentation System. The Lion Air pilots had lost control of their aircraft - MCAS had control, and tragically, it flew them into the sea at a high speed of more than 450 knots, with engines in high thrust accelerating them downward in a steep dive.

There was one other action the pilots could have taken to override the augmentation system, and that would have been to cut out the electrics to the stabilizer trim system, which was being used by MCAS to pitch the nose down. But, the action of "Stab Trim switches to cutout" is the emergency action necessary in *another type* of malfunction, namely "stabilizer trim runaway".

In the Lion Air 610 emergency, they *did not* have a "stabilizer trim runaway," and two happenings or goings-on pointed to that: (a) Their first and all-consuming indication of a malfunction was the stick-shaker and the noise and distraction which its activation precipitated. That warning pointed away from the trim system and rather indicated a check was needed on aircraft nose attitude, climb angle, airspeed, power settings, instrument cross reference between left and right side, and the like. (b) The second indication to the crew that pointed away from a "trim runaway" situation was the fact that when they pulled back on the control column, the electric trim system *was not* cut out, as it normally would have been in a trim-runaway situation. The latter feature was disabled by their activated MCAS.

Thus, in the Lion Air 610 emergency: (a) the pilots were not informed of the existence of the MCAS; (b) they were not informed of what flight controls that MCAS uses to pitch the nose of the aircraft down; (c) they were not informed that pulling back the control column under MCAS activation would in fact *not stop* the automatic nose-down trim; (d) they were not trained to recognize or to react to a malfunction in the MCAS; (e) they did not have any emergency procedures for the failure they were experiencing; (f) the activated stick shaker pointed to a different type of failure than the one they had; it made a noise, sowed confusion, and made it very difficult to recognize or analyze what the real failure was without having been informed of the new system and its malfunction modes.

Contributory Causes to the Crash of Lion Air 610

There were several strong contributing causes that were made known in the findings by the Indonesian National Transportation

Safety Committee. As is usual in air accidents, as mentioned before, more often than not, it takes a chain of contributing causes to ultimately cause a crash. Usually, breaking any one link in the chain of events could foreseeably prevent the accident from happening - and the crash of Lion Air 610 was no exception. The strong contributing causes identified early in the investigations were:

o *A Malfunctioning Angle of Attack Sensor:* The initiating incident in the crash of Lion Air 610 was the malfunctioning angle of attack sensor.

o *A Single Point Failure:* This 'single point' failure of a single angle of attack sensor could have been avoided if the second sensor (which was readily available) was designed and used by Boeing designers as backup sensor for the system, or as comparative sensor, which it was not on this aircraft. Thus, the faulty sensor engaged the Maneuvering Characteristics Augmentation System (MCAS), which then pushed the nose down, as it was designed to do, and did not allow the pilots to override it with the control yoke.

o *Lack of Technical Information and Failure to Train:* The pilots of Lion Air 610 were *not informed* of the existence of the MCAS or any failure modes in that system. They were not trained to recognize the malfunction mode and were not trained on emergency procedures in that system. No such procedures existed. The pilots of Lion Air 610, in turn, failed to disengage the malfunctioning augmentation system through the electric trim switches. They were unable to recognize the malfunction mode and therefore failed to use the trim cutout switches to disengage the stabilizer trim system. The obvious reason for their inability was that the pilots were not informed of the existence of MCAS and were not trained on the failure modes of that system. Therefore, the pilots do not bear the blame.

BOEING'S ROLE IN THE LION AIR 610 CRASH

Boeing's prior conduct contributed in five major ways to the causes of the accident, involving all three important points mentioned above, and two more. The Boeing Company's negative contributions are so compelling that the company bears *criminal culpability* in the Lion Air crash for the following reasons:

Criminally Negligent Decisions on MCAS

During the design and build phase of the 737 MAX, Boeing understood full well that MCAS was, quote, "a safety-critical system". The FAA Acting Administrator at the time confirmed that assessment. Boeing's own design requirements and coordination sheets of March 1, 2016, and June 11, 2018, said: "MCAS should not have any objectionable interaction with the piloting of the airplane", and "MCAS shall not interfere with dive recovery". Yet, the Boeing Company willfully ignored its own design requirements and coordination sheets. The MCAS indeed violated both these criteria. Boeing also initially included an MCAS enunciator in the cockpit, which would help the pilots in these situations, but later willfully discarded the plans in favor of commercial profits. Thus, under circumstances manifesting an extreme indifference to human life, Boeing engaged in conduct that created a grave risk of death to persons and thereby caused the death of 189 persons on Lion Air 610. Five short months later, Boeing caused the death of another 157 persons on Ethiopian Air 302.

Criminally Negligent Decisions on AOA Sensors for MCAS

Boeing's design of the MCAS, where a single-point failure could cause loss of control of an aircraft, exhibited a fatal flaw. Boeing knew that the 'single point' failure of a single angle of attack (AOA) sensor feeding the MCAS was an obvious weak link in the design of the MCAS. During 2015, a Boeing engineer warned the company that MCAS was not sufficiently redundant while using only one angle of attack sensor of the two available. Expressly, in Boeing's own internal "Airplane Level Safety Assessment", paper AVN-16, Boeing declared: 'loss of one AOA indicator followed by an erroneous AOA (on the other side) is deemed potentially catastrophic before crew recognition of the issue'. These assessments Boeing willfully ignored in favor of *cost considerations*.

Furthermore, Boeing knew that the 'AOA Disagree' light in the cockpit did not work unless airlines bought an upgraded package. Boeing deliberately failed to inform crews and the FAA of this issue. It is self-evident that (a) The decision made by Boeing to use a single angle of attack indicator for the augmentation system, instead of the two available, rendered Boeing criminally negligent and culpable - Boeing knew of the dangers; (b) Boeing knowingly and willfully cut corners on safety in favor of commercial profits, rendering the company criminally negligent and culpable.

Once again, under circumstances manifesting an extreme indifference to human life, Boeing engaged in conduct that created a grave risk of death to persons and thereby caused the death of 346 persons on Lion Air 610 and Ethiopian Air 302.

Deliberate Concealment of Pertinent Technical Information

In the first version of the flight manual, pilots were to be informed of MCAS. That logical decision was later reversed for Boeing's expediency, to the detriment of safety. On March 30, 2016, Boeing requested the FAA for permission to remove all reference to MCAS from the manuals since it was 'way outside of the normal operating envelope'. Boeing deliberately left a description of the Maneuvering Characteristics Augmentation System out of the technical, training, operations manuals, and non-normal checklists for pilots, so as to cut down the time and cost of 'differences training' between the older models and the new model of Boeing 737 aircraft. Deliberate concealment of technical information prevented emergency procedures from being formulated and trained for. Boeing's deliberate failure to inform pilots of the important new system was done for reasons of commercial profit – to be competitive in the marketplace with Airbus A320 Neo, so as to sell more aircraft. And that withholding of pertinent safety information proved fatal. Once more: under circumstances manifesting an extreme indifference to human life, Boeing engaged in conduct which created a grave risk of death to persons, and thereby caused the death of 346 persons on Lion Air 610 and Ethiopian Air 302. Boeing bears criminal culpability under Washington State law for that concealment.

Criminally Negligent Decisions on Pilot Training

Boeing knew that flight crew simulator training would enhance crew recognition and action on potential MCAS/Angle of Attack failures. However, not only did Boeing not inform pilots of the system, but Boeing deliberately did not train flight crews on how to recognize and how to deal with a failure mode in the MCAS. Boeing understood how important crew training was to prevent crashes, but actively worked against the training of crews. Boeing pushed the FAA and regulators around the world not to *require* simulator training. According to Boeing 737 Chief Technical Pilot Forkner, he "jedi mind-tricked" the FAA and foreign regulators (that is, subtly influenced the thoughts and actions of others) into accepting no simulator training for 737 MAX pilots.

That decision was motivated by commercial considerations concerning profit. Training of pilots on a new type or model, and training time and costs, feature heavily in the sales promotion of a new aircraft. Boeing deliberately (and criminally), under circumstances of extreme indifference to human life, avoided simulator training as a feature of its sale of the new B737 MAX aircraft. Boeing marketed the MAX 8 in part by telling customers that pilots would not need additional simulator training beyond that required for older models of B737.

That lack of knowledge and training on the augmentation system proved to be a major cause of loss of control of the aircraft and proved to be fatal to 346 people on Lion Air 610 and Ethiopian Airlines Flight 302. Boeing pleaded guilty to one count of defrauding the Federal Aviation Administration Aircraft Evaluation Group (and later withdrew its plea – as if that withdrawal would expunge the guilt). However, under Washington State law, RCW 9A.08.030(1)(b), Boeing bears criminal culpability for the deaths caused.

A Critically Flawed Engineering Policy

Boeing had an inverted and depraved engineering policy, where engineers reported safety concerns *to business leaders*, rather than to the chief engineer. Those safety concerns slowed down the development process of the new airplane, and the business leaders were strongly motivated to meet production schedules, to the detriment of fixing flight safety concerns.

A Criminal Corporate Culture

Boeing exhibited a strong history of criminality and a systemic pattern of extreme indifference to human life, as meticulously documented in the 'Dossier of Crimes' and discussed in previous chapters. That criminality and corporate culture were demonstrated in the air accidents of Lion Air 610 (and later Ethiopian Air 302), Asiana 214, and Air India IX-812. In each of the four accidents, the company put its own commercial decisions before flight safety considerations. In each case, it suppressed flight safety warnings and withheld pertinent technical information in favor of its own profits. That criminality and corporate culture are further demonstrated in Boeing's kidnapping and murder attempts upon me as a Senior Boeing Company Instructor Pilot and as a prime witness to Boeing's criminal conduct. That callous corporate culture places Boeing's commercial decisions regarding profit before flight safety considerations. After the accident of Lion Air 610, Boeing fought hard to avoid grounding the 737 MAX and to keep the fleet flying with an inadequate emergency procedure as an interim fix of the MCAS fault, while software fixes were being evaluated. Those hasty new emergency procedures proved inadequate for the task and led directly to the second fatal accident on a 737 MAX aircraft.

THE CRASH OF ETHIOPIAN AIRLINES 302

After the crash of Lion Air 610, knowledge of the new MCAS in the flight controls of the Boeing 737 MAX was made available to airlines and to 737 MAX pilots. The FAA and Boeing issued training advisories and warnings to all Boeing 737 MAX operators, and issued procedures on how to cope with and how to avoid the death dive that terminated Lion Air Flight 610. Those procedures and crew training were to constitute the interim fix while Boeing sought to rectify the MCAS control problem with software fixes. Boeing *did not* seek to ground the new 737 MAX until those problems were fully resolved. Instead, the company vehemently opposed such drastic action because that action would have affected the sale of aircraft and its bottom line - its profits. Boeing and its partner in crime, the FAA, pronounced the 737 MAX safe for flight. But was it indeed? As fate would have it, those hasty interim fixes proved totally inadequate and insufficient to solve the control problems on the new Boeing 737 MAX. Grave peril persisted from the same underlying causes. Thus, it took another accident from the same causes, and the death of another 157 people, for the international community to lead the way to the grounding of the Boeing 737 MAX.

Some five months after the tragic crash of Lion Air 610, on March 10, 2019, Ethiopian Airlines Flight 302 took off in a Boeing 737 MAX on an international flight between the Ethiopian capital,

Addis Ababa, and Nairobi, Kenya. The four-month-old aircraft was signed off as airworthy. The flight departed at 8:38 am local time with 149 passengers and eight crew members on board and crashed six minutes later, resulting in the destruction of the aircraft and the resultant death of all passengers and crew.

Upon investigation, it was found that the flight profile and events closely mirrored those of Lion Air 610. The captain, sitting in the left seat, was the flying pilot at the controls. Shortly after takeoff, the left angle-of-attack sensor became unserviceable and gave erroneous readings. Those erroneous high-angle readings in turn activated the stick-shaker, warning of an impending aerodynamic stall, and remained activated until near the end of the short flight. Also, airspeed and altitude readings differed between the left side of the cockpit readouts and those on the right side. The difference in readings lasted until near the end of the flight.

Within the first minute of flight, there were small amplitude roll and yaw oscillations, and slight heading changes, both with autopilot on and subsequently also with autopilot disengaged. The captain advised the first officer to report control problems and to request the air traffic controller for a clearance for them to maintain runway heading. The erroneous high-angle-of-attack indications on the left side also engaged the MCAS, which trimmed the nose of the aircraft down and arrested the climb and caused a slight descent. This precipitated a Ground Proximity Warning alert: "Don't sink". The captain opposed the nose-down movement by aft control column inputs and re-established a positive climb.

The MCAS again gave a second input of nose down trim, and this time, both pilots trimmed nose up to counteract the trim movement. As per their new emergency procedures, they switched off the stabilizer trim cut-out switches, which prevented a third nose-down trim input from the MCAS for the time being. They requested from air traffic control and were granted clearance to maintain an altitude of 14,000 feet, again reporting flight control problems.

For the next two and a half minutes, the stabilizer gradually moved in the nose-down direction, and both pilots exerted force on the control column simultaneously in order to oppose that nose-down movement. The airspeed increased and triggered the overspeed warning. The First Officer attempted to trim the stabilizer manually (as per their new emergency procedures) but was physically unable to move the trim wheel manually because of the high forces (which could have required as much as 50 pounds force to turn the manual trim wheel), due to their high speed. The crew requested a return to base, which was approved by air traffic control but was not attempted, just as in the case of Lion Air 610.

There must have been some pandemonium in the cockpit during the six minutes of flight after take-off. The pilots experienced: continuous noise and vibration from the left side stick-shaker; a Master Caution Anti-Ice Warning; un-commanded roll and pitch oscillations; airspeed and altitude disagreements between left and right side of the cockpit; noise from the auto-pilot disengaging; four separate aural "don't sink" Ground Proximity Warnings; the loud, continuous, and decidedly irritating noise from the over-speed clacker; communications between the two pilots and between the first officer and air traffic control; and all the while they were strenuously fighting heavy forces on the control yoke.

The captain requested the first officer to pitch up with him and remarked that the "pitch was not enough", indicating that they were starting to lose control of the plane. They must have put the trim-cut-out switches back on in a last-ditch effort to get more nose-up trim from the system to alleviate control yoke forces, since two short inputs of manually induced electric trim were recorded. But that switching back to 'on' of the trim cutout switches simultaneously gave the MCAS another chance, five seconds later, to respond with its erroneous and deadly nose down commands.

Again, both pilots responded to that trim input by simultaneously applying aft control column force, but the nose-down pitch continued, and the pilots soon lost control. In what must surely have been a terrifying sight for the pilots, and a terrifying feeling for the passengers and cabin crew, the aircraft reached 40 40-degree nose-down attitude and a speed of 500 knots, from which there was no recovery. The aircraft crashed into the ground some 28 nautical miles southeast of Addis Ababa near the village of Ejere with the sad loss of all 157 on board.

BOEING CRIMINAL CULPABILITY IN THE 737 MAX CRASHES

In addition to the reasons already mentioned above, the Boeing Company is criminally culpable in both the Ethiopian Airlines 302 catastrophe and the Lion Air 610 tragedies for several more reasons. The second accident confirms the following:

The 737 MAX Was Not Safe for Flight

Boeing built and sold the new model Boeing 737 MAX with inherent longitudinal (pitch) instability in certain flight regimes, which rendered the aircraft unsafe for flight. In an effort to counter that divergent stability in pitch, Boeing developed the 'Maneuvering Characteristics Augmentation System' or MCAS, and then, working with the FAA (and in certain arenas, in lieu of the FAA), 'wrongfully' certified the 737 MAX safe for flight. That conduct created a grave risk of death to persons and indeed led to the death of 346 people. Certification of the new aircraft was 'wrongful' because of the design flaw in the 'single point' failure of a single angle-of-attack sensor feeding the MCAS, and certification was wrongful for withholding pertinent technical information and emergency procedures from the pilots. The proof of 'wrongful *certification'* lies exposed in the causes of the two fatal accidents of the 737 MAX.

The MCAS Was Not Safe for Flight

It took 26 cycles of 'MCAS nose down trim and pilot nose up trim' to bring down Lion Air 610. Despite the new emergency procedures after the first accident, it took only four cycles of 'MCAS nose down trim and pilot nose up trim' to bring down Ethiopian Airlines 302. That is how critical the 'Maneuvering Characteristics Augmentation System' was to flight safety, and how perilous it turned out to be. Yet, before the first accident, Boeing and the FAA wrongfully certified the MAX *safe for flight* with the flawed MCAS as a fix for divergent pitch instability. That conduct created a grave risk of death to persons and indeed led to the death of 346 people in the two 737 MAX crashes.

The New Emergency Procedure Was Inadequate for Safe Flight

After the Lion Air accident, Boeing and the FAA approved a new (but hopelessly inadequate) emergency procedure and *'wrongfully'* re-approved the 737 MAX as safe for flight. Only pilot training and the inadequate new emergency procedure stood between safe flight and the next disaster, while a software fix was in the works for the five interim months between 737 MAX accidents. The new emergency procedure was 'wrongfully' approved because, as demonstrated by Flight ET 302, in certain high-speed regimes, it did not allow the pilots to use the manual trim system; the physical forces on the trim wheel were just too high.

The Ethiopian 302 crew ran out of aircraft pitch control, even after following the new procedure. It was only as a last-ditch maneuver towards the end of their flight that they re-engaged the electric trim when they could not overcome the control forces manually. Crew training on the MCAS, together with an emergency procedure for loss of reliable angle-of-attack sensors (provided after the Lion Air accident), proved inadequate to overcome the control column forces associated with repeated MCAS activation. Flight ET 302 pilots lost control after only four cycles of MCAS trimming. Yet, Boeing and the FAA approved that procedure as safe for flight. That conduct created a grave risk of death to persons and indeed led to the death of another 157 people.

Software Fixes Were Inadequate for Safe Flight

Boeing and the FAA failed to ensure that adequate software fixes were in place before resuming flight operations on the 737 MAX after the first 737 MAX accident. Those software fixes to MCAS were still in the works at the time of the Ethiopian Airlines crash, and yet Boeing (and the FAA) resisted and made no effort to ground the fleet while those fixes were made and were proven safe. If the proposed software fixes were installed, and if the system was using both angle-of-attack sensors in the Ethiopian Airlines case, the accident and the death of 157 people would in all likelihood have been prevented.

With Extreme Indifference

The combination of Boeing's perilous conduct regarding the Boeing 737 MAX manifested a culture of extreme indifference to human life in the following ways:

(i) certifying the 737 MAX for flight with known aerodynamic instabilities, countered only by a fatally flawed MCAS; (ii) designing an important control system (MCAS) without redundancy in a failure situation; (iii) before the first accident, deliberately failing to inform the pilots of the new flight control system (MCAS); (iv) before the first accident, deliberately failing to train pilots for failure modes of that system; (v) after the first accident, approving the flawed MCAS for flight with an inadequate interim fix; (vi) after the first accident, approving an emergency procedure for flight that was inadequate for the task.

Boeing's *indifference to human life*, relating to the 737 MAX and safety, was driven by its commercial desire to compete on par with Airbus in the marketplace. Further pertinent examples of Boeing's extreme indifference to human life include: (vii) repeatedly ignoring and suppressing safety warnings over several years; (viii) rushing the certification process of the 737 MAX; (ix) taking corrupt control from the FAA of elements of that certification process, corruptly overseeing its own compliance and non-compliance with federal standards (x) denial of aircraft problems on the 737 MAX and initially evading responsibility by blaming the pilots for the accidents, and (xi) attempting to delay the FAA mandated grounding of the 737 MAX fleet through a personal call by Boeing CEO Muilenburg to President Trump.

However, the most convincing, explicit, and reprehensible example of Boeing's extreme indifference to human life, remains: (xii) the series of attempts to inveigle a trusted Senior Instructor Pilot for the company, away from his normal place of work, there to kidnap and kill him, in an effort to silence his testimony in the courts on wrongdoing perpetrated by Boeing in combination with a senior government official, President George W. Bush. And then, covering up the foiled attempt. That foul deed alone is sufficient to come to the indisputable conclusion on Boeing's culture of extreme indifference to human life.

PATTERN OF CRIMINAL CONDUCT CREATED A GRAVE RISK OF DEATH

Consider for a moment the common thread that runs through all four of the air accidents described in the aforementioned chapters and pages, namely the crashes of Air India IX-812, Asiana Flight 214, Lion Air Flight 610, and Ethiopian Airlines 302. In these accidents, the Boeing Company's conduct formed a definite pattern of behavior which created peril to the international flying public and which, in time, played a crucial role in the accidents.

That pattern of nefarious conduct caused the death of many. Seen in combination with the incidents of attempted kidnap and murder of a prime witness, court litigant, and employee whistleblower, that pattern of conduct is considered criminal in terms of Washington State law. *In summary,* some of Boeing's pertinent actions are presented in juxtaposition, so as to clearly illustrate that pattern of criminality:

Flight Safety Warnings Suppressed

On May 25, 2005, Boeing was warned in a *'Flight Safety Report'* on Air India Express (written by me in my capacity as Senior Instructor Pilot) of the dangers of failing to abide by the aviation rules and regulations. Boeing violently suppressed and ignored those warnings and pertinent safety reports by violent retaliation against their own trusted instructor pilot (by attempts to kidnap and murder him and by retaliation against his employment). The direct result of that suppression of imperative flight safety information and remedial action was the crash of Air India Express Flight IX-812 and the death or injury of 166 people, with Boeing's criminal culpability therein.

On May 14, 2013, Boeing was sternly warned by me that, quote: *"Unless the existing lawlessness within the Boeing Company is addressed and known criminals in senior positions at Boeing are brought to justice, the catastrophic example of Flight IX-812 is most likely to be repeated with further loss of innocent lives in preventable aircraft accidents caused by ongoing criminality within the Boeing Company"*. Once more, Boeing ignored the prophetic warnings with callous indifference to human life, in favor of its commercial profits and public image. In turn, that conduct led to the fatal accident of Asiana Flight 214 in San Francisco on July 6, 2013 – with Boeing's criminal culpability therein.

On September 6, 2016, Boeing was again cautioned by me: *"not to take lightly my continual warnings to the Boeing Company; or your moral duties to society, to the Boeing Company, and to yourself, to address and correct what has been done amiss";* and furthermore that *"you have placed the future of your entire company at stake by your disreputable conduct and ongoing reluctance to take lawful corrective actions".* But still Boeing engaged in conduct which created a grave risk of death to persons, and thereby contributed in large measure to the death of 189 people in the crash of Lion Air 610, with Boeing's criminal culpability therein.

On November 19, 2018, I again entreated Boeing: *"to change the Boeing Company's criminal corporate culture, from the top down. That culture has played such a major destructive role in not only the recent crash of Lion Air 610, but also that of Air India IX-812, and Asiana 214; and in the attempted murder of me as prime witness to Boeing's criminality".* Boeing was forewarned to "heed the flight safety warning that the catastrophic examples of Air India IX-812, Asiana 214, and Lion Air 610, is almost certainly to be repeated with further loss of innocent lives in preventable aircraft accidents caused by the vile and ongoing criminality within the Boeing Company, as demonstrated by its extreme indifference to human life in the demise of these flights".

The criminality referred to in the warning was comprehensively addressed in the Dossier of Crimes, Volume III, Chapter 42, and Boeing officials, the Boeing Board of Directors, and the Executive Council were fully informed of it. Once again, Boeing failed to respond to the warning of criminality within the Boeing Company, and people paid with their lives in the crash of Ethiopian Airlines 302, with the loss of all 157 on board – with Boeing's criminal culpability therein.

On October 17, 2022, Boeing was again warned by me, acting as Prosecutor Qui Tam, to terminate its obstruction of justice in the criminal prosecution of the Boeing Company fraud and mass murder case; and to allow justice to be done. Boeing was warned that *"many more innocent people will die needlessly in inevitable air accidents on Boeing aircraft/spacecraft..."*, unless the ongoing criminality within the Boeing Company (and its US Government minders) is addressed and terminated. Little more than a year later, on January 5, 2024, a door plug blew off an Alaska Airlines Boeing 737 Max 9 in flight, causing a rapid decompression and some minor injuries. However, at higher altitudes, the incident could have been catastrophic with potential loss of life. The cause was attributable to a Boeing manufacturing error, where four bolts that were intended to secure the door were later found to be missing.

Nefarious Conduct by Boeing in the Crash of Air India Flight IX-812

In the accident of Air India Express Flight 812 on May 22, 2010, Boeing: (i) deliberately ignored and violently suppressed a pertinent flight safety report by one of its Senior Instructor Pilots; (ii) deliberately failed to respond to the safety warnings and to remedy known flight safety dangers reflected in that report; (iii) criminally suppressed reported dangers by retaliating against the author through terminating his employment and by attempts to kidnap and murder him.

Nefarious Conduct by Boeing in the Crash of Asiana Flight 214

In the accident of Asiana Flight 214 on July 6, 2013, Boeing conduct: (i) deliberately disregarded and suppressed a warning by an FAA test pilot, of autothrottle anomalies in its Boeing 777 aircraft; (ii) deliberately disregarded and suppressed a warning by the European Aviation Safety Agency, of autothrottle anomalies in its Boeing 777; (iii) deliberately disregarded and suppressed a warning of corporate crimes affecting flight safety, issued by a Senior Boeing Instructor Pilot; (iv) deliberately failed to warn B777

239

pilots of the known autothrottle anomalies; (v) deliberately failed to train Asiana (and other) B777 pilots on the known autothrottle anomalies; (vi) deliberately suppressed and ignored a series of relevant flight safety warnings.

Nefarious Conduct by Boeing in the Crash of Lion Air Flight 610

In the accident of Lion Air 610 on October 29, 2018, Boeing's conduct created grave risk of death: (i) by deliberately failing to inform pilots of an important new control system (MCAS) in the Boeing 737 MAX 8 aircraft, in an effort to avoid training time as a commercial selling feature; (ii) by deliberately failing to train pilots on that undisclosed new control system (MCAS), for the same reasons; (iii) by deliberately failing to provide emergency procedures on potential failures of the undisclosed new control system, for the same reason of avoiding training time for pilots; (iv) by deliberately failing to design redundancy and safety into the new control system, for penny-pinching economic reasons; and (v) by deliberately suppressing and ignoring a series of relevant flight safety warnings.

Nefarious Conduct by Boeing in the Crash of Ethiopian Airlines 302

In the accident of Ethiopian Airlines 302 on March 10, 2019, Boeing's conduct created grave risk of death: (i) by self-certifying the *aircraft,* coaxing, and rushing the certification of the *737 MAX* with extreme indifference, when it was not safe for flight; (ii) by self-certifying, coaxing, and rushing the certification of the *MCAS* on the 737 MAX with extreme indifference, when it was not safe for flight; (iii) by self-certifying, coaxing, and rushing the approval of the new emergency procedure on MCAS with extreme indifference, while that procedure was inadequate to ensure safe flight; (iv) by deliberately failing, with extreme indifference, to ensure that software fixes were in place *before* resumption of flight operations on the 737 MAX; and (v) by deliberately suppressing and ignoring a series of relevant flight safety warnings.

Nefarious Conduct by Boeing in the Alaska Air Door-plug Incident

In the mid-air emergency of Alaska Airlines on January 5, 2024, when a door plug blew out, Boeing's conduct created grave risk of injury and death: (i) by Boeing's failure to abide by its 'non-prosecution agreement with the Department of Justice, which prompted a criminal investigation by the DOJ; (ii) by breaching that non-prosecution agreement through 'failing to sufficiently design, implement, and enforce a compliance and ethics program to prevent and detect violations of the US fraud laws throughout its operations'; (iii) by Boeing 'failing to sufficiently integrate its ethics and compliance program with its safety and quality programs', according to the Department of Justice; (iv) by Boeing's failure to provide adequate training, guidance, and oversight (according to the National Transportation Safety Board Report of June 24, 2025); (v) by Boeing willfully failing to address unauthorized production that was identified in numerous Boeing internal audits, and in other forums, for at least ten years.

BOEING'S CONDUCT CAUSED DEATH

By the company's behavior described above, which created grave risk, Boeing indeed caused death and injury: (i) in the preventable accident of Air India Express IX-812, some 158 people were killed and another eight gravely injured; (ii) in the preventable accident of Asiana 214, another three people were killed and 181 gravely injured; (iii) in the preventable accident of Lion Air 610, another 189 people were killed; and (iv) in the preventable accident of Ethiopian Airlines 302, another 157 people were killed. (v) because of the attempts upon the life of a Boeing whistleblower, instructor pilot, and court litigant, and other related crimes perpetrated by Boeing, his crucial flight safety warnings were muted and suppressed, leading to a total of 507 deaths and 189 injured people; that is 696 people in total - and counting.

INDIFFERENCE TO HUMAN LIFE

The ongoing pattern of criminality within this large aircraft manufacturer and the impunity afforded to Boeing by the US Federal Government, Courts, and Washington State Government has engendered a strong and recognizable corporate culture within Boeing. In each case, the evidence shows that there is an active, constructive decision, deliberately made by Boeing management, to limit flight safety in favor of its profitability. There is also a repetitive pattern of deliberately withholding vital safety information in favor of profitability. Without fear of contradiction, it can be stated that: a company (Boeing) that engages in such criminal actions in a repeated and systematic pattern regardless of the consequences described above; and a company (Boeing) that made several attempts to kill one of its own trusted employees at managerial level - in favor of its $11 billion aircraft deal with India and in favor of its profits from a USAF tanker aircraft program - such a company exhibits an identifiable corporate culture of *extreme indifference to human life.*

MASS MURDER IN THE FIRST DEGREE

I have taken great pains to show in detail that the four crashes - that of Air IX-82, Asiana 214, Lion Air 610, and Ethiopian Airlines 302 - were not *random, unforeseen air accidents* caused by inescapable human error or other factors beyond human control. In fact, they were not 'accidents' per se. They *were not* unfortunate, unexpected, and unintentional incidents; they *did not* happen by chance or without apparent cause. In each case, it was known beforehand that the main contributory causes had a strong propensity to lead to accidents. Those potentials were discussed, were warned about, and were disregarded by Boeing in favor of its commercial profits. Again, to restate the benchmark, the Revised Code of Washington State, in statute RCW9A.32.030, states in relevant parts:

> *"(1) A person is guilty of murder in the first degree when: ... (b) Under circumstances manifesting an extreme indifference to human life, he or she engages in conduct which creates a grave risk of death to any person, and thereby causes the death of a person; ..."*

The questions should thus be asked: Did Boeing manifest an extreme indifference to human life in its decisions? Did Boeing engage in conduct that created a grave risk of death to persons? "Did Boeing thereby cause the death of persons?

The answers are an emphatic *'yes'* to all three questions. The abovementioned factors all combine to demonstrate ongoing and callous disregard by the Boeing Company and its top officials of the well-being and safety of individuals and of the international flying public, in favor of Boeing's commercial interests and profits. Boeing and its senior officials *did manifest* an extreme indifference to human life, and *did engage* in a systematic pattern of criminal conduct which *did create a grave risk of death* to passengers and crew - and thereby caused death or injury to 696 people. The Boeing Company's conduct violates, inter alia, the Revised Code of Washington, statute RCW 9A.08.030, *and constitutes mass murder in the first degree.*

The Boeing Company and its top officials do not carry sole culpability in their systematic pattern of criminal conduct. All United States Government officials and State officials who were informed of Boeing's criminality, who had a legal duty to act against it and to terminate such criminality, and who deliberately failed to act, are as culpable as the Boeing perpetrators in mass murder. *Since*

243

it was they who created the circumstances, offered Boeing the opportunity, furthered the commission of, or made it possible and enabled the Boeing offenders to commit murder. Still others assisted the offenders to escape justice, which served to perpetuate the concealment of the safety warnings. Pursuant the statutes 18USC2 & 18USC3, every criminal conspirator from the United States Government or State Government (and further afield) who aided in any way in the commission of this mass murder or who assisted the murderers to escape arrest, trial, and punishment, is also liable with Boeing officials in the murder of 507 and attempted murder of another 189 people. They are the 15,000 state and federal government officials implicated in the insurrection against the laws.

*****

Further to President Trump's presidential order of 21 Jan 2025, with regard to *'Keeping Americans Safe in Aviation',* on February 5, 2025, I warned President Trump that*: "No passengers flying on Boeing aircraft world-wide, including you, will ever be safe unless and until the Boeing Company's ongoing crimes are addressed and terminated once and for all".* President Trump was urged to heed my 'flight safety warning' and to address and terminate Boeing's criminal corporate culture that gives rise to flight safety dangers.

Acting as Prosecutor Qui Tam I filed criminal charges of mass murder against the Boeing Company after each of the accidents, with several government institutions tasked with law and order, including the White House, the Congress, and the US Supreme Court, et al. Where the US Department of Justice and FBI have up until now failed to investigate and prosecute, and the courts have failed to administer the laws, President Trump was requested to 'take care of the faithful execution of the laws', as the US Constitution demands. Failure to deal with the Boeing criminal matter according to the statutes will render President Trump complicit in the mass murder.

The delinquency, cruelty, corruption, brutality, and joint indifference, concerning the 'Boeing Company Mass Murder Case', should affront the senses of decent people everywhere and can accurately be described as *state-supported tyranny* upon the public.

Chapter 12
State-supported Tyranny

In a public address on the topic of Libya on March 19, 2011, President Obama declared: "We cannot stand by and do nothing when innocent men and women face brutality and death at the hands of their own government". But, having seen the splinter in another's eye, have we tended to the beam in our own eye?

Extract from Chapter 12.

ON HUMAN RIGHTS

Whilst considering the consequences of the Boeing Company's criminality and the impunity provided to Boeing by corrupt US Government officials, the question arises as to what rights and recourse the common man can practically and realistically invoke against such tyrannical consequences, if any? This chapter investigates that question.

Universal Declaration of Human Rights

The United Nations 'Universal Declaration of Human Rights' recognizes that *'the inherent dignity and the equal and inalienable rights of all members of the human family are the foundation of freedom, justice, and peace in the world'*. That noble Declaration further states that 'disregard and contempt for human rights have resulted in barbarous acts which have outraged the conscience of mankind'. It acknowledges that 'if man is not to be compelled to have recourse, as a last resort, to rebellion against tyranny and oppression, that human rights should be protected by the rule of law'.

State-supported Tyranny

The United Nations affirms its faith in fundamental human rights and in the dignity and worth of the human person and in the equal rights of all. Its Member States, including the United States, have pledged themselves to achieve the promotion of universal respect for and observance of human rights and fundamental freedoms as a common standard of achievement for all peoples and all nations. Article 3 of the Universal Declaration of Human Rights quite simply but very profoundly states:

Everyone has the right to life, liberty, and security of person.

Human Rights in the United States of America are essentially secured by the US Constitution, in particular by the Bill of Rights as Amendments to the Constitution. They are further secured by several other statutes of the United States Code. In addition, America is vociferous about, remains a champion for, and insists upon human rights worldwide. It proudly forms part of the United States' foreign policy. Concerning America's stand on human rights, the US Department of State publicly takes an active role and captivatingly declares:

> *The protection of fundamental human rights was a foundation stone in the establishment of the United States over 200 years ago. Since then, a central goal of U.S. foreign policy has been the promotion of respect for human rights, as embodied in the 'Universal Declaration of Human Rights'. The United States understands that the existence of human rights helps secure the peace, deter aggression, promote the rule of law, combat crime and corruption, strengthen democracies, and prevent humanitarian crises. Because the promotion of human rights is an important national interest, the United States seeks to:*
>
> > o *Hold governments accountable to their obligations under universal human rights*

> *norms and international human rights instruments;*
>
> o *Promote greater respect for human rights, including freedom from torture, freedom of expression, press freedom, women's rights, children's rights, and the protection of minorities;*
>
> o *Promote the rule of law, seek accountability, and change cultures of impunity;*
>
> o *Assist efforts to reform and strengthen the institutional capacity of the Office of the UN High Commissioner for Human Rights and the UN Commission on Human Rights; and coordinate human rights activities with important allies, including the EU, and regional organizations.*

These surely are very admirable goals for a country to exhibit, by any standard. But does the United States sincerely live up to these goals in practice? Does America practice what it preaches? Does the United States "promote the rule of law, seek accountability, and change cultures of impunity"? The matter under discussion in this book has put the United States to the test, and every reader may answer these questions for themselves, considering the facts presented in this narrative and briefly reviewed in this chapter.

In a public address on the topic of Libya on March 19, 2011, President Obama declared: *"We cannot stand by and do nothing when innocent men and women face brutality and death at the hands of their own government"*. But, having seen the splinter in another's eye, have we tended to the beam in our own eye?

THREAT TO PUBLIC SAFETY AND SECURITY

The 696 injuries and deaths which resulted from the demise of Air India IX-812, Asiana 214, Lion Air 610, and Ethiopian Airlines 302, occurred as a direct result of *systematic and willful suppression of flight safety warnings and vital technical information* by the Boeing Company - warnings pertinent to the safe conduct of each of these flights. In each case, the Boeing Company acted in concert with, and/or under the knowledge and sanction of senior US Government and judicial officials, to suppress the flight safety warnings and information that would otherwise have prevented the four accidents, if heeded. In each case, the loss of life and severe injury could most certainly have been avoided if lawful and timely corrective action had been taken on the dire safety warnings or on the suppressed technical information.

It may appear as an anomaly that a well-known and respected United States flagship corporation, the Boeing Company, stands accused in the United States Federal Courts of willfully breaching the most fundamental of human rights, that of *the right to security of person and life itself,* by demonstrating extreme indifference to human life and greatly contributing to the causes of the four preventable air accidents. The common response to air accidents normally assigns blame to the aircraft pilots for the accident, injuries, and deaths. However, with circumspect and comprehensive consideration in the four air accidents, and by tracking culpability only one step beyond that of the hapless pilots, it becomes patently evident that the accidents in all four instances occurred as a direct result of Boeing's suppression of vital flight safety warnings and technical information pertinent to the actions of those pilots and the safe conduct of those flights.

Sharing full culpability with the Boeing Company is the group of malevolent US Government executives, legislators, police, prosecutors, and judges, who banded together as one to violently prevent the faithful execution of the laws upon Boeing's criminal activities. Their unlawful enterprise has rendered meaningless the protections, rights, and freedoms enshrined in the United States Constitution. The peril posed to public safety by such a virulent criminal endeavor remains acute, and there will inevitably be more deaths and injuries resulting from the same known causes if those causes are not addressed and terminated.

The cruel and violent effect upon the lives of 696 people and upon their families and loved ones - and the international community at large - fits the International Criminal Court, Rome Statute, definition of *'crimes against humanity'*. Recounting the events of this case *in terms of the relevant statutes* leads one directly to that dictum. (See Appendix 4 for statutes).

Initial Offenses

The original criminal offenses from which the violence eventuated were those offenses perpetrated during corrupt legal proceedings in the case *Keyter vs. Keyter*, filed on August 25, 2000, in the Washington State Superior Court, Pierce County, case no. 00-3-02932-1. In that simple *'no fault'* divorce case, assets which were protected by an antenuptial contract and a legally binding settlement agreement were illegally seized by fraudulent court action. The presiding judge colluded with one of the litigants (Maureen Keyter) and her attorney (Michael Turner) to perpetrate a host of premeditated criminal offenses. Hard evidence, confessions under oath, and acknowledgement by the court of certain crimes are readily available to investigators. Crimes include, but are not limited to:

> *Burglary, Perjury, Fraud, Theft, Tampering with a Witness, Tampering with Evidence, and more.*

PROPAGATION OF OFFENSES

The breaches of law committed in the Washington State Superior Court were first reported to local law enforcement officers, and when no action was taken, they were reported to a wider circle of relevant Washington State officials tasked with law and order. The Washington State authorities simply ignored the reported crimes and refused to perform imperative legal obligations to investigate and prosecute - almost certainly because of the involvement of the malfeasant judge. These State authorities thus became embroiled in the crimes themselves. Those officials include the Washington State governor, lieutenant governor, attorney general, secretary of state, legislators, state police, prosecutors, and judges. Their willful failure of duty, both individually and collectively, violated the Revised Code of Washington (RCW) on numerous counts, including but not limited to:

> *Official Misconduct RCW 9A.80.010; Failure of Duty RCW 42.20.100; Rendering Criminal Assistance RCW 9A.76.080.*

That dereliction of law enforcement duty, cover-up, and associated offenses set a pattern for misconduct and lawlessness that would proliferate uninterruptedly through official circles across the length and breadth of the United States and into the top echelons of state and federal government. That proliferation is carefully detailed in the 240 criminal complaints contained in the 2,400 pages of the (three-volume) digest titled the 'Dossier of Crimes', USA.

Federal Offenses

The denial, by Washington State officials, of fundamental rights to due process of law, protection of the laws, and ownership of de jure property, not only violated the Washington State Constitution, but also the United States Constitution and several federal laws besides. The federal offenses were then reported to agents at the Federal Bureau of Investigation and prosecutors at the US Department of Justice for investigation and prosecution of the offenders where federal laws were found to be violated.

Once again, most certainly because of the involvement of government officials in the crimes, these two federal institutions of law enforcement simply ignored the blatant offenses and official misconduct. A wider search for justice was subsequently pursued within the US Federal Government, which included the United States Congress and judiciary committees, the White House, and the Cabinet. *All without success.* Each US Government official approached and presented with both evidence and a detailed description of the crimes simply ignored the multiple criminal complaints and contraventions of the Constitution and chose instead to protect delinquent state and federal officials from the consequences of any wrongdoing. By that dereliction of non-discretionary duty, each new official who was approached violated several federal laws themselves, including but not limited to:

> *Aiding and Abetting Known Criminals 18USC2; Accessory After the Fact to the crimes committed 18USC3; Misprision of Felony 18USC4; Conspiracy against Rights 18USC241; Denial of Rights 18USC242; Conspiracy to Commit Offense 18USC371; Reporting of Offenses of Government Officers 28USC535(b); Prosecutorial Duties 28USC547, oath of office, individual duties, and more.*

Obstruction of Justice

The criminal offenses committed by delinquent state and federal officials were, in turn, reported to the federal courts, which have a peremptory duty to deal with such reports pursuant to statutes 18USC3041, 18USC3046, & 18USC3060. Yet again, in order to assist the law-breaking officials to escape punishment, the official misconduct and dereliction of judicial duty advanced uninterruptedly through United States District Courts, Appeals Courts, and disgracefully, through the US Supreme Court. Although the cover-up of official wrongdoing was absolute, the number and severity of offenses committed in concealing the criminal endeavor kept escalating, and included, but are not limited to:

> *Obstruction of Justice 18USC1505; Theft of Court Record 18USC1506; Obstruction of Court Order 18USC1509; Tampering with and Intimidation of a Witness 18USC1512; Retaliating against a Witness 18USC1513; Interference with the lawful employment and livelihood of a Witness 18USC1513(e); Perjury 18USC1621; False Statements 18USC1001; Failure of Judges to Recuse 28USC144, or to disqualify 28USC455; on and on.*

Attempts to Kidnap and Murder a Witness

When the aforementioned crimes were imminently to be exposed in the US Supreme Court in case no. 05-140, a case against President GW Bush, the President swiftly instructed his agents who (on behalf of all the offending government officers) then attempted to kidnap and murder me in order to silence my testimony on felonies committed by government officials and by President Bush himself. The Boeing Company (my employer at the time), acting simultaneously at the behest of President Bush and Air India, facilitated the first (foiled) kidnap and murder attempt in return for government favors likely connected with the Air Force Tanker Aircraft Program. The second abortive kidnap and murder attempt followed shortly thereafter, and the conspiracy remains active today, via the Federal Aviation Administration, in violation of the following laws:

> *Attempt to Kidnap 18USC1201; Attempt to Murder 18USC1113; Conspiracy to Murder 18USC1117.*

Sedition against the State

Although the initial kidnap and murder attempts were foiled and were then reported to an ever-widening circle of officials tasked with law and order, at the time of writing, those crimes have yet to be investigated and prosecuted. Evidence at the FAA indicates that the conspiracy to murder has remained active during the terms of Presidents Bush, Obama, Trump, and Biden - with the knowledge and tacit consent of their Cabinets, the Congress, the Supreme Court, the Department of Justice, US Attorneys, the FBI and CIA, generals and admirals of the Armed Forces, and numerous state and federal judicial officers. The joint effort by these officials to neutralize me as a prime court witness to official wrongdoing, and to prevent, hinder, and delay, *by violence* (kidnap and murder), the execution of the laws of the United States upon law-breaking government officers, constitutes a clear violation of the statute on sedition:

Seditious Conspiracy 18USC2384.

Insurrection against the Laws

Not only are the top echelons of the United States Federal Government informed of the extensive seditious conspiracy within the government and the courts, but the 50 State Governments remain fully informed and were implored to deal with the seditious conspirators in terms of their legal obligations and their oath to preserve, protect, and defend the Constitution of the United States. State officials, who have a clear duty to address criminality in their States and in their ranks, include: state governors, lieutenant governors, secretaries of state, police chiefs, prosecutors, legislators, and judges of three levels of state courts. Twenty-three appeals for protection of the laws were made to an average of 9 institutions of government tasked with law and order in each of the 50 states.

State-supported Tyranny

To date, no action has been forthcoming from any of the state governments or courts to deal with the deluge of crime. The large number of state and federal officials, who collectively cooperated to provide a safe haven and passage to some 15,000 seditious conspirators, constitutes an *insurrection* against the authority of the United States and against the laws thereof.

Insurrection against the Laws 18USC2383;

Treason against the Nation

The subversive actions of more than 15,000 government officials, who have sworn their allegiance to this country, to assist the seditious conspirators and insurrectionists to escape justice, constitute aid and comfort to 'domestic enemies' of the United States, in violation of the statute on treason, namely:

Treason against the United States 18USC2381.

Mass Murder

The consequences of criminality with impunity, provided to the Boeing Company by some 15,000 government officers tasked with law and order, facilitated and enabled Boeing to play a fateful role in each of the four air accidents described in this narrative. Boeing's culpability in the death of 507 people and injury to another 189, analyzed in terms of the Revised Code of Washington (RCW), the United States Code (USC), the Indian Penal Code, constitutes mass murder and attempted murder:

> *Murder, Revised Code of Washington RCW 9A.32.030; Murder in the first degree, United States Code 18USC1111; Murder, Indian Penal Code Sections 300 and 301.*

Crimes against Humanity

Accidents are one thing, and they are bound to occur. However, crime in pursuit of profits, which leads to air accidents, is quite another. In all four crashes of Boeing aircraft mentioned, Boeing engaged in conduct that posed a danger to human life, and in fact, that conduct caused the loss of human life. Boeing and its Board of Directors ignored flight safety warnings before each of the four avoidable accidents mentioned in this chronicle. US Government and judicial officials similarly ignored flight safety warnings of the impact of unaddressed and ongoing criminality within the Boeing Company. The injuries and deaths occurred as a direct result of *systematic and willful suppression of vital flight safety warnings* by the Boeing Company - warnings pertinent to the safe conduct of each of those flights. In each case, the Boeing Company acted in concert with and/or under the consent of senior US Government and judicial officials to suppress the flight safety warnings that would otherwise have prevented the four accidents, if heeded. In all cases, the loss of life and severe injury could most certainly have been avoided if lawful and timely action had been taken on the dire warnings. The wrongful death (the mass murder) of 507 innocent people, and the grave injury (attempted murder) of another 189 people in the avoidable accidents, violate the Rome Statute of the International Criminal Court in The Hague:

> *'Crimes against Humanity of Mass Murder', Article 7(1)(a) of the Rome Statute; 'Crimes against Humanity of Other Inhumane Acts (Grave Injury), Article 7(1)(k) of the Rome Statute.*

A Case Made for 'Terrorism'

Within reason and law, a case can be made for domestic terrorism under the prevailing circumstances. The United States Code, Statute 18USC2331(1), defines "international terrorism" as follows:

256

Activities that- (A) involve violent acts or acts dangerous to human life that are a violation of the criminal laws of the United States or of any State, or that would be a criminal violation if committed within the jurisdiction of the United States or of any State; (B) appear to be intended— (i) to intimidate or coerce a civilian population; (ii) to influence the policy of a government by intimidation or coercion; or (iii) to affect the conduct of a government by mass destruction, assassination, or kidnapping; and (C) occur primarily outside the territorial jurisdiction of the United States, or transcend national boundaries in terms of the means by which they are accomplished, the persons they appear intended to intimidate or coerce, or the locale in which their perpetrators operate or seek asylum.

The activities of the state and federal officials implicated in the aforementioned criminal violations involve acts dangerous to human life, such as kidnapping *and murder.* The plot by government officials to murder me as a prime court witness to their crimes is active and ongoing at the time of writing. The threat of further and imminent attempts upon life and limb is factual and menacing. The activities are clearly intended to *intimidate and coerce*. Threats have been issued by several judges, all alluding to retaliatory action, including the implicit threat of false incarceration should my efforts to seek justice in the courts continue. Other criminal acts committed by federal judges and meant to intimidate include extortion, contempt of court, contempt of the laws, theft of evidence, tampering with a witness, and more. These offenses are aimed at silencing my testimony and obstructing efforts to bring the perpetrators to justice.

The acts dangerous to human life, the intimidation, extortion, coercion, threats of violence (false incarceration, retaliation, kidnap, and assassination), committed by a conspiracy of some 15,000 US government and industry officials, are clearly intended to influence, to establish, and to enforce by violence, *a corrupt United States government policy,* viz.: 'where government officials and/or Boeing Company officials are found to be implicated in crime, there to illegally shield them from investigation and prosecution by obstructing the administration of the laws, by defeating the course of justice, by providing protection to known criminals, and by denying constitutional rights to due process and protection of the laws'.

The author readily acknowledges that the insidious process of terror described in these pages does not conjure up the shocking images of a terrorist bomb blast in a crowded market square, or of the other awful forms of mass destruction and killing we have come to witness via television in recent years. Yet the gradual, subtle, and menacing threat to society of a corrupt government policy enforced by violence is just as dangerous to public safety worldwide as any visually appalling counterpart. The death (murder) of 507 and grave injury (attempted murder) to 189 innocent civilians internationally, 696 people in all in four preventable air accidents, and attempts upon the life of a prime witness, unambiguously demonstrate that.

The kidnap and murder attempts by US Government officials acting in conjunction with Boeing Company and Air India officials, intended to intimidate, coerce, establish, and enforce a corrupt government policy, and the resultant death and injury to innocent civilians which followed internationally, very likely violate the laws on terrorism, domestic and international:

> *Terrorism 18USC2331; Harboring and Providing Material Support to Terrorists 18USC2339; United States Code, statute 18USC1111 – Murder; Indian Penal Code, Section 301 – Murder; Revised Code of Washington, statute RCW9A.32.030 – Murder*

CORRUPT DISPOSAL OF THE BOEING COMPANY MASS MURDER CASE

Several court cases over the years, covering aspects of the violent criminal endeavor, have been conducted with the top echelons of the United States Government being fully informed of the corrupt proceedings in the courts and being fully involved in quashing those cases. One such case is the Boeing Company Mass Murder Case, which bears special mention as it consolidates other related cases into a single court case.

The *'Boeing Company Mass Murder Case'* was first filed on May 14, 2013, as case no. 13-2-19597-6KNT, in the Superior Court of the State of Washington in and for King County. The suit was filed as a class action for wrongful death and injury arising from the avoidable air accident of Air India Flight IX-812 and the Boeing Company's illegal suppression of crucial flight safety warnings regarding the safe conduct of that flight. The court case had a *civil component* concerning a restitution claim for Boeing's extreme indifference to human life regarding the 158 fatalities and eight injured survivors. The case also featured a *criminal component*, which addressed the murder charges filed in the case.

The case was immediately usurped by the Boeing Company and filed as case no. 13cv982 in the US District Court for Western Washington in Seattle, where the Boeing Company has a longstanding conspiratorial relationship with the judges of that court. The case was presided over by a District Judge, Ricardo Martinez, who was himself a named defendant in the case. The judge was rightfully accused as an accomplice in Boeing's felonies for facilitating and making it possible for Boeing and its officials to commit murder and thereafter to escape justice. He was also charged with being a co-conspirator in the underlying seditious conspiracy involving the Boeing Company and the government.

The US District Court case was illegally dismissed sans addressing the mass murder charges filed in the case regarding the death (murder) of 158 on board Flight IX-812 and three on board Asiana Flight 214; or the grave injury (attempted murder) of 8 on board Air India Flight IX-812 and 181 on Asiana Flight 214. The judge ignored a motion for arrest of the criminal offenders; ignored a motion to appoint a prosecutor; ignored a motion to compel Boeing to comply with Securities and Exchange Commission Regulations which the company was in breach of; ignored a motion for joinder; and ignored an urgent flight safety warning – just as if those documents were not filed. Judge Ricardo Martinez ruled that a motion for his disqualification (based on his being a defendant in the case) was *'frivolous'* and denied the motion. For his own nefarious reasons, Judge Martinez improperly suggested to the Lead Plaintiff that the complaint be rewritten with the Lead Plaintiff being the sole claimant, without the victims of the Air India crash being included in the suit.

An appeal against the illegal dismissal was lodged as Case No. 13-36056 in the Ninth Circuit Appeals Court on November 6, 2013. In order to save the Court time and effort, an 'Amended Appeal Brief' was filed on November 25, 2013, which combined all three related and pending cases against the Boeing Company (District Court case nos. 09cv962, 12cv474, and 13cv982) into a single *'Combined Boeing Company Mass Murder Case'*.

The Amended Appeal Brief in Ninth Circuit case no. 13-36056 not only addressed the harm caused by the criminal offenses of the Boeing Company and its law-breaking officials, but also that of *Boeing co-conspirators.* The respective roles of Boeing and its accomplices and accessories in their joint seditious conspiracy are completely intertwined and integrated, each being party to and sharing culpability in the other's criminal offenses.

To further save the Federal Courts' time and effort in addressing the joint seditious conspiracy, and to facilitate dealing with the individual roles of Boeing *and* its co-conspirators simultaneously as an integrated matter, the Ninth Circuit Appeal Brief was further amended in order to include the injurious criminal conduct perpetrated by *Boeing co-conspirators.* That criminal conduct was addressed in another 54 related and pending court cases at that time. The three pending cases against Boeing and the 54 pending cases against *Boeing co-conspirators* - totaling 57 court cases in all at the time - were thus consolidated into a single court case (the 58th) titled: *'The Consolidated Boeing Company Murder Case'.* All 57 associated cases of that date remained open and pending pursuant to FRCivP, Rule 60(b)(3)&(4) and Rule 60(d)(3), because of fraud and other crimes committed in the courts which have not yet been dealt with by the courts.

On March 13, 2014, Ninth Circuit Judges Fletcher, Smith, and Christen granted the Boeing Company's motion for summary affirmance of the District Court dismissal; they simultaneously summarily affirmed the District Court's judgment to dismiss the case. Likewise, in the Ninth Circuit Court, each Circuit Judge was a named party to the case for having previously assisted the defendants to escape justice for criminal wrongdoing. Without investigation or trial, and without the benefit of the evidence available to the court, the Circuit Judges ostensibly found that the questions raised in the Consolidated Boeing Company Murder Case - *concerning the death or injury of 350 people (at that time) - are so insubstantial as not to require further argument.* The willful neglect of Circuit Judges to address the murder charges violated 18USC3041, 3046, and 3060, rendered them accessories to the murder charges, and rendered their dismissal of the case illegal and void.

Throughout the dishonorable sojourn of the Consolidated Boeing Company Murder Case, the US Supreme Court Chief Justice and Associate Justices, all Members of Congress, and President Obama and his Cabinet, were once again kept fully apprised of the obstruction of justice in the courts as it occurred. They were requested to deal with the criminality within the judicial system while the criminal offenses were being committed, but tacitly and willfully refused to do so, rendering them complicit therein.

The 'Consolidated Boeing Company Murder Case' was appealed to the US Supreme Court on March 26, 2014 (as *the 60th case* in this matter) with a simple petition for due process and protection of the laws. The United States Supreme Court repeatedly refused the petition, failed to file the case on their docket, and corruptly returned the papers to the petitioner, just as the court had done in 11 of the 14 Supreme Court cases filed with them that address the broad underlying seditious conspiracy involving Boeing and the US Government. At the time of writing, the *'Consolidated Boeing Company Murder Case',* embracing 62 court cases addressing different aspects of the same extensive seditious conspiracy and insurrection against the laws, remains open and pending with the United States Supreme Court.

Return to the Hellhole of the US District Court in Seattle

After the Boeing 737 Max crashes, during May 2019, as Prosecutor Qui Tam, I went back to the hellhole they call the US District Court for Western Washington in Seattle. I was hoping beyond hope that, in the light of those crashes and the widespread polemic that it precipitated in the world press, the judges would experience some feeling of 'mea culpa' and remorse for their part in letting the obvious culprits go free, and would reconsider their own delinquency.

State-supported Tyranny

In a series of filings, the judges were informed of the first and then the second 737 Max crashes and requested to deal with the updated criminal complaint against the Boeing Company and its senior officials for their culpability in those crashes. The charges were *filed directly with the judges* as persons in authority pursuant to my duties under statute 18USC4. The petition was for the judges to follow the 'due process of law' and to secure the safety of the flying public. Rules 4 and 41, and 42(a)(2) of Federal Rule of Criminal Procedures, and statutes 18USC3041, 18USC3046, 18USC3060, would point their way along that path to due process of law.

Case number 3:19cv05379 was the 61st court case at that time, in the long series of related causes seeking justice and protection of the laws. The case also sought to enjoin the President and the DOJ to take care of the faithful execution of the laws on the criminal complaints filed with them, as the Constitution demands.

The full bench of judges of the United States District Court for the Western District of Washington was motioned to provide due process of law and protection of the laws to the flying public and the people of the United States in keeping with the United States Constitution, in keeping with relevant laws, and in keeping with the judges' oath of office. The *extraordinary step* to motion the full bench was taken since every judge on the bench was cognizant of, and was involved in, the matter before the Court.

Collectively and individually, the judges willfully failed to deal with the criminal reports and failed to ensure the public safety in the face of that criminality. The malevolent response of the US District Court judges/clerks was to corruptly employ the US Marshal Service to harass and intimidate me, to threaten me, and to try and coerce or corruptly persuade me in order to: *"hinder, delay, or prevent the communication to a law enforcement officer or judge of the United States of information relating to the commission or possible commission of a Federal offense".* Their acts constitute tampering with a witness, victim, or informant.

The Coup De Grâce of the Coup d' état

The coup de grâce (the intended death blow to the wounded informant) by the coup d'e état (the group of US government insurgents who have unlawfully usurped legal government in the United States of America) was destined to come from the hometown of the insurrection against the laws. It was on the outskirts of Seattle that the case under discussion had its beginnings, and it was there that the insurgents would later have the matter die a merciful death.

In response to my coming *full circle* in the search for justice, I received a threatening phone call from the US Marshal Service in Seattle, made on behalf of the judges, commanding me to lay off the pursuit of the Boeing case *and* the criminal charges. A US Marshal (Deputy Donrien Stephens), acting on behalf of the judges, threatened me with (false) incarceration if I did not comply. His actions amounted to witness tampering and coercion to violate the statute 18USC4, which requires reporting of known criminal offenses.

Because the actions commanded by the judges and executed by the US Marshal Service were in blatant violation of the laws, I went to see the US Marshal, the US Attorney, and the Clerk of the US District Court at their offices. They are all located in the same building in downtown Seattle. I sought to present them with the laws that compelled my actions and should have compelled their actions. Meeting first with the US Marshal Service (Deputy Michael Lee), *my* presentation was cordial, to the point, measured, and was conducted from prepared notes. *My demeanor* was not confrontational. *His demeanor,* on the other hand, was decidedly confrontational and aggressive. Deputy Lee clearly did not like to hear from me that the US Marshal Service was violating the laws by threatening me, a witness, and Prosecutor Qui Tam, with 'false' incarceration for reporting known crimes. In gross abuse of lawful authority, Deputy Lee took to force in order to curtail the conversation. For no reason other than unabashed intimidation, and catching me totally by surprise during the interaction, he gathered up a posse of five (presumably armed) US Marshals and security personnel to surround me and to escort me out of the offices and/or building. The threatening (and demeaning) armed posse 'escorted me' downstairs to the building entrance while limiting my freedom by the unlawful use of force in furtherance of their 'witness tampering'. As it happened, when we reached the building entrance hall, I simply turned to the posse and told them my business in that building was not done, and turned and walked off to the Court Clerk's Office, leaving them staring sheepishly after me and probably wondering what the show of armed escort was all about.

Nevertheless, the intent of the US Marshals was illegal. The intent was to intimidate and to harass. The effect was to *"hinder, delay, or prevent the communication to a law enforcement officer or judge of the United States of information relating to the commission or possible commission of a Federal offense"*. The unlawful use of force to escort or 'carry me away', by five law-enforcement officers, constituted *violent* deprivation of my liberty, or the threat thereof. I should have been allowed to go to my next meeting place on my own free will. I should not have been coerced by force. Exposed to the risk of violence and harm, there was no possibility for me to make other plans, for instance, to rearrange the sequence of my meetings. The posse of five guards had their orders from Lee and under threat of violence *their will applied* and not my own free will. I was being exposed to a risk of violence well above and beyond the normal course of a witness reporting and providing testimony on a crime. The unlawful and unwarranted restraint by five law-enforcement officers confined my movements to a controlled space between them. The intimidation and restrictive acts were perpetrated under the command of Deputy Lee, who was acting in concert and in protection of Deputy Stephens, who, in turn, was acting under orders from the judges. Their acts were later approved by Chief Deputy Michael Thomas and by US Marshal Jacob Green.

After reading the laws to the Clerk of the Court, he just shrugged his shoulders and indicated that the judges would not respond, and he had nothing more to say. The US Attorney simply complained of not having staff to investigate. In direct violation of the US Constitution and the laws, the full bench of judges ignored the criminal complaints against Boeing and its officials, and denied the motion for due process and protection of the laws for the American people and the flying public. The US District Court bench (all 22 judges) found the murder of 507 people and attempted murder of 189 a *"frivolous"* matter (quote) and dismissed the case on those grounds. The very obvious point made was: don't tackle our darling company - our partner in crime! Further criminal charges were filed with the US District Court against all 22 judges and the Clerk, as well as the US Marshals implicated, for the following crimes:

> *Witness Tampering on several counts, in violation of several sections of statute 18USC1512; Kidnapping, in violation of 18USC1201; complicity to and/or accessory after the fact to mass murder 18USC1111 and RCW 9A.32.30*

USA vs. The Boeing Company, Fort Worth, Texas

After the two fatal 737 Max crashes during 2018 and 2019, with the concomitant death of 346 people, the Department of Justice perversely charged Boeing with *one count of defrauding* the FAA Aircraft Evaluation Group – nothing more serious than that. On 7 January 2021, Boeing was fined a criminal monetary penalty of $243 million (in addition to payments to the airlines and crash victims for loss) and was offered a *'Deferred Prosecution*

Agreement' in the US District Court for Northern Texas in Fort Worth, case no. 4:21-cr-5-O. The Deferred Prosecution Agreement was to be in place for three years. Boeing violated that agreement during that time, and the DOJ and Boeing entered into a new 'Plea Agreement' on 24 July 2024. The US District Court, Judge Reed O'Connor, did not accept the Plea Agreement and set a trial date of 23 June 2025. However, before the trial, on 23 May 2025, Boeing was again let off the hook and reached a deal with the DOJ to altogether avoid prosecution for the crashes that killed 346 people. The non-prosecution agreement would allow Boeing, as a top US exporter and military contractor, to avoid being labelled a felon, which, of course, it is by its own admission of criminal conspiracy to defraud the United States. Boeing would pay another $243.6 million criminal fine; pay $444.5 million into a new fund for crash victims; and pay itself $444.5 million to invest it in its own compliance, safety, and quality programs. And the case would be dismissed.

Judge Reed O'Connor and the US District Court simply ignored the 19 criminal complaints that I filed in case no. 4:21-cr-5-O, as a Boeing crime victim and as Prosecutor Qui Tam regarding ongoing Boeing crimes. Judge O'Connor ignored my motion to arrest the Boeing criminal offenders; ignored my motion to disqualify the judge for his failure to obey the laws; ignored the motion to address ongoing criminality in the case; ignored the flight safety warning; and ignored the important joinder motion.

And here, in the US District Court for Northern Texas, we have a duplicate copy of the pantomime that played out in the Superior Court of Washington State, described in Chapter 2 of this narrative: *"The Kangaroo Court"*. Judge O'Connor criminally conspired with the defendant (Boeing) and with the government lawyers (the DOJ prosecutors) and allowed the Boeing Company and its officials to literally get away with murder, scot-free. I say 'criminally conspired' because:

- Judge O'Connor denied due process of law by blatantly violating statute 18USC3041, statute 18USC3046, and 18USC3060, and by not arresting the offenders or holding a preliminary hearing on the offenses filed in the case under affidavit, as the laws demand of him. He denied the American and international flying public and investing public the right to "protection of the laws" (those laws which Boeing is in breach of), in violation of 18USC241 - conspiracy against rights. (Boeing's violations are listed in my letter to President Trump, presented below in the next section). Judge O'Connor obstructed justice in the mass murder case by deliberately failing to deal with Boeing Company crimes, in violation of 18USC1512(c)(2) - obstruction of justice. Judge O'Connor thereby joining the insurrection against the laws, in violation of 18USC2383, violated his oath (28USC453) and court rules, showing contempt of court in violation of 18USC401.

- The Department of Justice prosecutors, who have a legal duty to 'prosecute for all offenses against the United States', willfully failed to perform their duty to prosecute, in violation of 28USC547.

- The Defendant Boeing, knowing of the guilt of its employees, failed to come clean and to work with the Prosecutor Qui Tam to address and terminate the ongoing crimes, willfully failed to make the needed reports to the Securities and Exchange Commission, the stock exchanges upon which they are listed, and to their shareholders in violation of statute 18USC371 (conspiracy to commit offense), and the Securities Act.

FLIGHT SAFETY WARNING ISSUED TO PRESIDENT TRUMP

While the Boeing Company enjoys impunity from prosecution; while corrupt United States authorities continue to cover up and refuse to address the Boeing criminal corporate culture; and while the United States authorities provide safe haven and passage to Boeing and its US Government co-conspirators, the dire peril posed to the international flying public and public at large remains real and imminent. Unless decisive action is taken, further crimes against humanity stemming from these same causes are a certainty. The following flight safety warning was issued to President Trump on February 5, 2025:

> *Dear President Trump,*
>
> *Re: Your Action is Needed to Keep Americans Safe in Aviation*
>
> *Further to your order of 21 Jan 2025, with regard to 'Keeping Americans Safe in Aviation', an immediate task for you in this regard would be to take action on the following flight safety warning:*
>
> **Urgent Flight Safety Warning:**
>
> *Four common causes, stemming from the Boeing Company, have caused the death of 507 people and grave injury to another 189 in the preventable air accidents of Lion Air Flight 610, Ethiopian Airlines Flight 302, Asiana Flight 214, and Air India Flight IX-812. Many more innocent people will die needlessly in inevitable aircraft or spacecraft accidents on Boeing aircraft/ spacecraft, attributable to these same avoidable causes:*
>
> o *Unless the ongoing criminality within the Boeing Company and its US Government co-conspirators is addressed and terminated.*

- o *Unless the impunity offered by the US Government (and DOJ) to the Boeing Company, for crimes committed, is ended forthwith.*
- o *Unless the Boeing Company's culture of 'extreme indifference to human life' is reigned in and eradicated for good. (See major contributory causes by Boeing in the accidents of Lion Air Flight 610, Asiana Flight 214, and Air India Flight IX-812.)*
- o *Unless Boeing's corporate culture of putting its financial interests first, well before flight safety considerations, is once and for all eliminated in full.*

The Boeing Company has committed a series of grave crimes that have not been addressed by the DOJ prosecutors under President Biden. Those crimes are listed below. The dangers posed to the flying public by those same Boeing crimes persist. The unattended criminal charges are herewith filed with you (on CD) for your action. (See Chapter 42.1 of the Dossier of Crimes, Volume III). Please take care of the faithful execution of the laws (as is your duty under the Constitution, Article II, Section 3) through your DOJ.

Not all 'manufacturer-involved' air accidents have their origin on the factory floor during assembly. In Boeing's case, many more 'factory-involved' incidents and accidents originate from expedient, unlawful decisions made in the boardroom and in company executive offices and stem from an overarching criminal corporate culture. This can be readily inferred from the list of Boeing's unaddressed crimes:

Boeing Unaddressed Past Crimes

Fraud on a large scale; obstruction of justice, 18USC1519; theft of court record; tampering with a witness; retaliation against a witness; contempt of court; perjury; conspiracy to commit offenses;

conspiracy to kidnap; conspiracy to murder a court witness; conspiracy against rights; deprivation of rights; misprision of felony; treason; misprision of treason; seditious conspiracy; insurrection against the laws; accessory after the fact to offenses of their government co-conspirators as detailed in the 'Dossier of Crimes'; crimes against humanity of mass murder in the death of 507 people; crimes against humanity of other inhumane acts in the grave injury of 189 innocent civilians.

Boeing Unaddressed Ongoing Crimes

Ongoing violation of: seditious conspiracy; fraud in the amount of $249.88 billion, plus a recent tranche of $21 billion, on three separate stock exchanges; Securities Act, Sections 17(a)(2) and 17(a)(3); Revised Code of Washington, RCW 9a.28.40; SEC 'cease-and-desist' order; {DOJ 'Plea Agreement', before it was rejected on 12/5/24}; USDC Northern Texas Order; Boeing ongoing criminal conspiracy with stock exchanges; Boeing ongoing criminal conspiracy with the US Government to cover-up fraud and unaddressed past crimes; Boeing ongoing criminal conspiracy with Alaska Airlines; Boeing 'ongoing' criminal conspiracy to defraud the United States; an ongoing criminal corporate culture as demonstrated by Boeing / US Government ongoing criminal conspiracy to murder the prosecutor qui tam, Anthony Keyter.

No passengers flying on Boeing aircraft worldwide, including you, will ever be safe unless and until the Boeing Company's ongoing crimes are addressed and terminated once and for all. For these reasons, you are urged to give heed to the 'Flight Safety Warning' and to address and terminate Boeing's criminal corporate culture that gives rise to the flight safety dangers.

Sincerely,
Anthony Keyter
Boeing Company Senior Instructor Pilot, Retired
Prosecutor Qui Tam of Boeing Crimes

Attachment CD:
Boeing's Unaddressed Crimes, the Dossier of Crimes, Vol III, Chapter. 42.1.

I am not a fear-monger. I take no perverse pleasure in having issued this warning. Rather, I am a concerned aviation professional, an instructor pilot and test pilot (retired), who has dedicated much of my life's labors to flight safety. I am the one who has time and again forewarned many US officials of obvious dangers, *before* those dangers extinguished 507 lives, maimed another 189, and forever changed the lives of hundreds of dependents and loved ones. I am he who has suffered intimidation and assassination attempts aimed at silencing my testimony in the courts on these matters. No one is immune to that continuing but needless danger warned of – including you, the reader, the next time you say goodbye to family and loved ones at the airport to fly on a Boeing aircraft.

That which I have painstakingly tried to illustrate in these pages and in the flight safety warnings – the *unattended and unchecked* danger thrust upon the American people and the international flying public by the Boeing Company – is merely one side of the manifested tyranny. But the lawless Boeing Company is *'supported'* in its tyranny upon the population. The support is provided by the United States federal and state institutions and officials in protecting the commercial company and its officials from prosecution. And how did that situation come about? Remember that it was Boeing who acted on behalf of President George W. Bush in the attempt to kidnap and murder the President's Supreme Court opponent, a Senior Boeing Company Instructor Pilot. Two sides of the same coin. It is in quid pro quo that the state repays its partner in crime, the Boeing Company, by providing impunity against prosecution for any crime the company or its officials indulge in. In fact, providing impunity for all crimes committed, including mass murder and major stock exchange fraud.

And there you have it, the consequences of crime with impunity: *'State-supported tyranny in the land of the free!'* There is no known practical recourse against it or remedy available to the common man - yet.

THE US GOVERNMENT-BOEING IMPASSE

The US Government is at an impasse in dealing with its partner in crime. It cannot prosecute Boeing without incriminating itself. And, as partner in crime, Boeing has powerful extortion and blackmail capability over the US Government, over its prosecutors and its courts, and over the Federal Aviation Administration. That is a fact of life.

Still, nobody wants to see Boeing go down under the weight of its own criminality – myself included. The company plays too vital a role as one of Americas biggest exporters and as large supplier of military and civilian aircraft and spacecraft alike. It is 'too big to fail', to use a colloquial term; more accurately put, Boeing is too strategically important to be brought down. Yet, nobody wants to see more avoidable accidents and deaths due to Boeing's unaddressed criminal corporate culture. And to have Boeing shareholders pay the price of huge fines for corporate criminality, as the US Department of Justice is dealing with the matter, has no effect upon Boeing's delinquent decision-makers. And to hold the inert Boeing Company, quote, 'responsible for the crimes of its employees', as the Department of Justice philosophy advocates, has no deterrent value upon those law-breaking employees.

The solution to the dilemma is obvious. Boeing employees who have committed crime should be prosecuted for the crimes of those

Boeing employees. The decision-makers of decisions made with callous indifference - decisions that cause death and injury - should be punished for their indifference to human life. Such an objective policy to hold individuals responsible for their own crimes, should include the Boeing Board of Directors and Boeing's executive leadership team. Then only, will flight safety and respect for human life and the law triumph over the single-minded pursuit of profits by Boeing's leadership. Then only, will Boeing's role in ongoing stock exchange fraud be terminated and its investors be secure.

Boeing's part in that massive fraudulent stock exchange scheme, and that of US Government institutions enabling the fraud, is discussed in the next chapter.

Chapter 13
$1.42 Trillion Stock Exchange Fraud

"Acting as Prosecutor Qui Tam in this matter, I believe that the massive fraudulent scheme in the amount of $1.42 trillion will have a major detrimental effect on the financial markets worldwide. The loss of $1.42 trillion to investors could be sudden and will cause great financial harm and loss to ordinary people across the globe".

Extract From Chapter 13.

A further impact upon public security, caused by the government not prosecuting large law-breaking companies, including Boeing, is the instability it will in time bring upon the world's financial markets. United States Government authorities were informed of the build-up to $1.42 trillion stock exchange fraud and were requested to deal with that major international crime, as was their duty. Those authorities and institutions turned a blind eye to the serious ongoing crime, deliberately failed to investigate and prosecute, and callously left investors and the public at the mercy of the criminals.

SYNOPSIS OF THE CRIME

Seven public companies willfully failed to share material facts with their investors, which facts will materially affect their share price and reputation when those facts become public knowledge. In failing to make that mandatory report, the seven companies, individually, violated the law.

Four stock exchanges, on which those seven companies are listed, were informed of the material facts affecting the companies' share prices. The stock exchanges knew that, legally, the information needed to be shared with investors and knew that the seven law-breaking companies deliberately failed to share that information. The four stock exchanges willfully and expediently acquiesced to the unlawful scheme and condoned and sanctioned the breaches of the securities regulations.

The combined result of the actions of the seven companies and four stock exchanges represents *'concealment of important information'* in a deliberate scheme to obtain financial gain for the companies and for the stock exchanges. The individual actions by the seven companies and one unlisted subsidiary company (effectively eight companies in total), *and* the actions taken together with the stock exchanges, *constitute fraud.* In this case, the combined value of that fraud is equal to the sum of the peak market capitalization value of the seven errant companies and four stock exchanges during the period, which amounts to $1.42 trillion in US dollars.

The fraud on the four stock exchanges was reported to the financial authorities of the three countries involved: the United States, the United Kingdom, and South Africa. The financial authorities, in turn, sanctioned and condoned the fraud, protected the well-known, strategically important companies and stock exchanges from prosecution, and enabled the massive fraudulent scheme to continue unabated, with their knowledge and consent. The heads of state of the three countries housing the stock exchanges were on several occasions informed of the extensive fraud on the stock exchanges and fraud in their financial watchdog institutions, and were requested to address and terminate the international fraudulent scheme. Instead of protecting the international public from the massive fraud, the three heads of state, one head of government, and the government institutions under their command, who are tasked with law and order, gave their support to the fraudulent scheme. Together, the Heads of State and their government institutions provided the perpetrators a safe haven and passage and protected the seven companies and four stock exchanges from prosecution for the crime of stock exchange fraud.

Underlying the fraud were serious crimes perpetrated by the seven listed companies. Those underpinning crimes, and the likely consequences to the boards of directors, were the material facts affecting their stock price, which the seven companies and their stock exchanges did not report to their shareholders. The Heads of State and/or Government of the three countries also protected the seven companies from prosecution for their *underlying crimes,* which the companies failed to report to their shareholders and to the authorities. Addressing and terminating the underlying crimes would have terminated the ongoing fraud of $1.42 trillion. In willfully failing to terminate the underlying crimes, the three heads of state and one head of government, together with their failed institutions, were rendered accomplices to the international fraud *and* to the underlying crimes which gave rise to the fraud charges.

Acting as Prosecutor Qui Tam in this matter, I believe that the massive fraudulent scheme in the amount of $1.42 trillion, will have a major detrimental effect on the financial markets worldwide. The loss of $1.42 trillion to investors could be sudden and will cause great financial harm and loss to ordinary people across the globe. As Prosecutor Qui Tam, I strongly recommend that the unlawful scheme to defraud the investing public and global financial markets be terminated and that the perpetrators be brought to justice - regardless of their social or diplomatic standing.

During his time in office, President Biden and his Cabinet, including the FBI and DOJ, were fully informed of the fraud and underlying crimes, which underpinned the $1.42 trillion fraud case.

They were requested to address and terminate the fraud and those underlying crimes. Biden and his Administration deliberately failed to act on the crimes and thereby assisted and enabled the seven companies to continue their crime spree and fraud. Biden and his Administration Members, who were addressed, were rendered accomplices to the international fraud *and* to the underlying crimes which gave rise to the fraud charges.

Since the new Administration under President Trump's second term has come into power, they too have been informed and requested to deal with the criminal matter. At the time of publishing, it remains to be seen whether President Trump and his Administration will take care of the faithful execution of the laws and will terminate the major international fraud and underlying crimes.

The '$1.42 trillion Stock Exchange Fraud Case' is filed as Chapter 50.11.5a of Volume III of the tome titled: the Dossier of Crimes, USA. As a reminder, the Dossier of Crimes serves as a collection of criminal complaints and as a source of evidence of the underlying crimes in the criminal complaint regarding 'Stock Exchange Fraud'. The Dossier of Crimes is filed at the United States Supreme Court with the Chief Justice and the Associate Justices. The dossier is also filed in the criminal case 'United States vs. the Boeing Company', in the US District Court for Northern Texas, case number 4:21-CR-5-O. Thus, the criminal complaint on the $1.42 trillion stock exchange is public knowledge and can be accessed from the docket of the Texas case, in docket number 229, or from the US Supreme Court.

STOCK EXCHANGE FRAUD

The principal perpetrators in the fraud include seven internationally renowned companies, four well-known stock exchanges, the most prestigious financial and government institutions in three countries, and four 'ostensibly respectable' world leaders, all of whom are enabling and are part of the criminal enterprise by providing the enterprise a safe haven and passage. The seven large and well-known companies are at the center of the virulent international criminal enterprise emanating from the stock exchanges. They include the following companies:

o The Boeing Company;
o The Ford Motor Company;
o Alaska Air Group;
o Berkshire Hathaway Inc. and
o Insurance Auto Auctioneers Inc. / Ritchie Bros.
o Barclays Plc, a large banking and financial institution from the United Kingdom;
o Barclays Africa Group Ltd (BAGL)/ (now named Absa Group) and its subsidiary Absa Bank, a prominent South African bank;

The four international stock exchanges upon which these seven companies trade, who are well-informed and who are committing the massive fraud on the international investment markets in concert with the corrupt companies, are:

o The New York Stock Exchange (NYSE);
o The National Association of Securities Dealers Automated Quotations (NASDAQ);
o The London Stock Exchange (LSE); and
o The Johannesburg Stock Exchange (JSE).

US Government Institutions Enabling the Fraud

o US Presidency and Cabinet (under former President Biden)
o US Congressmen
o US Supreme Court Justices
o Securities and Exchange Commission

- US Department of Justice and Attorney General
- Federal Bureau of Investigation

There are 722 company and government perpetrators from the United States, who are implicated in the $1.42 trillion stock exchange fraud case.

The underlying crimes committed by the quoted companies are many, are known, and are supported and covered up by the aforementioned stock exchanges on which they trade. Some of the seven companies, including the Boeing Company, have in the past been found guilty of gross dishonesty and have been fined by their respective financial authorities on a number of occasions.

The fraud committed by the NYSE and NASDAQ, in concert with the American companies mentioned above, is further endorsed, enabled, and protected from prosecution by the very institution tasked with preventing fraud on the financial markets, namely: the US Securities and Exchange Commission (SEC). That supposed 'financial watchdog' is fully informed of, and shamefully integrated into, the criminality on the two American stock exchanges mentioned. The US Securities and Exchange Commission forms an integral part of the criminal enterprise, without which the criminal scheme would not be possible.

The US Securities and Exchange Commission is not partaking in the international fraud scheme in isolation or on its own whim or authority. The supposed financial 'supervisory body' has, in turn, been given the green light and is protected from prosecution for their criminal activity by the fully informed United States President and cabinet - namely that of President Biden from the former Administration. President Biden and his cabinet were fully engaged in the criminal enterprise and rendered criminal assistance to the US Securities and Exchange Commission (SEC) and the companies involved. President Biden and his cabinet enabled the respective stock exchanges (NYSE, NASDAQ) and the offending American companies of: Boeing, Ford, Alaska Air, Berkshire Hathaway, and Insurance Auto Auction, and provided a safe haven and passage and escape from justice to the criminal enterprise. At the time of publishing this book, it remains to be seen if President Trump will take the needed legal actions in a timely manner.

The US Securities and Exchange Commission has the ability to terminate the known and ongoing fraud. However, it is instead protecting the fraudsters from apprehension, trial, and punishment – thus enabling the ongoing fraud, amongst other crimes, with impunity.

The evident success of this sweeping criminal enterprise, in defrauding the world's financial markets and investors, stems from the fact that heads of state and heads of government across the world are seldom, if ever, held to account for their criminality, including United States Presidents. World leaders assist each other to escape justice. In their own countries, world leaders control the prosecutors, who, in turn, assist their leaders to escape justice by failing to prosecute law-breaking leaders. Additionally, in the United States, presidents enjoy impunity – by decree of the US Supreme Court. It is these facts that have hitherto ensured exemption to the dangerous and escalating criminality in the world's financial systems, as acutely demonstrated by this case of $1.42 trillion fraud, international organized crime, and crimes against humanity.

THE CRIMES

The $1.42 trillion international stock exchange fraud is ongoing and is facilitated by the host governments in which the companies and stock exchanges operate. From the crime of international fraud, the criminal enterprise has progressed on to other crimes in order to silence witnesses and cover up the ongoing fraud. Those crimes can be grouped as *crimes against the administration of justice* in the fraud case. A second grouping of crimes is the nationally *subversive crimes* of 'rebellion against the laws', and treason, stemming from the large number of perpetrators in each country acting in concert to defeat justice and to undermine the laws of their own country. A third group of crimes constitutes the *underlying crimes* of the 'international criminal enterprise'. These crimes underpin the $1.42 trillion fraud charges in that they were the crimes *not reported* to shareholders, *not investigated* by the authorities, and *not prosecuted* by willful prosecutors, so as to protect the criminals from the consequences of their crimes.

The continuing fraud and the continuing underlying crimes have yet to be terminated. These crimes will affect the share prices of the companies involved when they are eventually brought to light.

A comprehensive rendition of the underlying crimes of the 'international criminal enterprise', lying at the bottom of the $1.42 trillion international stock exchange fraud, is available to all serious investigators in *'The Dossier of Crimes'*. That digest comprehensively covers the history and impunity of the international criminal endeavor over a period of two and a half decades and comprises several thousand pages. Separate volumes cover the United States (USA), the United Kingdom (UK), and the Republic of South Africa (RSA).

Criminal charges were first filed with the authorities of each of the three countries involved, for their imperative action, as early as December 21, 2022. Charges have since been updated and include the following crimes or groups of crimes:

- o $1.42 trillion Stock Exchange Fraud.
- o Obstruction of Justice, in the fraud case.
- o Insurrection against the Laws and Treason, in the fraud case.

o Complicity in / Accessories After the Fact to the underlying crimes which gave rise to the ongoing fraud of $1.42 trillion, including crimes against humanity.

BOEING COMPANY / NYSE / NASDAQ / LSE FRAUD

The Boeing Company has a long history of criminal conduct. In the past 25 years alone, since 2000, Boeing has had 124 violations of the law. Its officials have not been taken to court criminally. Liability has been borne by its shareholders. The Boeing Company has paid $4.219 billion in fines for fraud, false claims, investor protection violations, benefit plan violations, aviation safety violations, financial offenses, government contracting offenses, employment-related offenses, and more. Boeing is, at the time of publishing, embroiled in a criminal case brought by the United States in the US District Court for the Northern District of Texas, on account of defrauding the Federal Aviation Administration Aircraft Evaluation Group. Trial and prosecution have at this time been set aside.

The Boeing Company trades its shares on the New York Stock Exchange, the NASDAQ, and the London Stock Exchange. The Boeing Company is presently, at the time of writing, committing massive fraud upon the international investing public and financial markets, in two ways:

1. A Failure to Report

Boeing and the Boeing Board of Directors have played a leading role in a broader and virulent criminal conspiracy involving the following unaddressed crimes:

> *Fraud on a large scale; obstruction of justice (20 years imprisonment for 18USC1519); theft of court record (5 years); tampering with a witness (20 years); retaliation against a witness (10 years); contempt of court; perjury; conspiracy to commit*

offenses (5 years); conspiracy to kidnap (life imprisonment); conspiracy to murder (life imprisonment); conspiracy against rights (10 years); deprivation of rights; misprision of felony (3 years); treason (imprisonment up to life or the death penalty); misprision of treason (7 years); seditious conspiracy (20 years); insurrection against the laws (10 years); accessory after the fact to offenses of their government co-conspirators as detailed in the 'Dossier of Crimes'; crimes against humanity of mass murder in the death of 507 people (life imprisonment or the death penalty); crimes against humanity of other inhumane acts in the grave injury of 189 innocent civilians.

None of the crimes committed by Boeing have been investigated and remain pending. These Boeing Company offenses are meticulously detailed in the 2,400-page 'Dossier of Crimes', USA, Volume III, Chapter 42.1. The dossier is filed with the courts, and the criminal offenses are public knowledge. The crimes and their cover-up have been perpetrated with the full knowledge and tacit consent of the United States President and Government, and the Washington State Government. The above offenses have not been investigated or prosecuted despite being filed with Presidents GW Bush, Obama, Biden, Trump, and their Administrations, the US Supreme Court and Chief Justice Roberts, and the US Congress. Boeing is illegally 'protected by the US Government' against prosecution for this lawlessness.

The Boeing Company has willfully failed to advise its investors that the above criminal charges are pending against the company and against the Board of Directors, as is their legal duty to report, pursuant Sections 17(a)(2) and 17(a)(3), and Item 401(f) of the US Securities Act. The Boeing Company has deliberately failed to advise its shareholders and prospective shareholders that its Board of Directors and multiple other officials could be arrested at any moment (bar for the illegal protection and impunity granted by US government officials). The Boeing Board of Directors willfully failed to advise its investors (and traders in its shares) of *all material facts* that impact, or potentially impact, its share price. That deliberate failure to report constitutes fraud.

2. Debarred from Doing Business

The Boeing Company and the Boeing Board of Directors have also played a leading role in a criminal conspiracy relating to the Boeing 737 MAX accidents and two further air accidents involving the death (mass murder) and injury (attempted murder) of 696 people. The US Congressional Committee investigating the MAX accidents confirmed that, quote: *"Boeing had a criminal conspiracy"* which precipitated the 737 MAX accidents. As Prosecutor Qui Tam prosecuting the above charges, I personally have significant evidence of *criminal conspiracy* perpetrated by Boeing in Washington State, in Boeing's attempts to kidnap and murder me. The Department of Justice charged the Company with one count of 'Conspiracy to defraud the United States' in its earlier non-prosecution agreement, which was violated by Boeing. Boeing pleaded guilty to one count of defrauding the FAA Aircraft Evaluation Group in its former Plea Agreement with the Department of Justice.

A major division of the Boeing Company, namely *Boeing Commercial Airplanes,* is located in Washington State. Washington State law forbids any company that has taken part in a *criminal conspiracy* to do business in that state. The Revised Code of Washington (RCW) clearly states in statute RCW 9A.08.030(5), quote:

> *"Every corporation, whether foreign or domestic, which shall violate any provision of RCW 9A.28.40, shall forfeit every right and franchise to do business*

in this state". [RCW 9A.28.40 refers to criminal conspiracy].

The Boeing Company is thus debarred from doing business in Washington State for violating the prohibition against criminal conspiracy. Yet, the Boeing Company and Boeing Commercial Airplanes (division) continue to do business there illegally, in flagrant violation of the law. Boeing continues to unlawfully build and sell aircraft, offer shares, pay salaries, do business with vendors, and so forth. And with every aircraft sold and every share offered or sold, they are in violation of the criminal statutes.

The Boeing Company has willfully failed to advise its shareholders and prospective shareholders that it is illegally doing business in Washington State, and that the unambiguous law requires it to forthwith close down its commercial airplane division in that State. That deliberate failure to advise its shareholders constitutes fraud.

Boeing's criminality and that of its directors *will undeniably devastate* its share price when these facts become public knowledge, as inevitably they must. These undisclosed and hidden facts, materially affecting the Boeing share price, constitute unmistakable *fraud committed* with every Boeing share that is offered and traded. The quantum of the fraud in respect of Boeing shares is equal to the value of the sudden investment loss, that is, the peak market capitalization value of the company over the period of fraud. That market capitalization, and thus the fraud, amounts to an astronomical $249.88 billion (the peak value taken on 21 December 2022).

THE FORD MOTOR COMPANY / NYSE / NASDAQ FRAUD

The Ford Motor Company has a history of criminal conduct. Ford Motor Company Directors and the Corporate Officers were informed by me, as Prosecutor Qui Tam, on September 15 and 28, and November 2, 2006, that their President and CEO of that time, Mr. Alan Mulally, had committed multiple and serious felonies acting in a major criminal conspiracy together with other conspirators from the Boeing Company. They were advised that information about the illegal conspiracy had been suppressed and that the crimes of the conspiracy had not been investigated or prosecuted.

Having been so informed, the Ford Directors and Officers were requested to take immediate steps in terms of their statutory duties under statute 18USC4, to report the criminal conspiracy to the appropriate law enforcement agencies that would take action thereon. Moreover, Ford Directors and Officers were requested to advise the Ford Motor Company's shareholders of the situation that very likely would have a material impact on the Company's share price when the issue becomes public knowledge – as corporate law dictates.

Ford Company Directors and Officers failed to report the crimes to the appropriate law enforcement agencies that would take action thereon, and failed to advise their shareholders and the public of the matter that would have a material impact on the company's share price. Ford Motor Company Directors and Officers conspired amongst themselves to suppress the information of the felonies and to cover up the crimes. The crimes committed by the former Ford President and CEO, Mr. Mulally, and his co-conspirators continued unchecked with the full knowledge and acquiescence of the Ford Directors. The criminal conspiracy within Ford to suppress information material to the Ford share price continued unabated. Consequently, on November 6, 2006, criminal charges were filed with the Department of Justice against the Ford Motor Company Directors and Corporate Officers at the time. Criminal charges were filed for violations of the following criminal statutes:

A Dirty U.S. Government Secret

18USC4 (Misprision of Felony); 18USC371 (Conspiracy to commit offense); 18USC3 (Accessory After the Fact, to the crimes of Ford President, Mr. Mulally); and for failure to inform shareholders of material information which could and would affect the share price; and for failure to ensure that shareholders be informed. (Documented with the US Supreme Court in the Dossier of Crimes, Volume III, Chapter 43).

None of the crimes have been investigated and remain pending. Details of the broader criminal conspiracy in which Ford's President was implicated and to which the Ford Board Members and Corporate Officers had become accessories to, can be found in the Dossier of Crimes USA, Volume III, Chapters 42.1.2 and 43, filed with the US Supreme Court. The Ford Motor Company's criminality was also reflected in the papers filed in the United States Supreme Court in the following two corruptly stifled cases: Case No. 05-140 (Anthony P. Keyter vs. George W. Bush), and Case No. 06-284 (*Anthony P. Keyter vs. 230 Government Officers*). These documents are a matter of public record.

Ford Company Directors and Officers were informed of the criminal charges that had been filed against them and against the Ford Motor Company. When the law takes its proper course, the criminal charges against the entire Board will have a profound impact upon the operations and the share price of the Ford Motor Company. The Directors were *again reminded* of their statutory and fiduciary duties to report that new fact to the investor public and to the shareholders and prospective shareholders of the company, and to the Securities and Exchange Commission.

At the time of publishing, the Ford Board of Directors has not reported the known material irregularities, despite the fact that the Board has been aware of criminal charges against Directors *since December 8, 2006.* They have not reported the fact that they have taken part in a 'conspiracy' and that Ford, like Boeing, may not do business in Washington State, yet they continue to illegally do business there. Their acts, and inaction where action was legally due, constitute fraud upon the international investing public. That fraud *has been ongoing for years since 2006* and takes place on a daily basis with every share that is traded. Indeed, every Ford tranche of shares traded is one count of fraud. That ongoing fraud has been entrenched in the Ford Motor Company since December 8, 2006, with the knowledge and consent of all Ford Motor Company Directors since that time, up to the present day.

Such unrepentant and sustained criminality over almost two decades will in all likelihood lead to the loss of the Ford Motor Company business license when the criminality is finally brought to book, with the subsequent loss to shareholders of the value of the peak Ford Market Capitalization value during the period (less the break-up value of the company).

The Ford Motor Company (Ford) is listed on both the New York Stock Exchange and the NASDAQ exchange. On 21 December 2006, both the NYSE and NASDAQ were informed of material irregularities at the Ford Motor Company, which the Ford Directors failed to report to the police and financial markets. The Directors and Corporate Secretary of the NYSE and NASDAQ were informed that: those unreported material irregularities were very likely to have a profound impact upon the Ford Motor Company share price, that it represented a large potential loss to stockholders, and that intervention was urgently required.

The two stock exchanges failed to act to caution the markets or to suspend trading until the material irregularities were removed or publicly reported. A further reminder and warning of fraud perpetrated by the Ford Motor Company went out from me, as Prosecutor Qui Tam, to the NYSE and NASDAQ exchanges on 20 September 2007; and a third caution was sent to the NYSE on 11

March 2008. Each time, no action was taken by the exchanges regarding the fraud being perpetrated by the Ford Motor Company. Hence, the fraud is continuing unremittingly to this day (the time of publishing) with the knowledge, sanction, and participation of the two stock exchanges, by them providing a safe haven and passage.

The highest market capitalization during the period occurred on 10 January 2022, and the NYSE / NASDAQ / Ford Motor Company fraud is valued at $100.96 billion.

ALASKA AIR GROUP / NYSE FRAUD

Alaska Air Group is listed on the NYSE. Alaska Air Group has a history of criminal conduct. On 14 March 2022, criminal charges were filed in the US Supreme Court against the Alaska Air Group for willful criminal interference and obstruction of the United States judicial process, in the 'Boeing Company Mass Murder Case' filed in the US Supreme Court. The obstruction of justice was committed through retaliation against a court witness in the Boeing case. This section addresses crimes committed by Alaska Airlines through its Board of Directors and Executive Leadership, on behalf of (and it is believed at the behest of) the Boeing Company. Those crimes joined the Alaska perpetrators to the crimes of the Boeing Company in the aforementioned case. The charges are detailed in the Dossier of Crimes, USA, Volume III, Chapter 42.3, filed in the US Supreme Court and are public knowledge. The charges include violations of the following United States Code and Revised Code of Washington statutes:

> *18USC1513 – Retaliating against a witness, victim, or an informant; 18USC371 – Conspiracy to commit offense; 18USC241 – Conspiracy against rights; 18USC2384 – Seditious Conspiracy; 18USC2383 – Insurrection against the laws of the United States; 18USC4 – Misprision of Felony; 18USC1001 –*

$1.42 Trillion Stock Exchange Fraud

Fraud; RCW 9A.08.030(5) Corporate liability concerning conspiracy.

None of the crimes have been investigated and remain pending. Alaska Air Board of Directors and Executive Leadership Team acted in concert to commit the offense of retaliating against a Supreme Court witness, victim, or an informant (see statute 18USC1513), and such persons did act in unison, or omitted to act where action was necessary, to effect the object of their combined conspiracy (to defeat the course of justice in the Boeing Company Murder Case), in violation of statute 18USC371 addressing conspiracy. Their conspiracy also violated the Revised Code of Washington (RCW) where they are headquartered. Again, statute RCW 9A.08.030(5), addressing corporate liability concerning conspiracy, states:

> *Every corporation, whether foreign or domestic, that shall violate any provision of RCW 9A.28.40 shall forfeit every right and franchise to do business in this state. [RCW 9A.28.40 refers to criminal conspiracy].*

Thus, statute RCW 9A.08.030(5) forbids Alaska Air to do business in Washington State. The serious charges against the entire Alaska Board of Directors and executive team will most certainly affect the company's share price when their arrest takes place. The knowledge that Alaska Air, headquartered in Washington State, may not do business in that state and is continuing to illegally do business there will certainly affect their stock price when that news becomes public knowledge.

The Alaska Air Group Board of Directors and Executive Leadership Team had a legal duty under SEC Regulations S-K, Item 401(f) to report to the SEC and shareholders irregularities that could profoundly affect the Alaska Air stock price. The Alaska Air Board of Directors and Executive Leadership Team had a duty to advise their shareholders, potential future investors, the SEC, and the

NYSE that, pursuant to Washington State law RCW 9A.08.030(5), Alaska Air was prohibited from doing business in Washington State.

Knowing that there were material irregularities that would affect the Alaska Air share price when the criminality (and likely arrest) of the Alaska Air Board of Directors and Executive Leadership Team comes to public attention, as inevitably it will, Alaska and its Board failed to make the announcements required by law. That concealment of material facts constitutes *fraud* upon shareholders and any potential buyers and the public, in violation of statute 18USC1001 regarding fraud. Continuing to do business in Washington State while the law disbars Alaska Air from doing so *constitutes fraud* upon their shareholders and upon the State.

As mentioned, that fraud upon shareholders was eventually reported to the Securities Exchange Commission (and by implication to the NYSE) by me on 29 July 2022, while acting as Prosecutor Qui Tam. Neither institution took affirmative action to terminate the fraud. That combined fraud by Alaska Air and the SEC and NYSE continues day after day with SEC and NYSE sanction and knowledge, with every share that is traded since 25 February 2022; with every airline ticket sold since that date; with every new aircraft bought from Boeing; with every aspect of business done illegally by Alaska Air in Washington State. Every business transaction is one count of fraud. The highest value of the fraud is taken as the highest market capitalization of the company since 25 February 2022.

The value of the Alaska Air/ NYSE fraud equates to $7.24 billion on 21 March 2022.

BERKSHIRE HATHAWAY / IAA-RITCHIE BROS FRAUD

Berkshire Hathaway Inc. and its 67 subsidiary companies, including the insurance company Geico, together with International

Auto Auctions (IAA) Inc., acted in concert in a criminal enterprise to cover up insurance fraud and criminal profiteering.

Criminal charges were filed in the US Supreme Court on 22 September 2023, against the Berkshire Hathaway Company board of directors and the boards of 67 of its subsidiary companies (including the Geico company), for their role in the cover-up of a fraudulent criminal enterprise. Criminal charges were also filed against Insurance Auto Auctions Inc (IAA)-Ritchie Bros, its directors, and some personnel, who acted in criminal conspiracy with Geico insurance in repeated and deliberate attempts to steal and resell a Toyota Highlander sports utility vehicle, and for criminal conspiracy to cover up that offense. The charges stem from criminality in connection with Geico insurance company claim # 0174417660101012 and IAA Stock # 37271117.

Beyond the initial attempts at auto theft and actual insurance fraud, a slew of other criminal offenses followed sequentially. Beyond the initial perpetrators, several other employees, managers, company directors, and executive team members of Berkshire/Geico/IAA-Ritchie Bros also acted to cover up the crimes and to protect the initial perpetrators from investigation and prosecution. The criminal endeavor thus spread and multiplied rapidly into a potent criminal enterprise.

Criminal charges that were filed on September 20, 2023, with the FBI in Seattle, Washington, and with Gig Harbor Police in Washington State, against the initial perpetrators and board of directors of the companies, include:

Attempted car theft on six counts, in violation of the Revised Code of Washington: Theft RCW 9A.56.020(b); Theft of motor vehicle RCW 9A.56.065; Theft with Intent to Resell - RCW 9A.56.340; Trafficking in Stolen Property - RCW 9A.82.050; Criminal Profiteering - RCW

9A.82.010(r). In violation of the United States Code: 18USC2312 - Transportation of Stolen Vehicles; 18USC2313 – Sale of Stolen Vehicles.

Theft by false pretenses of an estimated $50,000 in insurance premiums over 34 years, in violation of: RCW 9A.56.020; Illegal dealing in Premiums – RCW 48.30.190(1); Misrepresentation of Policies – RCW 48.30.090; False Information and Advertising - RCW 48.30.040; Misconduct of Officers and Employees - RCW 48.30.120(3); Unfair Practices - RCW 48.30.010. US Code violations: Wire Fraud – 18USC1343.

Washington Administrative Code Violations: WAC 284-30-390 (7) - Re additional loss discovered during repair; WAC 30- 392 – All information on initial inspection; WAC 284.30.380 (7) - Insurer responsible for Fair Market Value.

Misprision of Felony in violation of the United States Code, statute 18USC4.
Conspiracy to Commit Offense: in violation of the Revised Code of Washington, RCW9A.28.040; and United States Code 18USC371.

Securities and Exchange Act Violations: Item 401(f); Sections 17(a)(2) and 17(a)(3); Securities and stock exchange fraud of $813.14 billion.

These crimes are detailed in the charges filed with the US Supreme Court in the Dossier of Crimes, USA, Volume III, Chapter 50.11.5b. None of the crimes have been investigated and remain pending. As directors, executives, and managers under the Berkshire Hathaway holding company, and directors of IAA/ Ritchie Bros, the perpetrators had a duty, pursuant the Securities Act Item 401(f), to report and disclose to the public, to shareholders and to prospective future shareholders, to the Securities Exchange Commission, and to stock exchanges on which they are listed, the fact that their directors and executives are named subjects of a pending criminal proceeding. That fact will have a devastating effect on each company's share price and should have been reported. The directors deliberately failed to perform that legal duty to the detriment of all those concerned and to whom those reports should have gone, especially the stock exchanges upon which their companies are listed and trading.

The omissions of the directors of the Berkshire Hathaway companies, and of Geico, and the IAA/ Ritchie Bros directors, their deliberate failure to make the needed reports violate of the Code of Federal Regulations and the Securities Act, namely: (a) The Code of Federal Regulations, 17CFR§229.401(f), {or Item 401(f) of SEC Regulations S-K}; and (b) Sections 17(a)(2) of the Securities Act – Misstatement liability; and (c) Section 17(a)(3) of the Securities Act – Scheme liability.

Section 17(a) of the Securities Act

Section 17(a) is the key anti-fraud provision in the Securities Act. Section 17(a) makes it unlawful to 'employ any scheme to defraud, or obtain money or property, by using misstatements or *omissions*'. Section 17(a)(2) applies "in the offer or sale of any securities".

As stated, the directors and executive officers of the companies omitted to report to the public that their directors / executive officers are named in criminal proceedings (a copy of the charges of which they had in their possession). That also means that the directors and executive officers omitted to report that fact to their prospective shareholders, to the SEC, and to the stock exchanges upon which some of them trade. Again, Section 17(a)(2) of the Securities Act applies "in the offer or sale of any securities".

The public reports stating that directors are named subjects in criminal proceedings, and the fact that Berkshire / IAA-Ritchie Bros will be under investigation for criminal conduct of a systematic pattern of fraud/theft and other criminal violations, will significantly impact their share price. The omission to report those material facts to the markets and to the authorities, in violation of Item 401(f) of SEC Regulations S-K, constitutes fraud, as stated above. That fraud will potentially cause harm and loss to investment markets to those unsuspecting buyers or sellers of the shares in the perpetrator companies who do not possess knowledge of those material facts. The potential quantum of that fraud is equal to the maximum market capitalization of the company on the stock exchanges.

In the case of *Berkshire Hathaway*, the stock exchange market capitalization and fraud figure is $807.81 billion, as established on September 18, 2023, at 4:03 pm. In the case of *Insurance Auto Auctions-Ritchie Bros.*, the stock exchange market capitalization and fraud figure is $5.33 billion, as established on September 18, 2023.

The stock exchange fraud perpetrated by this criminal enterprise is $807.81 billion plus $5.33 billion, giving a *total fraud figure on the* stock exchanges *of $813.14 billion.*

FRAUD COMMITTED BY THE STOCK EXCHANGES

There were three stock exchanges (the New York Stock Exchange, the NASDAQ, the London Stock Exchange) that were advised of the criminal enterprise involving the *five listed* American companies (Boeing, the Ford Motor Company, and Alaska Air Group, Berkshire Hathaway, IAA-Ritchie Bros), as follows:

$1.42 Trillion Stock Exchange Fraud

In the case of the Boeing Company's Material Irregularities and Fraud:

- o The London Stock Exchange (LSE) was informed as far back as 22 October 2013 of Boeing fraud on the LSE; and again on 7 June 2021, 22 November 2022, and 27 November 2022.
- o The New York Stock Exchange (NYSE) was informed regarding Boeing Company fraud and other irregularities that would affect their stock price on 8 March 2006, 5 September 2007, 11 March 2008, 22 October 2013, 7 June 2021, 12 December 2022, and 14 December 2022.
- o The NASDAQ Stock Exchange was informed regarding Boeing Company fraud and other irregularities that would affect their stock price on 8 March 2006, 5 September 2007, 11 March 2008, 22 October 2013, 7 June 2021, and 14 December 2022.

In the case of the Ford's Material Irregularities and Fraud:

- o The NASDAQ was informed on December 21, 2006, of Ford's criminality and their failure to report irregularities to stockholders.
- o NYSE was informed on December 21, 2006, of Ford's criminality and their failure to report irregularities to stockholders.

In the case of the Alaska Air Group's Material Irregularities and Fraud:

- o The Securities Exchange Commission and, by implication, the NYSE were informed on July 29, 2022, of Alaska's criminality and their failure to report irregularities to stockholders.

In the case of the Berkshire Hathaway/ Geico/ IAA-Ritchie Bros fraud:

○ The NYSE, NASDAQ, and LSE were informed of the fraud and criminal endeavor on September 22, 2023.

Once knowing that the five quoted American companies had committed serious crimes which needed a cautionary statement to be issued to the markets, and knowing that the five delinquent quoted companies or groups had not issued these 'cautionaries' and were thus defrauding the markets, these stock exchanges had an unequivocal duty to suspend the share-trading in those companies or to delist the companies. The stock exchanges willfully failed to do that in consideration of their own profitable financial situation with those companies. Instead, they provided the five corrupt, quoted, American companies a safe haven and passage within which to continue their fraud. The stock exchanges covered up the crimes and placed an enormous business risk upon unsuspecting shareholders. The stock exchanges themselves thus became co-perpetrators in the listed American companies' fraud upon the international financial / investment markets.

In most cases, the fraud by the stock exchanges lingered for many years and is still active at the time of publishing. Every tranche of shares sold fraudulently by sanctioning the failure to report material facts concerning those shares is a new count of fraud. At any time, when the underlying crimes of the five American companies are exposed, investigated, and prosecuted by the authorities, investors and prospective investors potentially face very large losses.

Fraud perpetrated by the three Stock Exchanges regarding their own companies

Similarly, the stock exchanges, having perpetrated enormous fraud for many years and facing a severe risk of *collapse,* shareholders in the stock exchange companies themselves (NYSE, NASDAQ, LSE), face very large losses. A stock exchange company that has defrauded the markets and defrauded its own shareholders by tens of billions of dollars over so many years cannot expect to retain a business license. That would be most unwise.

The stock exchanges (as companies) in turn have a duty to issue a cautionary to their own shareholders and prospective shareholders, but have willfully failed to do so. The potential losses to those shareholders in the stock exchange companies are equal to the highest market capitalization of each stock exchange company over the fraud period. Those figures are:

- o New York Stock Exchange / ICE: 25 October 2021$77.81 billion
- o NASDAQ: As of 1 November 2021, $35.31 billion
- o London Stock Exchange $ 49 billion

US GOVERNMENT ACCOMPLICES IN THE STOCK EXCHANGE FRAUD

Government Officials were Informed

Through a series of letters that I addressed to the US government authorities, they were informed them of the ongoing crimes and fraud committed by the five lawbreaking American companies and the three stock exchanges. In particular, they were informed of the fraud relating to the unlawful offering and trading of Boeing, Ford, Alaska, Berkshire, and IAA-Ritchie Bros shares on the three stock exchanges involved, namely: the New York, the NASDAQ, and the London stock exchanges. Over a period of almost two decades, consecutive United States Presidents and their cabinets were informed in a long series of communications and criminal charges of *ongoing crimes, including fraud,* perpetrated by Boeing and Ford. Those institutions include but are not limited to the White House, the Department of Justice, the Federal Bureau of

Investigation, the US Supreme Court, all Members of the US Congress, and the Securities and Exchange Commission. During 2022, these same US institutions were informed of the Alaska Air Group crimes, including stock exchange fraud. These same institutions were also advised of the New York Stock Exchange and NASDAQ fraud, and on 22 September 2023, of the Berkshire Hathaway, IAA-Ritchie Bros fraud.

A Legal Duty to Act

Having been informed of fraud on the three stock exchanges and fraud perpetrated by the five lawbreaking American companies upon the investing public, the US government officials and their institutions had a statutory and a moral duty to suspend the fraudulent sale of shares; to terminate the fraud upon international investors; and to bring the fraudsters (the five companies and two US stock exchanges) to justice in the USA.

The President(s) in turn had a duty to tend to the faithful execution of the laws upon the unlawful operations of the five American companies; and the execution of the laws upon the errant NYSE and NASDAQ exchanges. The FBI has a duty to investigate potential offenses against the United States. The US Attorney General and the Department of Justice have a duty to prosecute *for all offenses* against the United States. Congress has a duty to oversee the upholding of the rule of law and the performance of duties by the executive branch. The Supreme Court Justices had a duty to address the crimes under statute 18USC4 and other statutes. It is the very raison d'être of the Securities and Exchange Commission to prevent fraud.

Deliberate Failure to Act

Despite being informed on numerous occasions of the crimes and fraud on the NYSE, NASDAQ, and LSE, the US Government institutions and officials ignored that fraud, condoned the crimes committed by these malevolent companies, provided safe haven and passage to those companies and their law-breaking officials, and rendered criminal assistance to them to continue to defraud the investing public in concert with the stock exchanges. The United States Government perpetrators have willfully taken no action to terminate the fraud or to suspend the unlawful trading of shares on the stock exchanges involved.

THE COMBINED QUANTUM OF FRAUD

The original fraud figure presented in a criminal complaint filed on 21 December 2022, of "$144 billion, was amended and increased by additional fraudsters and by considering the highest potential fraud during the period under consideration. As of 22 September 2023, the total fraud on four stock exchanges, perpetrated by the seven listed companies (Boeing, Ford, Alaska Air, Barclays, and BAGL/Absa, Berkshire Hathaway and IAA-Ritchie Bros) and by the four corrupt stock exchange companies (NYSE, NASDAQ, LSE, and JSE), is as follows:

1. The Boeing Company / NYSE /NASDAQ / LSE fraud: $249.88 billion
2. The Ford Motor Company / NYSE / NASDAQ fraud:$100.96 billion
3. Alaska Air Group / NYSE fraud: $7.24 billion
4. Berkshire Hathaway/ IAA-Ritchie Bros $ 813.14 billion
5. Barclays / NYSE / NASDAQ / LSE fraud: $75.71 billion
6. Barclays Africa Group / Absa Group / JSE fraud: $11 billion
7. New York Stock Exchange / ICE – 25 Oct 2021)$77.81 billion
8. NASDAQ: (as of 1 November 2021) $35.31 billion
9. Johannesburg Stock Exchange $ 0.55 billion
10. London Stock Exchange $ 49 billion

TOTAL FRAUD: $1.4206 TRILLION

THE LAWS VIOLATED

Fraud is defined as a deliberate scheme to obtain financial or similar gain by using false statements, misrepresentations, ***concealment of important information,*** or deceptive conduct. In the case of Boeing, Ford, Alaska Air, Barclays, Berkshire, and IAA/Ritchie Bros (and their government enablers), it is the concealment from their shareholders or prospective shareholders of important information, in order to obtain financial gain, which constitutes the fraud. Boeing, Ford, Alaska Air, Barclays, Berkshire, and IAA/Ritchie Bros fraudulent offer and sale of shares are addressed by the following statutes.

> ***18USC1343 - Wire Fraud:*** *"Whoever, having devised or intending to devise any scheme or artifice to defraud, or for obtaining money or property by means of false or fraudulent pretenses, representations, or promises, transmits or causes to be transmitted by means of wire, radio, or television communication in interstate or foreign commerce, any writings, signs, signals, pictures, or sounds for the purpose of executing such scheme or artifice, shall be fined under this title or imprisoned not more than **20 years,** or both....."* [Note: the federal wire fraud statute specifically mentions wire, radio, and television communications, but it also includes many fraud offenses involving computers and the internet].

> ***15USC77Q – Fraudulent Interstate Transactions***
> *It shall be unlawful for any person in the offer or sale of any securities ... or any security-based swap agreement ... by the use of any means or instruments of transportation or communication in interstate commerce or by use of the mails, directly or indirectly – (1) to employ any device, scheme or artifice to defraud, or (2) to obtain money or property by **means of any untrue statement of a material fact or any omission to state a material fact***

302

necessary in order to make the statements made, in light of the circumstances under which they were made, not misleading; or (3) to engage in any transaction, practice, or course of business which operates or would operate as a fraud or deceit upon the purchaser.

Securities Act, Section 17(a)(2); *[and/or, The Exchange Act, Rule 10b-5].*
Section 17(a)(2) of the Securities Act of 1933 prohibits obtaining money or property by means of an untrue statement of a material fact; or an omission of a material fact necessary to make statements not misleading in the offer or sale of securities.

18USC371 - Conspiracy to Commit Offense
If two or more persons conspire either to commit any offense against the United States, or to defraud the United States, or any agency thereof in any manner or for any purpose, and one or more of such persons do any act to effect the object of the conspiracy, each shall be fined under this title or imprisoned not more than seven years, or both.

The company fraudsters committed fraud as principal offenders in terms of the US statutes 18USC1343, and 15USC77q, the Securities Act 17(a)(2); and 18USC371. The Government officials who had a duty but deliberately failed to address and terminate the fraud were rendered accomplices to the ongoing Boeing, Ford, Alaska Air, Berkshire, and IAA/Ritchie Bros fraud. As stated above, there are 722-plus United States company and government principal perpetrators implicated in the $1.42 trillion stock exchange fraud case. Each principal perpetrator directly took part in the fraud. Each accomplice sanctioned the fraud, enabled it, gave safe haven and passage to the fraudsters; or assisted by covering up the crime and assisting the perpetrators to escape justice. Again, they include but are not limited to the White House, the Department of Justice, the Federal Bureau of Investigation, the US Supreme Court, all Members of the US Congress, and the Securities and Exchange Commission.

The lawless acts committed en masse by the more than 722 United States principal perpetrators, and then their accomplices, join with and augment an underlying, widespread, and virulent *'insurrection or rebellion against the laws of the United States'* in violation of statute 18USC2383, as described across the pages of this chronicle. It is part and parcel of the United States government and industry modus operandi.

Each United States perpetrator in this matter has deliberately failed to address and terminate the fraud and thus the underpinning insurrection against the laws; or is otherwise party to the rebellion for adding to the group lawlessness. Each United States perpetrator has protected his/her fellow perpetrators from prosecution for failing to report the crimes or failing to bring them to justice. And each US perpetrator has thereby given aid and comfort to domestic enemies of the United States – the insurrectionists in the rebellion against the laws of the United States (not the 6th of January 2021 insurrection). And thereby, each US perpetrator has violated the statute on treason, 18USC2381, prohibiting the giving of aid and comfort to domestic enemies of the United States. And, pursuant to the United States Code 18USC2381, each US perpetrator is guilty of treason and *"shall suffer death, or shall be imprisoned not less than five years and fined under this title but not less than $10,000; and shall be incapable of holding any office under the United States"*. That is the law of the land.

In accordance with statutes 18USC2381 concerning treason, 18USC2383 concerning insurrection against the laws, and the 14th Amendment of the Constitution, Section 3, the US perpetrators may not hold office under the United States. Considering the top government positions presently held by a large number of the United States perpetrators - by President(s) and their cabinet(s), by Attorney Generals and DOJ officials, by Congressmen, by Justices of the Supreme Court - the United States Government will continue to be unlawful in terms of the US Constitution if the stock exchange fraud and insurrection against the laws is not addressed and terminated.

The US Government's dirty secret, as summarized in the next chapter, must be exposed and dealt with, by the full force of the law.

Chapter 14
A Dirty Government Secret

'The number of crimes committed in this seditious conspiracy is thus 15,000 x 67 x 15,000 = 15 billion crimes – and counting. These are sobering statistics and represent a powerful insurrection within the government, against the laws of the United States'.
Extract From Chapter 14.

SUBVERSIVE AND VIOLENT CRIMES BY GOVERNMENT OFFICIALS

What then, in summary, is the disgraceful United States Government secret that lends title to this real-life account? Simply, it is the legal verities, collectively, which I have been talking about. 'The dirty secret' in plain language, in legal definition, in shame to this otherwise ethical nation, and in dishonor upon the good-natured American people, is this:

> *The United States Government and more than 15,000 of its malfeasant officials are culpable in a large series of grave and unaddressed criminal offenses, perpetrated with impunity.*

> *The offenses of these top government officials include complicity in, and enabling, Boeing's mass murder of 507 people, attempted murder of 189; and ongoing conspiracy to kill a U.S. Supreme Court witness. Concealed financial crimes include $1.42 trillion in stock exchange fraud. Concealed subversive crimes include seditious conspiracy, insurrection against the laws, and treason against the nation.*

A Dirty Government Secret

These latter subversive crimes render the United States Government and its top officials illegitimate in terms of the highest law of the land - the United States Constitution.

The sweeping insurrection against the laws, active within the government and the courts of the United States and described in the pages of this book, started with the 'unaddressed' crimes of a single judge. The situation existing today shows how far that unaddressed deed has travelled. Through some 14,000 appeals to the malfeasant government officials, to address and terminate the ongoing criminality, I have kept the government officials fully informed of the escalating criminal endeavor. It has been allowed to continue with impunity for two and a half decades and through the Administrations of four presidencies. Originating as it did in a Washington State court case filed in August of 2000, the 25-year-old rebellion from within the government, against the United States of America, against its constitution, its laws, and its people, is *ongoing and thriving* and has yet to be terminated. Some 352 proceedings in 62 court cases have failed to bring an end to the lawlessness.

Officials implicated over the past 25 years include President George W Bush and his Administration and every president and cabinet member from him on forward, including: every FBI Director, every US Attorney General, every FAA Director; every Congressman, every US Supreme Court Justice and many more state and federal judges, to name but a few.

Those government officials, acting in concert with industry officials, have combined and cooperated to provide *'impunity'* to common criminals in their midst. Consecutive Administrations, Congress, and the Courts, have suppressed all investigation of the extensive criminal endeavor and have shielded the perpetrators from punishment, because these institutions and their officials, themselves, are implicated in the crimes.

At the time of publishing this book, there remains in American society a large parcel of criminal offenses which has yet to be investigated and prosecuted. The crimes are meticulously detailed in the 2,400 pages of Volumes I to III of the tome titled: *'The Dossier of Crimes'*. Some 240 criminal complaints covered in the dossier provide meticulous details of the 67 different offenses (not counting the number of counts of each offense). The crimes have been perpetrated in the methods of a criminal conspiracy, as defined by statute 18USC371. By the nature of such criminal conspiracy, one party performed one part of the criminal act, and another performed the other part. Every conspirator knew about the other's crimes and had a legal duty to address them. Having willfully failed their legal duty to terminate it, every conspirator is thus culpable under the law for the offenses of every other conspirator in the extensive criminal endeavor.

> *The number of crimes committed in this seditious conspiracy is thus 15,000 x 67 x 15,000 =* **15 billion crimes** *– and counting. These are sobering statistics and represent a powerful insurrection within the government, against the laws of the United States. Combined with the proclivity to violence, such acts constitute seditious conspiracy and treason against the United States.*

Despite this dire state of affairs, there has been no investigation or prosecution, the trap set for my kidnap and murder remains firmly in place, and the criminal conspiracy continues unabated at the time of publishing. The ongoing, but concealed, crimes pose a definite danger and acutely affect the flying public and investing public.

The Dossier of Crimes, a document open to the public, lies hidden in the White House and the Cabinet, the Department of

Justice and the FBI, the Securities Exchange Commission, both houses of Congress, and numerous courts, including the US Supreme Court, which has 34 copies. The Department of Justice has 93 concealed copies of that Dossier of Crimes.

THE ESSENCE OF TREASON

The US Constitution defines treason as specific acts, namely "levying war against the United States", **OR** "adhering to their enemies, giving them aid and comfort". Enemies of the United States, as applied in this case, are persons who have engaged in subversive acts such as the seditious conspiracy against the United States and engaged in the insurrection against its laws, as described in the earlier chapters of this book. Aid and comfort to those enemies is taken to be: providing a safe haven and passage, protection from prosecution, cover-up of their crimes, and assisting their escape from punishment for criminal wrongdoing.

These acts, and the hostile intent with which they were committed, have impaired and undermined the legal authority and power of the United States. Even the omission to perform legal duty, the willful failure to report known offenses; the willful failure to provide constitutional due process of law, and to provide for the protection of the laws to the American people, demonstrates the hostile intent of malfeasant officials towards the country. The statute addressing treason, 18USC2381, unambiguously states:

> **Treason, 18USC2381:** *"Whoever, owing allegiance to the United States, levies war against them or adheres to their enemies, giving them aid and comfort within the United States or elsewhere, is guilty of treason and shall suffer death, or shall be imprisoned not less than five years and fined under this title but not less than $10,000; and shall be incapable of holding any office under the United States".*

The obligation for allegiance of the government conspirators to the United States is evident from their government oath of office. The obligation of allegiance for all conspirators, government officials or otherwise, is to be found in the tacit agreement between individuals and the United States, in terms of which the United States confers its protection upon the individual citizens in return for their undertaking to obey the laws of the country. Each one of the more than 15,000 US government officials involved in this insurrection against the laws has taken an oath before God and the nation to avow their allegiance to the United States.

Each of the government officials involved has an individual and undivided collective duty to defend the United States against its enemies, foreign or domestic. Each government official involved has willfully failed to defend the United States and its people against subversive insurgents from within, domestic enemies, who are bent on rebellion against the laws of the country. Each has instead given aid and comfort to the insurrection against the laws and has protected the insurrectionists from prosecution, assisting known criminals to escape justice. And every one of the 15,000 officials so implicated has committed an unmitigated act of treason against the United States of America.

Charges of treason were thus compiled by me acting as Prosecutor Qui Tam, and taken directly to the courts pursuant to my duties under the statute on misprision of treason, 18USC2382, in the absence of any intention shown by the constituted authorities to investigate or prosecute.

DEBARRED FROM HOLDING OFFICE

The United States Constitution is clear on the matter: no person who has taken part in an insurrection against the laws shall hold any government office.

The 14th Amendment of the United States Constitution
unambiguously states in Section 3:

> *No person shall be a Senator or Representative in Congress, or elector of President and Vice President, **or hold any office,** civil or military, under the United States, or under any state, who, having previously taken an oath, as a member of Congress, or as an officer of the United States, or as a member of any state legislature, or as an executive or judicial officer of any state, to support the Constitution of the United States, shall have engaged in insurrection or rebellion against the same, or given aid or comfort to the enemies thereof. But Congress may, by a vote of two-thirds of each House, remove such disability.*

In addition to the Constitution, ***Statute 18USC2383 on Insurrection or Rebellion against the laws*** unambiguously states:

> *Whoever incites, sets on foot, assists, or engages in any rebellion or insurrection against the authority of the United States **or the laws thereof,** or gives aid or comfort thereto, shall be fined under this title or imprisoned not more than ten years, or both; and shall be **incapable of holding any office** under the United States.*

And again, the statute on ***Treason 18USC2381,*** quoted above, unambiguously states that anyone:

> *"guilty of treason .... shall be **incapable of holding any office** under the United States."*

At the time of writing, more than 15,000-plus US federal and state officials have breached these statutes, yet they have illegally remained in their positions of power, masquerading as legitimate government officials, from whence they continue to rebel against the United States and its laws. Holding office, as they do or as they did, in disregard and violation of the United States Constitution and criminal statutes, rendered or renders the top office holders in the former or present Administrations, in the Judicial Branch, and in Congress, **unlawful.** Holding office illegally, in violation of the Constitution and the laws forbidding such an act, renders the actions of their office *illegitimate.*

AN UNLAWFUL U.S. GOVERNMENT

Pursuant to the succinct definition in the Constitution of the United States of America, the United States Government has been *'illegitimate'* and is so at the time of publishing, and has held *no lawful power*, nationally, over several Administrations. All actions, transactions, treaties, laws, decisions, and agreements made or taken by the United States Administration, Supreme Court, and Congress during the unlawful government period are unlawful and thus null and void, including all court rulings.

This veritable fact also has international ramifications. Under an illegitimate United States Government, the Permanent Membership of the United States to the UN Security Council is unlawful. Furthermore, the United States' presidency of the UN Security Council in March 2021 and in August 2023 was unlawful. These facts rendered the UN Security Council unlawful during those months of illegitimacy and at any other time while it had or has an unlawful Permanent Member or President. That includes all actions, all transactions, all treaties, and all agreements and decisions made or taken by the UN Security Council under an illegitimate Security Council President or Permanent Member.

The United States Government is not illegitimate because of fraudulent elections, as was controversially claimed in recent times. The United States Government is illegitimate because of subversive crimes perpetrated against the United States by its top officials. The top officials from all three branches of the United States Government under former Presidents George W Bush, Barack

Obama, Joe Biden, and Donald Trump, blatantly and willfully engaged in the crimes and may not hold or may not have held office under the United States.

As stated, this situation has attendant ramifications internationally, in particular where the United States plays a leading role in organizations like the United Nations Security Council, NATO, and global financial institutions. Lest the illegitimacy of the United States Government affect the legitimacy of those institutions, an illegitimate United States is compelled to withdraw from those institutions until such time as lawful government is restored under the dictates of the United States Constitution.

FURTHER CONSEQUENCES

The US Government, being an illegitimate government, which is maintaining an illegitimate armed force, causes that armed force to be *a mercenary force.* The Geneva Conventions, in Article 5, avers that States Parties (in this case, the United States) shall not recruit, use, finance, or train mercenaries and shall prohibit such activities in accordance with the provisions of the present Geneva Convention.

Any deaths that occur involving the illegitimate United States armed forces, including NATO operations, is a war crime of willful killing in terms of the Rome Statute of the International Criminal Court, Article 8 (bis 3) (g), which states:

> *"The sending by or on behalf of a State of armed bands, groups, irregulars or mercenaries, which carry out acts of armed force against another state of such gravity as to amount to acts listed above [willful killing], or its substantial involvement therein".*

Thus, pursuant to the Geneva Conventions, the illegitimate US Government will be held culpable of war crimes if US (mercenary) forces cause any deaths in willful killing, as described above.

The United States is an illegitimate government in the informal 'G20 grouping of nations', in the World Trade Organization, and in multiple other world forums. On these international platforms, the United States promotes its unlawful, iniquitous agendas, as opposed to the benign universal inclusiveness sought by these organizations.

For the sake of the United States' and the world's economy, for the safety and security of people everywhere, and for the universal principle of the rule of law, this lawless situation can only be addressed and terminated by bringing all insurrectionists against the laws of the United States to justice.

*****

Incumbent state and federal officials, including President Trump and his Administration, and including U.S. Attorney General Pam Bondi, have the duty to address and correct this aberration in government and law, and the cataclysmic consequences facing the American nation today, with its concomitant violent impact upon society.

The question is: Will they? Or will they swell the ranks of the government insurrection against the laws?

A CONSTITUTIONAL CRISIS

The conclusions discussed hitherto, unambiguously point to the United States of America being in the midst of a *constitutional crisis.* This constitutional crisis has existed since the ongoing 'insurrection against the laws' first appeared in the ranks of United States Government officials and in the ranks of 627 state and federal government institutions, some 25 years ago.

A Dirty Government Secret

Enquiringly, one may ask: what is a *'constitutional crisis'*? Although there is no legal definition for the term, or even an agreed-upon informal definition, legal experts and historians often point to any one of several factors that can create a 'constitutional crisis'. Some of those factors referred to, are:

o A systemic failure, where the system of checks and balances fails to resolve a serious political dispute. This can occur when one branch of government oversteps its legal authority, and the other branches are either unwilling or unable to stop it.

o Defiance of law or court orders by a branch of government, where that branch openly refuses to comply with the law or a binding judicial order.

o Gaps in a constitution, or vagueness which causes ambiguity that prevents institutions from resolving a problem between them.

o Systematic violations of fundamental constitutional principles and constitutional order, such as the separation of powers, the rule of law, and due process and equal protection clauses of the U.S. Constitution and the laws.

In the particular adverse situation under discussion in this book - meticulously underscored with the aid of the laws - the constitutional crisis has occurred through state and federal government institutions and officials being *unwilling and/or unable to address the major insurrection against the laws that remains active within their ranks.*

The corollary or consequence of that long running and unattended insurrection against the laws of the United States, being perpetrated by state and federal government officials, is the likely collapse of American democracy. Both the Democratic Party and Republican Party have contributed thereto and presently remain involved therein – with their eyes wide open. No party should blame the other. Both parties are implicated.

A WARNING: DANGER TO AMERICAN DEMOCRACY

As pilot and as aviation professional, I have for many years warned that unattended and ongoing criminality within the Boeing Company can and will lead to air accidents. (See Chapters 6, 9, and 11). Those stern warnings have been ignored and Boeing has been allowed to continue its criminal spree with the concomitant death and/or injury to 696 innocent people in four *avoidable* air accidents to date. That count will continue, until Boeing's crimes are addressed and their dire effect on flight safety is terminated.

Similarly, as naturalized American citizen, as the intended murder victim of US Government/ Boeing Company assassins, and as compassionate observer of man's follies, I herewith extend a plea to an informed electorate and to all Americans with concern for the demise of our democracy and way of life:

> *Legally tend to the 'insurrection against the laws',*
> *active within state and federal government. Since,*
> *failing to terminate the ongoing insurrection against*
> *the laws will in due course lead to* ***a legal***
> ***dictatorship.***

Again, that insurrection is described in detail in the Dossier of Crimes, Volumes I to III, filed with the White House, the Congress, and the Courts, including the US Supreme Court. The US Government crimes, left hidden and unattended to continue unabated, allows any present or future President of the United States to *legally* transform the United States Government into a one-man dictatorship. *In fact, under the existing laws, the statutes demand that of a U.S. President.* Under the prevailing circumstances, any present or future US President need only to obey the laws to legally become a dictator. I shall present those laws to you for your sober scrutiny.

Insurrection or rebellion is a refusal of obedience to the laws or orders of the established authority: the 'United States'. The 'Posse Comitatus Act' outlaws the willful use of any part of the Army or Air Force to execute the law unless expressly authorized by the Constitution or an act of Congress. On the other hand, the *Insurrection Act of 1807* is a major exception to the Posse Comitatus Act. The Insurrection Act expressly gives the U.S. President the authority and lays upon him the duty to act concerning a rebellion against the authority and the laws of the United States:

> ***Statute 10USC332:*** *Use of militia and armed forces to enforce Federal authority: Whenever the President considers that unlawful obstructions, combinations, or assemblages, or rebellion against the authority of the United States, make it impracticable to enforce the laws of the United States in any State or Territory by the ordinary course of judicial proceedings, he may call into Federal service such of the militia of any State, and use such of the armed forces, as he considers necessary to enforce those laws or to suppress the rebellion.*

> ***Statute 10USC333:*** *Interference with State and Federal law: The President, by using the militia or the armed forces, or both, or by any other means, shall take such measures as he considers necessary to suppress, in a State, any insurrection, domestic violence, unlawful combination, or conspiracy, if it- - (1) so hinders the execution of the laws of that State, and of the United States within the State, that any part or class of its people is deprived of a right, privilege, immunity, or protection named in the*

Constitution and secured by law, and the constituted authorities of that State are unable, fail, or refuse to protect that right, privilege, or immunity, or to give that protection; or (2) opposes or obstructs the execution of the laws of the United States or impedes the course of justice under those laws. In any situation covered by clause (1), the State shall be considered to have denied the equal protection of the laws secured by the Constitution.

Statute 10USC334: *Proclamation to disperse: Whenever the President considers it necessary to use the militia or armed forces under this chapter, he shall, by proclamation, immediately order the insurgents or those obstructing the enforcement of the laws* **to disperse** *and retire to their abodes within a limited time.*

Those officials and institutions of government who have perpetrated these deeds, addressed above and described in this book, who have: (a) engaged in "unlawful obstructions, combinations, or assemblages, or rebellion against the authority of the United States"; (b) who have engaged in insurrection and unlawful combination or conspiracy; (c) who have failed or refused to protect the rights of the American people to due process and protection of the laws; and who have (d) obstructed the execution of the laws of the United States and impeded the course of justice under those laws – those institutions and officials are subject to statute 10USC334: the proclamation to disperse. Their acts of insurrection against the laws have been well-described in this narrative and in its companion document: The Dossier of Crimes.

The many judges and courts involved, all Congressmen involved, and all 15,000 government officials involved, and the institutions through whom they have operated, ***shall by***

proclamation of the President, be ordered to disperse, to disband, to break-up, to dissolve, and to retire to their abodes. That means ***dissolution, by law,*** of the Courts, Congress, the DOJ, the FBI, and all other state and federal institutions involved in the insurrection against the laws through their insurgent officials - 627 state and federal institutions and more than 15,000 officials in all.

SYNOPSIS

A brief summary of these striking points mentioned above may be in order here, to drive home the profound corollary to this narrative:

> ***There is an ongoing seditious conspiracy and virulent 'insurrection against the laws', active within the government and the courts of the United States of America, today. The crimes committed collectively by this subversive conspiracy (where each conspirator is complicit in the crimes of the others), number more than 15 billion crimes, and counting. Pursuant the Constitution and the laws, the federal government and state governments implicated, are unlawful. Their officials who are drawn in may not hold office. A constitutional crisis exists in which there are systematic violations of fundamental constitutional principles and the rule of law.***
>
> ***The Insurrection Act of 1807 demands that the President use the armed forces to dispel the insurrectionists. Those insurrectionists happen to be 15,000-plus unlawful government officials populating the Courts, Congress, and the Administration.***
>
> ***Under the present circumstances, should the present or any future President decide to obey the***

Constitution and the Insurrection Act, which they are by law compelled to do, that U.S. President will find himself/herself as sole survivor of the proclamation to disperse the participants in the insurrection against the laws.

What will be left, is a dictatorship by the one person left standing, the President of the United States. Such a dictatorship would be protected and enforced by law. Such a dictatorship is demanded by law: by statute 10USC334!

*****

This is the profound result of the willful failure by government officials, to bring to justice the extensive and harmful 'insurrection against the laws', which is active within the government and the courts of the United States. This, then, is the most likely consequence of keeping *'A Dirty U.S. Government Secret',* secret.

Chapter 15
Restitution

"A nation can have no greater shame than to have the custodians of its morals fall foul of the very principles they are the custodians of. As long as we give away our power to leaders who sway public opinion by the dexterity of their tongues and not with the sincerity of their hearts, we will suffer the consequences of this misdirection".

Extract From Chapter 15.

CONCLUSIONS

Tyranny upon the Populace

Aptly, it has been stated that *"despotism sits nowhere so secure as under the effigy and ensigns of freedom"*. (Walter Savage Landor, 1775-1864). The notion of *'freedom and justice'* in America today does not reflect the harsher realities. There can be no more perverse an example of state-supported tyranny upon an outwardly *'free society'* than is presented by this case - and indeed in a country which is vociferous about human rights.

Fiercely has the United States establishment and its partner in crime, the Boeing Company, protected errant ones in their midst, by fair methods and foul, heedless of the crimes committed. The staggering level of collective criminal activity casts a dark shadow upon our brand of democracy in the United States. The government officials implicated have violated their duties and the laws with callous indifference to the suffering they are causing to those they have pledged to serve. They have had one overriding objective in mind: to shield law-breaking colleagues from prosecution and to conceal the crimes of their colleagues and their own crimes. Since there exists no viable restraining mechanism to curtail the abuses of power in spite of the tenets of the United States Constitution, unbridled oppression is frequently inflicted upon the common man. Given these circumstances, can one in truth claim that there is any difference between the United States of today and Brezhnev's Russia or Hitler's Germany?

It is in opposing this clear trend towards state-supported tyranny and in addressing the scourge of impunity against prosecution that I have risked my all. I have suffered slander of my good name, unlawful tapping of my communications, destruction of my career and livelihood, and theft of incriminating evidence from the courts. I have endured intimidation and retaliation against my testimony and my employment, denial of justice, threats of false incarceration, attempted kidnapping, and a series of abortive attempts upon my life. It is in my efforts to eradicate this dark stain upon the nation and to reveal the worthlessness of *'a just and a fair Constitution'* under such prevailing circumstances, that I have brought this matter to the attention of our leaders who are in a position to change this state of affairs but who have for two and a half decades steadfastly refused to do so.

Impunity Afforded to our Leaders

The scourge of impunity afforded to government and industry leaders has caused much suffering in our day. Despite a benign constitution and platitudes of protection of the laws; despite institutions dedicated to law and order; and notwithstanding profuse rhetoric on freedom from oppression and the virtues of the rule of law; despite all the false pledges, impunity remains strongly entrenched in the United States Government:

> *In practice, law-breaking US Government officers are, for the most part, beyond the reach of the law. Impunity afforded to our leaders engaged in all*

322

manner of crimes against humanity remains a potent force for evil upon our society.

The case presented herewith demonstrates the far-reaching tentacles and harsh effects of such impunity.

Neglect of Official Duty

The laws, and mandated official duties to enforce, to administer, to execute, and to oversee the laws should have ensured that this calamitous situation facing the nation today never occurs. And it would not have ever occurred but for grand-scale dereliction of duty.

The neglect of official duty in the United States stretches from the most junior policeman to the chief executive of the nation. In the Office of the President, in the position of the greatest responsibility that can be undertaken in this country, that neglect measures equal in power and strength to the neglect of all the other delinquents combined. *In practice*, the rights of the individual, enshrined in the US Constitution, have been denied on an ostentatious scale. If those rights, so freely spoken about, are only there to protect a favored few, the political elite, then never should we as a self-respecting people grant such treachery the freedom to rule over us. That is not the intention of a democracy, and that was not the intention of the laborers upon a fair and just constitution. Such treachery must be attacked head-on.

Those amongst us who have the propensity to take on the responsibility of a government position, or the grave responsibility of the Oval Office, must learn to honor that position; must learn to honor the subjects over whom they have power and responsibility. And every government officer who has crossed the bounds of decency into immorality and criminality, who has lost the essence of human-ness and love and compassion for fellow man, must learn that lesson towards greater human relations.

Whilst one recognizes the misguided tendency of humanity to band together in groups to protect the mostly selfish interests of the group or of individuals in the group, much of the time, such protection is provided at the expense of the interests of another group and/or individuals in that other group. However, the nobler principles of love for fellowman and selfless service to humanity stretches beyond the protection of an errant or law-breaking colleague, beyond any group interest, beyond party-political inclinations to the rest of the citizens of our nation; even beyond the generally selfish interests of nations, further onwards to the rest of humanity.

Dishonesty in Government

Savaging the truth is a particularly abhorrent pastime. Since what is a word worth if you cannot rely upon that word? Dishonesty in government is a fundamental cause of many an evil and lies at the root of many of the failures described in this book. Dishonesty lies deeply entrenched in the modus operandi of so many government officials in their dealings with the public, with the press, or with world leaders - the truth of their intent masked by falsities. That dishonesty is acutely displayed from the time many (if not most) elected officials start campaigning for public office, and it continues uninterruptedly from there on forward. Dishonesty is simply a standard from top to bottom in the government of the United States. As a society, we are all very familiar with the phenomenon. That dishonesty is what has led to the widespread mistrust of our leaders, not just nationally but also internationally, where American diplomacy is seen as diplomacy of deceit.

Of course, it should be recognized that dishonesty is not only a characteristic of government officials in isolation, but is rampant in business, in advertising, in the media, and in almost every department of life in the rest of our society as well. It is this human shortcoming that was the cause of the 2008 global financial crisis and suffering, with the near-collapse of the world's financial system – originating as it did, with profound dishonesty in the United States subprime mortgage market.

It is also this vice of dishonesty that underpins the role of the United States Courts in the defeat of justice under discussion in this book. It is dishonesty that underpins the incalculable suffering of so many who are unfortunate enough to come within the ambit of the hellholes that serve as our courts. The judgments in 62 court cases and 352 proceedings attest to that deceit, for example, where one judge was accused of 47 false and perjurous statements, another of 64 perjurous statements in their rulings. Again, these cases are not unique, but merely reflect what happens day after day, in court after court across the nation.

Dishonesty by United States Government officials has caused much anguish upon the populace of this nation. Yet it need not be so. Simple and sure remedies exist. Laws are in place to prevent such bedlam - the laws need only to be applied. For example, statute 18USC1001 refers to ***fraud and false statements*** and states that:

> *"Whoever, in any matter within the jurisdiction of the executive, legislative, or judicial branch of the Government of the United States, knowingly and willfully (a) falsifies, conceals, or covers up by any trick, scheme, or device a material fact; (b) makes any materially false, fictitious, or fraudulent statement or representation; or (c) makes or uses any false writing or document knowing the same to contain any materially false, fictitious, or fraudulent statement or entry; shall be fined under this title, imprisoned not more than 5 years ..."*

This repugnant characteristic of man can be corrected by teaching honesty in the formative years so that politicians and diplomats of the future gag upon their own false utterings, and so that any false statement by a government official results in swift retribution. Then, perchance, can we again *with meaning* sing the Battle Hymn of the Republic: "Mine eyes have seen the glory of the coming of the Lord…. *'His Truth'* is marching on".

Failure of the Constitution, the Courts, and the Laws

Unyielding refusal to deal with the anarchy within the government by consecutive US Presidents and their Cabinets, by the Supreme Court and the Federal Court System, by Members of Congress, the Armed Forces, and by the 50 State Governments, bears ultimate witness to the stern reality summed up in the following conclusions:

- o ***The United States Code,*** *for all its elevated laws and theoretical protections afforded to the American public, does not, in practice, apply to law-breaking government officials. This corrupt policy covers all possible harmful criminal acts against the state or its citizens, including attempted kidnapping and murder, insurrection against the laws, sedition, and treason. Government officers who violate the laws at the expense of the common man are well-nigh unassailable.*

- o ***The Courts*** *tend strongly to protect executive and legislative branch officials from prosecution for any wrongdoing. In turn, the courts enjoy the protection of the executive and legislative branches from misdeeds they may have committed. This incestuous relationship between the three branches of the United States government is unequivocally demonstrated in three Supreme Court cases against President Obama, the Congress, and the Supreme Court Justices. (Appealed from First Circuit case nos. 09-2617, 09-2618, and 09-2619). The notion of an 'independent judiciary' does not exist in practice.*

Restitution

- o ***The United States Constitution,*** *for all its noble principles of justice and fairness, remains a hollow promise when its tenets are not applied: to secure the rights of the common man; to prosecute law-breaking government officials who violate the Constitution; or to prevent insurrection against the laws and state-supported tyranny upon the American populace.*

The degeneracy in the institutions of the United States government stands deeply exposed in this case - a governmental and judicial system corrupt to the core, where even the most moral who enter are besmirched by the system. A nation can have no greater shame than to have the custodians of its morals fall foul of the very principles they are the custodians of. As long as we give away our power to leaders who sway public opinion by the dexterity of their tongues and not with the sincerity of their hearts, we will suffer the consequences of this misdirection. It is only with discretion and enlightened choices by an informed electorate that we can keep common criminals off the honorable court bench and out of the esteemed White House.

As members of that electorate, it is our individual and collective duty to ensure that those whom we give our power to in democratic elections, nevermore abuse that power to perpetrate crime upon the ordinary good-natured man on Main Street, who elected them. Not ever again. Should this anarchy in the United States government not be arrested and reversed, and should government officials be allowed to continue unchecked to fuel this debauchery, it will entrench repressive government and will inflict untold suffering upon the citizens of tomorrow. Yet again, it need not be so if proper corrective action is taken.

The laws were promulgated to benefit society as a whole, not for the control of the governed by those who govern. Law, consistently applied throughout all levels of society, makes freedom possible without license and makes governance possible without tyranny.

THE REMEDIES

Need for Profound Overhaul

Yet, a rare opportunity presents itself in this debacle that faces the American nation. If we can face the lessons of the present and understand their nature and negative ramifications upon future generations, if we can rectify our errors and the fatal flaws in our judicial and governmental systems, then we will sow the seeds of a brighter tomorrow. If our justice system can rid itself of the common criminals in its midst, then we may begin to redesign a more nurturing, just, and fair jurisprudence. And, if we can inculcate in public servants the attributes of responsibility and true service - without selfish ambition, malice, dirty political maneuvering, and the iniquitous protection of malfeasant colleagues - then the seeds of a more benevolent society, truly free from tyranny, will have been planted.

Then can we usher in an era of improved human relations and a more just and honest society that can lead the world, not by sham and showmanship, nor by force, but by superlative example, deserving of God's rich blessings. *That* will be a legacy worthy of future generations and deserving of our invocation: "God Bless America". The time has come to restore our self-respect and honor as a nation. But in order to do that, we will have to take the required medicine, bitter as it may be.

A More Perfect Union

The 'Founding Fathers' of the United States established a fair Constitution in order to 'form a more perfect union, to establish justice, to promote the general welfare, and to secure the blessings of liberty to ourselves and our posterity'.

Restitution

Nearly 240 years after ordaining and establishing that profoundly noble document in 1787, events have come full circle, and the menace of government tyranny must once again be confronted. The passage of time has made it necessary for scholars, philosophers, politicians, and free men alike to revisit the founding principles and to determine where the Constitution, the laws, and our system of democracy as practiced today have so profoundly failed us as a nation.

And *'failed us'*, they have. The only thing that seems to have changed since the repression that caused the American Revolution (1765-1783) is the way in which we come by the tyrants who govern. Today, we elect them. Once in power, their methods of rule remain the same as in far-off days. We have not yet been able to lift the yoke of enslavement from the masses of men. However, the time has come to lay the foundations of a *'more perfect union'* for the next 240 years, and then some. The occasion calls for the brightest minds amongst us, calls for our most forward-thinking leaders and high-minded politicians, philosophers, and honorable judicial officials, to re-establish and secure *'the blessings of liberty to ourselves and our posterity'*.

The aim of sharing this very personal story is to expose some of the noticeable failures in the present government and judicial systems of the United States by unambiguously demonstrating aspects of what exists in practice. The plot only touches upon the volume of information available. It has gathered strands from several different arenas and has attempted to harness them into a single, coherent storyline in order to show the dire need to rectify the broad failures. Comprehensive and sound solutions to the breakdown of law and order will, however, require much study over a number of years by many dedicated scholars and researchers - more than what a single man (the author) working with limited resources (as a result of his ordeal) can accomplish. Nevertheless, some obvious proposals are made to initiate corrective actions and to indicate the way forward towards remedy.

The Lawlessness Punished

Foremost, the widespread criminal endeavor operating with impunity within the government and the courts of the United States must be addressed in full and with the full force of the law. *All perpetrators* must be arrested and brought to trial without delay, in keeping with the applicable laws and federal rules of criminal procedure. There can be no claim of ignorance, excuse, clemency, immunity, or pardon.

Justice must be administered impartially, without respect to persons or their high positions in government. All offenders must be treated equally under the law, and there must be no exceptions. Justice must apply throughout our entire society and not just in the domain of the common people, neglecting to address the rampant anarchy within officialdom. Each government officer implicated must be punished according to their level of responsibility and scope of dereliction of duty, and their role in the criminal offenses associated with this case. For verily I say to you, the sun must not set upon this iniquity until each offender has paid for the suffering that they have caused their fellow countrymen.

The Causes Analyzed

The data on *'the practical application of the laws'*, meticulously gathered over two and a half decades, must be examined and analyzed by academics and government task forces alike. The likely causes that gave rise to the breakdown of our judicial and government systems must *a posteriori* be scrutinized and tabulated. The full impact of our deviant judicial and government system must be laid bare in order that infallible remedies to the failures in our democracy may be generated. The impunity afforded to our leaders, their failure of duty, their relentless dishonesty, their protection of iniquitous colleagues against prosecution, and the arbitrary application of the laws are just some of the areas that will need to be addressed in full.

RE-ORIENTATION OF GOVERNMENT FOR THE PEOPLE

This nation is at the forefront of human development. However, if the paradigm exposed in this case is the best example we have to offer the world, then we must rethink our position of world leadership. The ongoing criminal behavior of more than 15,000 of our top government officials, as documented in the case, negates any suggestion of a *'true democracy'* existing in the United States of America.

An elementary principle such as *'responsibility'* amongst officials is sadly lacking in practice - and not just in government, but in society as well, which takes its cue from our political leaders. Basic civility, helpfulness, truthfulness, and respect for their subjects; these are essential traits that will have to be inculcated in public servants, ere our system will work as was intended by the 'founding fathers'.

The time has come to seek an enhancement of the United States Government and our form of democracy – improvement beyond that which exists today and which gave rise to the extensive lawlessness, disorder, dishonesty, and the malicious attempts to kidnap and murder a witness to that lawlessness. In short, a *'re-orientation of government for the people'* is needed. I hold in my prayers a brighter vision of:

    a. A truer democracy of *'cooperative unity'* between government and the people, made possible through the right use of the systems of education, of communication, of law, and of justice.

b. A responsible and free community, not victimized by those who rule.

c. A leadership element of illumined minds, driven by high ideals, sincerity, and goodwill, and chosen for their selflessness and sacrifice to fellow man.

d. Rulers chosen to rule by a community of developed men and women, thinking men and women, who remain oriented to a world of right values and human virtues.

e. A purification of the political field and political consciousness, to a consciousness oriented towards service which honors the freedom and the rights of the individual, free from selfish ambition and dirty political maneuvering.

f. A cleansing of our processes of representation and an exact accounting by officials to the people whom they represent.

g. The complete abolishment of the system of legalized bribery and blackmail of special interest groups, regardless of how sophisticated that bribery and blackmail may appear to be. Dishonest inducements and unfair manipulations, where money buys influence, have entirely corrupted our system of democracy, and that corruption runs throughout the establishment.

h. Inescapable disciplinary action when a servant of the people steps out of line.

i. A benevolent *'public service'*, intent upon serving the public.

I hold in my mind's eye a new era of government premised upon the higher principles of responsibility, selfless service to fellow countrymen, care, respect for the governed, and respect for the sanctity of life.

A NEW JURISPRUDENCE

The wayward judicial system must be corrected - a system that for many years colluded with and sanctioned the lawlessness of more than 15,000 government officials and industry officials. Corrective actions should include:

a. Introduction of federal legislation that renders *failure of duty by public officials'* a felony. The harsh consequences and cumulative effects of deliberate failure of duty are amply demonstrated in the pages of this exposition.

b. Strict application of federal legislation which renders *false statements by an official'* a felony (18USC1001). The dire consequences of unbridled dishonesty by government officials are clear for all to see.

c. A failsafe system must be found for the 'faithful application of laws', *involving the citizenry in the loop,* where government officials are implicated in wrongdoing.

d. The laws must be applied without prejudice - in practice, and not just in theory.

e. Judges must be held accountable for breaching their oaths - in practice, and not just in theory.

f. The corrupt liaison between judges and clerks, and their assistants, must be terminated. Today, that liaison is misused and abused to obfuscate, prevaricate, delay, prevent, and obstruct the very course of justice they are there to administer.

g. The problem of 'jurisdiction' must be resolved, and a flawless transition must be found from one jurisdiction to the next. The responsibility for finding the correct jurisdiction in the courts and in problems relating to government must lie with the courts or with the relevant government departments, and not with members of the public seeking their assistance.

h. The frivolous and arbitrary application of so-called 'case law' must be corrected and formalized. At present, any decision, even decisions with totally opposing viewpoints and principles, can be found to the heart's content and quoted as 'case law'.

i. An infallible set of checks and balances, *involving the citizenry in the loop,* must be introduced.

I hold in my mind's eye a benign, more nurturing, more practical, and more honest jurisprudence - a system premised upon the higher principles of justice, founded in love, according to God's plan for humanity.

Epilogue

The account is complete. The facts are on the record. History shows that governments rarely admit their darkest deeds. This book has pulled back a curtain. What was hidden is now exposed. It is up to citizens to demand answers and to protect the ideals of justice, democracy, and accountability.

Throughout my long and arduous odyssey in pursuit of justice, the question has lingered upon my mind: 'When shall one arise from the heart of this nation, enlightened and courageous, who will take on the prosecution of this systemic tyranny and wave of crime amongst government officials; and when shall arise a political leader who has the vision to see that the legal system and governmental system of the United States are deeply flawed and in need of profound overhaul'?

When such one arises, I shall say: 'My task is done!'

Appendices

Appendix 1

LIST OF UNITED STATES INSTITUTIONS THAT FAILED TO TAKE ACTION

Some 15,000 US government officers from **627 United States federal and state government institutions** have been approached over the years, but have failed to address the subversive criminal activities within the government and the courts of the United States. These institutions are listed below:

Number of Institutions

US Presidency	1
US Cabinet	1
US Department of Justice: Civil Rights Division, Criminal Division, AG Office	3
US Attorneys	90
US State Department	1
US Police: US Marshals, Secret Service, Supreme Court Police, FBI	4
US Senate, Committees on Judiciary, Homeland Security & Govt. Affairs	3
US House, Committees on Judiciary, Government Oversight	3
US Armed Forces	1
US District Courts	51
US Appeals Courts	11
US Supreme Court	1
State Governors	50
State Cabinet/Executive	50
State Attorneys General	50

State Senate	50
State House of Representatives	50
State Police/Patrol	50
State Superior Courts	54
State Appeals Courts	35
State Supreme Courts	50
State Committees: Ethics, Judicial Conduct, Gender and Justice	3
State Bar Associations	2
County Sheriffs	2
County Prosecutors	2
County Councils	2
County Ethics Committee	1
City Police	2
City Prosecutors	2
City Councils	2

627

Appendix 2

Proceedings in the following 63 United States court cases (and one case in India) substantiate the verity of the facts presented in the 'Dossier of Crimes'. These cases have in vain attempted to address the proliferation of the international criminal endeavor, only to be thwarted before trial by corrupt judges and intervening government officials.

List of International Court Cases
Criminal Plaint against Directors of Air India
1. Supreme Court of India, Diary Nos. 5352/2006/SC/PIL and 13690/SC/PIL/2010.

List of United States Court Cases (6.15.25)
In Re: International Terrorism Plot
1. U.S. District Court, Delaware, Case # 10-802
2. U.S. 3rd Circuit, Case # 10-4296
3. U.S. Supreme Court, case number not assigned.

In Re Anthony Keyter, Complaining Witness in Domestic Terrorism Plot
4. U.S. District Court, Eastern District of Virginia, Case # 10mc5
5. U.S. Court of Appeals, 4th Circuit, Case # 10-1267

In Re: Domestic Terrorism Plot
6. U.S. District Court, Delaware, Case # 10-36
7. U.S. Court of Appeals, 3rd Circuit, Case # 10-2209.
8. U.S. Supreme Court, case number not assigned.

In Re: Terrorism Plot
9. U.S. District Court, Rhode Island, Case # 10-MC-36-S-DLM

10. U.S. District Court, Rhode Island, Case # 10-MC-130-LDA

United States vs. Bush, Roberts, Gonzales, Mueller

11. U.S. District Court, District of Colorado, Case # 08-cr-00085-ZLW

12. U.S. Court of Appeals, 10th Circuit, Case # 08-1064

United States vs. 443 Known Insurgents

13. U.S. District Court, District of Colorado, Case # 08-cr-00086-ZLW

14. U.S. Court of Appeals, 10th Circuit, Case # 08-1063

United States vs. 535 Members of the 110th Congress

15. U.S. District Court, District of Colorado, Case # 08-cr-00087-ZLW

16. U.S. Court of Appeals, 10th Circuit, Case # 08-1061

United States vs. 14,164 Seditious Conspirators

17. U.S. Supreme Court, case number not assigned.

[United States of America] vs. 111th Congress

18. U.S. District Court, Maine, Case # 09-516

19. U.S. First Circuit Appeals Court, Case # 09-2617

20. U.S. Supreme Court, case number not assigned.

[United States of America] vs. Justices of the US Supreme Court

21. U.S. District Court, Maine, Case # 09-517

22. U.S. First Circuit Appeals Court, Case # 09-2618

23. U.S. Supreme Court, case number not assigned.

[United States of America] vs. Pres. Obama and the Cabinet

24. U.S. District Court, Maine, Case # 09-518

25. U.S. First Circuit Appeals Court, Case # 09-2619

26. U.S. Supreme Court, case number not assigned.

United States vs. The Boeing Company

27. U.S. District Court, Northern District of Texas, Case # 4:21-CR-5-O

28. U.S. Fifth Circuit Appeals Court, Case # 25-10457

Anthony P. Keyter vs. Obama/Cabinet/Congress/ Supreme Court Justices
29. U.S. District Court, Massachusetts, Case # 09-11700

Anthony P. Keyter vs. Bush, Roberts, Gonzales, Mueller
30. U.S. District Court, District of Delaware, Case #1:08cv97

Anthony P. Keyter vs. The Boeing Company
31. U.S. District Court, Western District of Washington, Case # 09cv962
32. U.S. Supreme Court Appeal on 09cv962, case number not assigned.
33. U.S. District Court, Western District of Washington, Case # 12cv474
34. U.S. Court of Appeals, 9th Circuit, Case # 12-72265
35. U.S. Supreme Court Appeal on 12-72265, case number not assigned.
36. King County Court, Case # 13-2-19597-6 KNT
37. U.S. District Court, Western District of Washington, Case # 13cv982
38. U.S. Court of Appeals, 9th Circuit, Case # 13cv-36056
39. U.S. Supreme Court Appeal on 13-36056, case number not assigned.

Anthony P. Keyter vs. The Ford Motor Company
40. U.S. District Court, Western District of Washington, Case # 09-897

Anthony P. Keyter vs. Air India
41. U.S. District Court, Western District of Washington, Case # 09-825

Combined Appeal: Anthony P. Keyter vs. Boeing, Ford, and Air India
42. U.S. Supreme Court, case # not assigned.

Anthony P. Keyter vs. United States of America
43. U.S. District Court, Northern District of Texas, Case # 3:08cv260

Anthony P. Keyter vs. George W. Bush
44. U.S. District Court, District of Columbia, Case # 03-cv-2496 (EGS)
45. U.S. Court of Appeals, D.C. Circuit, Case # 04- 5324
46. U.S. Supreme Court, Case # 05-140

Anthony P. Keyter vs. Senator John McCain, et al
47. U.S. District Court, District of Arizona, Case # CV05-01923- PHX-DGC
48. U.S. 9th Circuit Court of Appeals, Case # 06-15253
49. U.S. Supreme Court, Case # 06-1069

Anthony P. Keyter vs. 230 Government Officers
50. U.S. District Court, Western District of Washington, Case # 3:04cv5867
51. U.S. Court of Appeals, 9th Circuit, Case # 05- 35717
52. US Supreme Court, Case # 06-284.

Anthony P. Keyter vs. John Ashcroft, et al.
53. U.S. Court of Appeals, D.C. Circuit, Case # 04-5392

Anthony P. Keyter vs. Vice President Dick Cheney, et al.
54. U.S. Court of Appeals, D.C. Circuit, Case # 04-5365

Anthony P. Keyter vs. Haggerty et al.
55. US District Court, Oregon, Case # 08-cv-00545

Anthony P. Keyter vs. Maureen E. Keyter
56. Washington State Superior Court, Case # 00-3-02932-1
57. Washington State Superior Court, Case # 04-2-13977-1
58. Washington State Court of Appeals, Case # 2737- 6-II
59. Washington State Supreme Court, Case # 76972-9
60. Washington State Supreme Court, Case # 76956-7
61. US Supreme Court, case # not assigned.

Anthony P. Keyter vs. President Trump
62. U.S. District Court, Western District of Washington, Case # 3:19cv05379
63. U.S. Court of Appeals, DC, Case # 19-5159

Appendix 3

AN OVERVIEW OF EVIDENCE

Prima Facie Proof

Despite the complete and willful absence of official investigations, three primary sources of information provide strong evidence of the crimes committed by more than 15,000 conspirators engaged in the widespread criminal endeavor. A fourth source binds the first three together into a single coherent document comprising some 55,000 pages. The four sources of prima facie evidence are:

1. Appeals for protection of the laws.
2. Court documents in 63 United States court cases and two further cases abroad.
3. The 'Dossier of Crimes'.
4. 'Constitutional Crisis: A Treatise on the Legality of U.S. Government'. (Not yet published as of this date.)

These sources of information are briefly described herewith, and an indication of how to access that evidence is also given.

1. Appeals for Protection of the Laws

Dating back to early 2002, some 14,000 appeals for due process and protection of the laws against the conspirators in the ongoing criminal endeavor have been made over a period of more than two decades to, amongst others, the following institutions and individuals or groups of United States government officials:

- Six (7) Presidents and their Vice Presidents - Carter, GHW Bush, Clinton, GW Bush, Obama, Biden, Trump.
- The Cabinets of Presidents George W. Bush, Barack Obama, Joe Biden, and Donald Trump.

- Nine (9) consecutive Attorneys General – Ashcroft, Gonzales, Mukasey, Holder, Lynch, Sessions, Bar, Garland, and Bondi.
- Consecutive US Congresses since February 2003.
- Consecutive US Supreme Court Justices since May 2004
- Some 3950 Judges - 1252 federal judges and 2689 state judges.
- Two hundred and eight (208) Courts - US Supreme Court; all 13 Circuit Appeals Courts; 54 Federal District Courts (out of 89 total); and 140 State Courts
- All ninety-three (93) US Attorneys and their staff.
- Fifty-eight (58) Generals and Admirals of the US Armed Forces, including the Joint Chiefs of Staff
- FAA Administrators and several other FAA officials.
- The US Ambassadors to the UN of several consecutive Administrations.
- The Comptroller and 13 Managing Directors of the Government Accountability Office.
- Three Directors of the CIA and 10 top officials.
- Several Directors of the FBI and 37 Agents in Charge of FBI Field Offices.
- The Director of the US Marshals and 89 US Marshals.
- The Director of the US Secret Service and several special agents.
- US Supreme Court Police Chief and several policemen.
- The 50 State Governments - all 50 Governors, Lt. Governors, Attorneys General, Secretaries of State, Police Chiefs, Senators and Representatives of the legislatures, and three levels of state courts.
- And more.

Ultimately, some *15,000 officials* from *627 US institutions* tasked with law and order had been approached individually and/or in groups, in a series of more than *14,000 letters* and reports of criminal offenses. In the end, 82 appeals had been made to President

Bush; 111 appeals to President Obama; 215 to Members of Congress; 121 to the FBI in Seattle and to their headquarters in DC; all tallied, some 1000 appeals to the Department of Justice; 644 appeals to officials from Washington State; on and on.

Correspondence with and appeals to government and industry officials are bound in the comprehensive treatise by the same author: *'The Defeat of Justice: A Treatise on the Practical Application of the Laws in the USA'*, in Part II: *Evidence.*

2. Corrupt Court Proceedings

Sixty-three (63) US court cases sought in vain to address different aspects and groupings of the virulent seditious conspiracy within the government of the United States. (See *Appendix 2*). These cases were lodged in federal courts across the length and breadth of the country and included courts in the following States: Arizona, Colorado, California, Delaware, D.C., Massachusetts, Maine, Oregon, Pennsylvania, Rhode Island, Texas, Virginia, and Washington. The cases and the proceedings in those cases provide a representative example of the corrupted modus operandi of the entire United States judicial system.

The court cases were motivated by the criminal neglect of government officials in dealing with a deluge of criminal offenses within their ranks. Some cases sought civil restitution for harm and loss caused directly by delinquent officials. Other cases were entirely criminal in nature, based on affidavits which reported criminal offenses to the courts in terms of statutes 18USC4 and 18USC2382. All cases sought protection of the laws against crimes committed by government officials and the administration of the laws against lawbreaking officials.

More than *352* corrupt proceedings in the cases provide unambiguous evidence of the subversive activities of law-breaking judicial officers. Court records are, for the most part, available online via 'Public Access to Court Electronic Records' (PACER).

344

However, the official court record does not represent a full set of documents because of the prolific theft of court records and incriminating evidence in the cases. A comprehensive set of records in each case will only be gleaned by complementing official court records with the set of documents presented in Part II of the exposition: *'The Defeat of Justice: A Treatise on the Practical Application of the Laws in the USA'.*

3. The Dossier of Crimes

The *'Dossier of Crimes'* measures the criminal actions of offenders (and their inaction where action was due) against the laws of the United States. Criminal offenses, committed by individual conspirators and by natural groupings within the 15,000-plus conspirators, are meticulously documented, and *prima facie* evidence is provided in some 2,400 pages of the dossier and 240 criminal complaints. The dossier was prepared to serve as a basis for the investigation and prosecution of the criminal conspirators in accordance with the appropriate jurisdiction and the applicable laws.

The dossier was first compiled on January 17, 2003, and has been continuously updated over the years since then. The latest revision of the dossier available to investigators and prosecutors at the time of writing is dated *January 1, 2025.* Since the unlawful conspiracy has not been arrested and is continuing unimpeded at the time of writing, the dossier is dynamic and is continuously updated to keep abreast of the escalating saga.

The *'Dossier of Crimes'* has been presented to the courts and government institutions listed in *Appendix 1* on some 700 occasions. The undeniable evidence has also been presented to the US Supreme Court on some 34 occasions. Earlier versions of the dossier remain filed in each of the 63 United States court cases listed in *Appendix 2,* and can be accessed online in those cases via 'Public Access to Court Electronic Records' (PACER).

A version of the dossier dated January 1, 2025, is available under the Freedom of Information Act from the Department of Justice, the White House, Congress, or the US Supreme Court.

4. 'Constitutional Crisis: A Treatise on the Legality of U.S. Government' – By Anthony P. Keyter. *(Soon to be published.)*

The fourth source of information combines the appeals to officials, court cases, and proceedings, and the Dossier of Crimes, into a single account comprising an estimated 55,000 pages, and provides a broader overview in terms of how the laws are applied in practice. The treatise reveals the complete failure of the American justice system to administer the laws in a consistent manner across the full spectrum of the population. It reveals how politicians, officials, and judicial personnel contrive with one another to prevent and hinder, at times by means of violence, the execution of the laws upon law-breaking colleagues. The work demonstrates how this situation has led to a constitutional crisis in government and warns against a potential dictatorship, perversely demanded by the laws.

The impunity enjoyed by government officials against prosecution for crimes committed is contrasted with the accountability exacted from the common man for those very same crimes. The breakdown of a theoretically 'independent and impartial' justice system is demonstrated in unassailable terms. The treatise exposes the arbitrary nature in which the laws are administered at the whim of pernicious judicial officials working in collusion with, and oft under the influence of, malevolent government executives and legislators.

The treatise recommends that, for the sake of future generations of Americans, the acute problems in the courts be investigated and analyzed in depth by the many talented legal minds of this country, and that enduring solutions to the waywardness be found. Hand in hand with an improved United States judicial system will spring forth an enhancement of the system of government that has corruptly sanctioned and colluded with the lawlessness uncovered in this exposition. The treatise further recommends that a more benign and 'just' legal system be introduced - a system that reaches for a deeper understanding of what is, in truth, meant by the universal concept of *'justice'*.

This comprehensive work is not yet published as of this date, but will soon be available to serious investigators and researchers, directly from the writer.

Appendix 4

EXTRACT OF STATUTES

UNITED STATES CONSTITUTION

US Constitution, Article II, Section 3
In relevant part: "The president ... shall take care that the laws be faithfully executed."

US Constitution – 5th Amendment:
No person shall be ... deprived of life, liberty, or property, without due process of law ....

US Constitution – 14th Amendment, Section 1:
In relevant part: ".... Nor shall any state deprive any person of life, liberty, or property, without due process of law; nor deny to any person within its jurisdiction the equal protection of the laws".

US Constitution – 14th Amendment, Section 3:
No person shall be a Senator or Representative in Congress, or elector of President and Vice President, or hold any office, civil or military, under the United States, or under any state, who, having previously taken an oath, as a member of Congress, or as an officer of the United States, or as a member of any state legislature, or as an executive or judicial officer of any state, to support the Constitution of the United States, shall have engaged in insurrection or rebellion against the same, or given aid or comfort to the enemies thereof. But Congress may, by a vote of two-thirds of each House, remove such disability.

FEDERAL STATUTES

§5 Government organization and employees

5USC3331 - Oath of office:
An individual, except the President, elected or appointed to an office of honor or profit in the civil service or uniformed services, shall take the following oath:

"I, AB, do solemnly swear (or affirm) that I will support and defend the Constitution of the United States against all enemies, foreign and domestic; that I will bear true faith and allegiance to the same; that I take this obligation freely, without any mental reservation or purpose of evasion; and that I will well and faithfully discharge the duties of the office on which I am about to enter. So help me God."

This section does not affect other oaths required by law.

§18 Crimes and Criminal Procedure

18USC2 – Principals:
(a) Whoever commits an offense against the United States or aids, abets, counsels, commands, induces, or procures its commission is punishable as a principal. (b) Whoever willfully causes an act to be done which, if directly performed by him or another, would be an offense against the United States, is punishable as a principal.

18USC3 – Accessory after the Fact:
Whoever, knowing that an offense against the United States has been committed, receives, relieves, comforts, or assists the offender in order to hinder or prevent his apprehension, trial, or punishment, is an accessory after the fact.

18USC4 – Misprision of Felony:
"Whoever, having knowledge of the actual commission of a felony cognizable by a court of the United States, conceals and does not as soon as possible make known the same to some judge or other person in civil or military authority under the United States shall be fined under this title or imprisoned not more than three years, or both".

18USC241 - Conspiracy against Rights:

In relevant part: "If two or more persons conspire to …oppress…any person in any State…in the free exercise or enjoyment of any right or privilege secured to him by the Constitution or laws of the United States…they shall be fined under this title or imprisoned not more than ten years".

18USC242 - Deprivation of Rights:

In relevant part: "Whoever, under color of law…. willfully subjects any person in any State… to the deprivation of any rights… secured by the Constitution or laws of the United States, … shall be fined under this title or imprisoned not more than one year".

18USC371 – Conspiracy to Commit Offense

If two or more persons conspire either to commit any offense against the United States, or to defraud the United States, or any agency thereof in any manner or for any purpose, and one or more of such persons do any act to effect the object of the conspiracy, each shall be fined under this title or imprisoned not more than five years, or both.

18USC401 - Contempt of Court:

"A court of the United States shall have power to punish by fine or imprisonment, at its discretion, such contempt of its authority, and none other, as-- (1) Misbehavior of any person in its presence or so near thereto as to obstruct the administration of justice; (2) Misbehavior of any of its officers in their official transactions; (3) Disobedience or resistance to its lawful writ, process, order, rule, decree, or command".

18USC1001 – Fraud and False Statements or entries generally

(a) Except as otherwise provided in this section, whoever, in any matter within the jurisdiction of the executive, legislative, or judicial branch of the Government of the United States, knowingly and willfully -- (1) falsifies, conceals, or covers up by any trick, scheme, or device a material fact; (2) makes any materially false, fictitious, or fraudulent statement or representation; or (3) makes or uses any false writing or document knowing the same to contain any materially false, fictitious, or fraudulent statement or entry; shall be fined under this title, imprisoned not more than 5 years or, if the offense involves international or domestic terrorism (as defined in section 2331), imprisoned not more than 8 years, or both. If the matter relates to an offense under chapter 109A, 109B, 110, or 117, or section 1591, then the term of imprisonment imposed under this section shall be not more than 8 years.

(b) Subsection (a) does not apply to a party to a judicial proceeding, or that party's counsel, for statements, representations, writings, or documents submitted by such party or counsel to a judge or magistrate in that proceeding. **(c)** With respect to any matter within the jurisdiction of the legislative branch, subsection (a) shall apply only to-- (1) administrative matters, including a claim for payment, a matter related to the procurement of property or services, personnel or employment practices, or support services, or a document required by law, rule, or regulation to be submitted to the Congress or any office or officer within the legislative branch; or (2) any investigation or review, conducted pursuant to the authority of any committee, subcommittee, commission or office of the Congress, consistent with applicable rules of the House or Senate.

<u>18USC1111 - Murder</u>

(a) Murder is the unlawful killing of a human being with malice aforethought. Every murder perpetrated by poison, lying in wait, or any other kind of willful, deliberate, malicious, and premeditated killing; or committed in the perpetration of, or attempt to perpetrate, any arson, escape, murder, kidnapping, treason, espionage, sabotage, aggravated sexual abuse or sexual abuse, child abuse, burglary, or robbery; or perpetrated as part of a pattern or practice of assault or torture against a child or children; or perpetrated from a premeditated design unlawfully and maliciously to effect the death of any human being other than him who is killed, is murder in the first degree. Any other murder is murder in the second degree. (b) Within the special maritime and territorial jurisdiction of the United States. Whoever is guilty of murder in the first degree shall be punished by death or by imprisonment for life; Whoever is guilty of murder in the second degree, shall be imprisoned for any term of years or for life.

18USC1117 - Conspiracy to Murder

If two or more persons conspire to violate section 1111, 1114, 1116, or 1119 of this title, and one or more of such persons do any overt act to effect the object of the conspiracy, each shall be punished by imprisonment for any term of years or for life.

18USC1201 – Kidnapping:

In relevant parts: (a) Whoever unlawfully seizes, confines, inveigles, decoys, kidnaps, abducts, or carries away and holds for ransom or reward or otherwise any person, except in the case of a minor by the parent thereof, when---(2) any such act against the person is done within the special maritime and territorial jurisdiction of the United States;---such person shall be punished by imprisonment for any term of years or for life; --- (c) If any two or more persons conspire to violate this section and one or more of such persons do any act to effect the object of the conspiracy, each shall be punished by imprisonment for any term of years or for life.

18USC1505 - Obstruction of Justice

In relevant part: "Whoever corruptly... .... influences, obstructs, or impedes ....the due and proper administration of the law under which any pending proceeding is being had before any department or agency of the United States... shall be fined under this title, or imprisoned not more than 5 years..."

18USC1506 – Theft of Record

States in relevant part: Whoever feloniously steals, takes away, alters, falsifies, or otherwise avoids any record, writ, process, or other proceeding, in any court of the United States, whereby any judgment is reversed, made void, or does not take effect...; -- Shall be fined under this title or imprisoned not more than five years, or both.

18USC1512 - Tampering with a witness, victim, or an informant:

In relevant parts:

(a)(1) Whoever kills or attempts to kill another person, with intent to-- (A) prevent the attendance or testimony of any person in an official proceeding; (B) prevent the production of a record, document, or other object, in an official proceeding; or (C) prevent the communication by any person to a law enforcement officer or judge of the United States of information relating to the commission or possible commission of a Federal offense or a violation of conditions of probation, parole, or release pending judicial proceedings; shall be punished as provided in paragraph (3): The punishment for an offense under this subsection is-- (A) in the case of murder (as defined in section 1111), the death penalty or imprisonment for life, and in the case of any other killing, the punishment provided in section 1112; (B) in the case of-- (i) an attempt to murder; or (ii) the use or attempted use of physical force against any person; imprisonment for not more than 20 years; and (C) in the case of the threat of use of physical force against any person, imprisonment for not more than 10 years.

(b) Whoever knowingly uses intimidation, threatens, or corruptly persuades another person, or attempts to do so, or engages in misleading conduct toward another person, with intent to-- (1) influence, delay, or prevent the testimony of any person in an official proceeding; (2) cause or induce any person to-- (A) withhold testimony, or withhold a record, document, or other object, from an official proceeding;(B) alter, destroy, mutilate, or conceal an object with intent to impair the object's integrity or availability for use in an official proceeding; (C) evade legal process summoning that person to appear as a witness, or to produce a record, document, or other object, in an official proceeding; or (D) be absent from an official proceeding to which such person has been summoned by legal process; or (3) hinder, delay, or prevent the communication to a law enforcement officer or judge of the United States of information relating to the commission or possible commission of a Federal offense or a violation of conditions of probation, supervised release, parole, or release pending judicial proceedings;

(c) Whoever corruptly-- (1) alters, destroys, mutilates, or conceals a record, document, or other object, or attempts to do so, with the intent to impair the object's integrity or availability for use in an official proceeding; or (2) otherwise obstructs, influences, or impedes any official proceeding, or attempts to do so, shall be fined under this title or imprisoned not more than 20 years, or both.

<u>18USC1513 - Retaliating against a witness, victim, or an informant:</u>
In relevant parts:

(a)(1) Whoever kills or attempts to kill another person with intent to retaliate against any person for-- (A) the attendance of a witness or party at an official proceeding, or any testimony given or any record, document, or other object produced by a witness in an official proceeding; or (B) providing to a law enforcement officer any information relating to the commission or possible commission of a Federal offense or a violation of conditions of probation, supervised release, parole, or release pending judicial proceedings; shall be punished as provided in paragraph (2): The punishment for an offense under this subsection is—(A) in the case of a killing, the punishment provided in sections 1111 and 1112; and B) in the case of an attempt, imprisonment for not more than 20 years; …

(e) Whoever knowingly, with the intent to retaliate, takes any action harmful to any person, including interference with the lawful employment or livelihood of any person, for providing to a law enforcement officer any truthful information relating to the commission or possible commission of any Federal offense, shall be fined under this title or imprisoned not more than 10 years, or both … Whoever conspires to commit any offense under this section shall be subject to the same penalties as those prescribed for the offense the commission of which was the object of the conspiracy.

<u>18USC2331 (1) International Terrorism</u>
As used in this chapter— (1) the term *"international terrorism"* means activities that— (A) involve violent acts or acts dangerous to human life that are a violation of the criminal laws of the United States or of any State, or that would be a criminal violation if committed within the jurisdiction of the United States or of any State; (B) appear to be intended— (i) to intimidate or coerce a civilian population; (ii) to influence the policy of a government by intimidation or coercion; or (iii) to affect the conduct of a government by mass destruction, assassination, or kidnapping; and (C) occur primarily outside the territorial jurisdiction of the United States, or transcend national boundaries in terms of the means by

which they are accomplished, the persons they appear intended to intimidate or coerce, or the locale in which their perpetrators operate or seek asylum.

18USC2331 (5) Domestic Terrorism
In relevant part: (5) "domestic terrorism" means activities that a) involve acts dangerous to human life that are a violation of the criminal laws of the United States or of any State; b) appear to be intended (i) to intimidate or coerce a civilian population; (ii) to influence the policy of a government by intimidation or coercion; (iii) to affect the conduct of a government by mass destruction, assassination, or kidnapping; and (c) occur primarily within the territorial jurisdiction of the United States.

18USC2339 - Harboring or concealing terrorists (Summarized)
Whoever harbors or conceals any person who he knows, or has reasonable grounds to believe, has committed, or is about to commit, an offense under .... section 2332b (relating to acts of terrorism transcending national boundaries) of this title, ... shall be fined under this title or imprisoned not more than ten years, or both.

18USC2381 – Treason
Whoever, owing allegiance to the United States, levies war against them **or** adheres to their enemies, giving them aid and comfort within the United States or elsewhere, is guilty of treason and shall suffer death, or shall be imprisoned not less than five years and fined under this title but not less than $10,000; and shall be incapable of holding any office under the United States.

18USC2382 - Misprision of Treason
Whoever, owing allegiance to the United States and having knowledge of the commission of any treason against them, conceals and does not, as soon as may be, disclose and make known the same to the President or to some judge of the United States, or to the governor or to some judge or justice of a particular State, is guilty of misprision of treason and shall be fined under this title or imprisoned not more than seven years, or both.

18USC2383 - Rebellion or Insurrection

Whoever incites, sets on foot, assists, or engages in any rebellion or insurrection against the authority of the United States <u>or the laws thereof,</u> or gives aid or comfort thereto, shall be fined under this title or imprisoned not more than ten years, or both; and shall be incapable of holding any office under the United States.

18USC2384 - Seditious Conspiracy

If two or more persons in any State or Territory, or in any place subject to the jurisdiction of the United States, conspire to overthrow, put down, or to destroy by force the Government of the United States, or to levy war against them, or to oppose by force the authority thereof, <u>or by force to prevent, hinder, or delay the execution of any law of the United States,</u> or by force to seize, take, or possess any property of the United States contrary to the authority thereof, they shall each be fined under this title or imprisoned not more than twenty years, or both.

18USC3041

States in relevant part: "for any offense against the United States, the offender may, by any justice or judge of the United States … be arrested and imprisoned".

18USC3046 – Warrant or Summons (Rules)

Issuance upon complaint, Rule 4. Issuance upon indictment, Rule 9. Summons on request of government; form; contents; service; return, Rules 4, 9.

18USC3060 – Preliminary Examination

(a) Except as otherwise provided by this section, a preliminary examination shall be held within the time set by the judge or magistrate judge pursuant to subsection (b) of this section, to determine whether there is probable cause to believe that an offense has been committed and that the arrested person has committed it. (b) The date for the preliminary examination shall be fixed by the judge or magistrate judge at the initial appearance of the arrested person. Except as provided by subsection (c) of this section, or unless the arrested person waives the preliminary examination, such examination shall be held within a reasonable time following initial appearance, but in any event not later than— (1) the tenth day following the date of the initial appearance of the arrested person before such officer if the arrested person is held in custody without any provision for release, or is held in custody for failure to meet the conditions of release imposed, or is released from custody only during specified hours of the day; or (2) the twentieth day following the date of the initial appearance if the arrested person is released from custody under any condition other than a condition described in paragraph (1) of this subsection. (c) With the consent of the arrested person, the date fixed by the judge or magistrate judge for the preliminary examination may be a date later than that prescribed by subsection (b), or may be continued one or more times to a date.

§28 *Judiciary and Judicial Procedure*

28USC144 (Recusal of Judges)
"Whenever a party to a proceeding in a court makes and files a timely and sufficient affidavit that the judge before whom the matter is pending has a personal bias or prejudice either against him or in favor of any adverse party, such judge shall proceed no further therein, but another judge shall be assigned to hear such proceeding."

28USC453 – Judge's Oath of Office
Each justice or judge of the United States shall take the following oath or affirmation before performing the duties of his office: ``I, ___ ___, do solemnly swear (or affirm) that I will administer justice without respect to persons, and do equal right to the poor and to the rich, and that I will faithfully and impartially discharge and perform all the duties incumbent upon me as ___ under the Constitution and laws of the United States. So help me God."

28USC455 – Disqualification of a Judge
"(a) Any justice, judge, or magistrate of the United States shall disqualify himself in any proceeding in which his impartiality might reasonably be questioned."

28USC509 – Functions of the Attorney General:
In relevant parts: "All functions of other offices of the Department of Justice and all functions of agencies and employees of the Department of Justice are vested in the Attorney General ..."

28USC535 (b) (Reporting of offenses of government officers)
States: "Any information, allegation, or complaint received in a department or agency of the executive branch of the government relating to violations of title 18 involving Government Officers and employees shall be expeditiously reported to the Attorney General by the head of the department or agency, unless (1) the responsibility to perform an investigation with respect thereto is specifically assigned otherwise by another provision of the law".

28USC547 (Prosecutor Duties)
In relevant part: "Except as otherwise provided by law, each United States Attorney, within his district, shall (1) Prosecute for all offenses against the United States ...."

28USC591
States in relevant part: (a)...."—The Attorney General shall conduct a preliminary investigation in accordance with section 592 whenever the Attorney General receives information sufficient to constitute grounds to investigate whether any person described in section (b) may have violated any Federal criminal law other than a violation classified as a Class B or C misdemeanor or an infraction." (b)....."The persons referred to in subsection (a) are : (1) The President and Vice President;"

Federal Rules of Criminal Procedure

Federal Rules of Criminal Procedure, Rule 4.
Rule 4 (a) states: "If the complaint or one or more affidavits filed with the complaint establishes probable cause to believe an offense has been committed and that the defendant committed it, the judge must issue an arrest warrant to an officer authorized to execute it. Rule 4 (c) states: Such warrant must "command that the defendant be arrested and brought without unnecessary delay before a judge".

Federal Rules of Criminal Procedure, Rule 41
After receiving an affidavit or other information, a magistrate judge or a judge of a state court must issue the warrant if there is probable cause to search and seize a person or property under Rule 41(c). {Rule 41(c) – Evidence of a crime}.

Revised Code of Washington (RCW)

RCW 9A.32.30 – Murder in the First Degree:
In relevant part (1) A person is guilty of murder in the first degree when: (b) Under circumstances manifesting an extreme indifference to human life, he or she engages in conduct which creates a grave risk of death to any person, and thereby causes the death of a person; ....

RCW 9A.76.080 – Rendering Criminal Assistance: As used in RCW 9A.76.080, a person "renders criminal assistance" if, with intent to prevent, hinder, or delay the apprehension or prosecution of another person who he knows has committed a crime, he prevents or obstructs, by use of deception, anyone from performing an act that might aid in the apprehension of such person.

RCW 9A.80.010 - Official Misconduct: states that a public servant is guilty of official misconduct if, with intent to deprive another person of a lawful right or privilege, he/she intentionally refrains from performing a duty imposed upon him/her by law.

RCW 42.20.040 - False Report by public officer: states that every public officer who shall knowingly make any false or misleading statement in any official report or statement, under circumstances not otherwise prohibited by law, shall be guilty of a gross misdemeanor.

---

www.ingramcontent.com/pod-product-compliance
Lightning Source LLC
Chambersburg PA
CBHW052107030426
42335CB00025B/2881